W9-BBW-562

AFTERWORDS

Previous Salon Books

Salon.com's Wanderlust: Real-Life Tales of Adventure and Romance
Edited by Don George

The Salon.com Reader's Guide to Contemporary Authors
Edited by Laura Miller with Adam Begley

Mothers Who Think: Tales of Real-Life Parenthood
Edited by Camille Peri and Kate Moses

Stories and
Reports
from 9/11
and Beyond

AFTERWORDS

Compiled by the Editors of

Salon.com

WASHINGTON SQUARE PRESS

New York   London   Toronto   Sydney   Singapore

The sale of this book without its cover is unauthorized. If you purchased this book without a cover, you should be aware that it was reported to the publisher as "unsold and destroyed." Neither the author nor the publisher has received payment for the sale of this "stripped book."

 WSP A WASHINGTON SQUARE PRESS *Original* Publication

Copyright © 2002 by Salon, Inc.
Foreword copyright © 2002 by David Talbot

All rights reserved, including the right to reproduce this book or portions thereof in any form whatsoever. For information address Washington Square Press, 1230 Avenue of the Americas, New York, NY 10020

ISBN: 0-7434-5612-2

First Washington Square Press trade paperback printing September 2002

10 9 8 7 6 5 4 3 2 1

WASHINGTON SQUARE PRESS and colophon are registered trademarks of Simon & Schuster Inc.

Printed in the U.S.A.

For information regarding special discounts for bulk purchases, please contact Simon & Schuster Special Sales at 1-800-456-6798 or business@simonandschuster.com

CONTENTS

COLLATERAL DAMAGE

START MAKING SENSE

FOREWORD

Nothing would ever be the same. And yet it was. The World Series was played at Yankee Stadium, just miles from ground zero—and the president even threw out the first pitch. Christmas shoppers thronged the department stores and malls. Planeloads of passengers again lifted into the air, despite the continued flaws in airport security and the occasional headline-blaring breach. Soon enough, the live, in-color immolation that mesmerized the entire world on September 11 was packaged into an extravagant kitsch fest, with tear-streaked Statues of Liberty and Old Glory refrigerator magnets replacing the stunned disbelief, rage, and unspeakable loss that initially swept over us. Life went on in America. Same as it ever was.

And yet everything did change. Emergency rescue workers most of us once regarded as a faceless part of the urban landscape suddenly achieved mythic stature. Lovers, spouses, and children on their way out the door in the morning were held to the chest a beat or two longer. Americans, long complacent or ignorant about their country's role in the world, began speaking knowledgeably about radical Islam's case against the West, the fateful bond between the United States and Israel, and the ancient tribal demarcations of Afghanistan. The political and cultural effluvia that had once enthralled us now seemed "so September 10." We no longer felt immune to the world's madness and mayhem—on one bright and terrible morning it had come swooping down and torn a hole in our sky.

Like most Americans, *Salon*'s editors and writers quickly realized we were living in a strange new world, and we rushed to explore it. In the days and weeks and months following the terror attacks on America, we fanned out across the country and the world to capture this epic story. *Salon*'s ragtag army of staff reporters, freelancers, essayists, and average citizens filed stories from New York, Washington, Berkeley, St. Louis, Paris, London, Brussels, Islamabad, Mazar-e-Sharif, Kabul, and many other far-flung cities. Our medium, the World Wide Web, was the best vehicle to get on top of this global, fast-changing story. The Web allows for an immediate, intimate, and reflective type of journalism not easily replicated by other media. This was the first major war in which Americans used the Web to follow the news as it happened, logging on from work during the day instead of waiting for the evening TV news.

Most of the articles collected in this anthology have a deeply personal tone, from the eerie first-person account of a ground zero volunteer to the story of a World Trade Center widower who must learn to brush his daughter's hair for the first time to a war correspondent's harrowing escape from a murderous band of Afghan soldiers. *Salon* also turned to novelists such as Rick Moody, Jeffrey Eugenides, and Janet Fitch, as well as humorists, to help make sense of this unique moment in the world's history. And while some of the pieces here attempt to put September 11 and its aftermath in a broad geopolitical context, others take a street-level view, looking, for instance, at how the war amped up sexual relationships in Manhattan, coining the term "terror sex." *Salon* has always avoided party-line journalism, preferring a mix of voices and opinions to the political monotone of the left or right. And that diversity is represented here as well, with my own account of my hawk-ish transformation placed alongside a spirited conversation with American foreign policy's most implacable critic, Noam Chomsky. And finally, we have included some of *Salon*'s best in-depth reporting on the war, including staff writer Eric Boehlert's chilling account of how a law-abiding Palestinian professor at a Florida university was lynched by a hysterical media in the weeks after September 11.

Since its founding in 1995, *Salon* has prided itself on tak-ing a fearless and iconoclastic look at the news events of the day, crawling behind the headlines in ways that our corporate media counterparts often find grubby and distasteful. We like to ask questions no one else is asking; we see the wisdom in the unconventional. And we're not embarrassed to let our emotions show. This enterprising, if sometimes jagged, approach to journalism is on full display in this anthology.

The stories collected here span the period between September 11 and President Bush's January 29 "axis of evil" State of the Union speech, an address that marked the end of the "firefighters' war," as political pundit Chris Matthews termed it, and the beginning of a much broader and more controversial campaign to eradicate America's enemies. *Afterwords* is not the official account of this horrid and heroic chapter in history. This anthology may lack the seamless and authoritative feel of the works of scholarship that are certain to come in future years. But I think you will agree that the vivid reports here bring these times fully to life. Here, in these pages, is a scrapbook of living history, eyewitness accounts, and impassioned essays that capture that millennial fever of 9/11 and the days that followed.

—David Talbot
Salon Editor
February 2002

AFTERWORDS

Ground Zero

RUNNING AGAINST THE GRAIN: A SURVIVOR'S TALE

ANN MARSH

SEPT. 14, 2001—At the time the first airplane strikes Tower One of the World Trade Center, David Boyle is working on the ninety-third floor of Tower Two, for a Cupertino, California–based start-up called Oblix. David doesn't hear the impact, but sees thousands of white papers fluttering in the air, traveling in a northeasterly direction outside his window. "At first," David tells me later, "I thought, Maybe this is a ticker-tape parade." People in the office are milling around, drinking coffee, perplexed, but not particularly concerned. David wanders from window to window looking for the source of the paper. His windows look out on the Brooklyn Bridge, away from Tower One. He notices that the papers are substantially larger than confetti. Looking down on the streets, he sees debris covering the ground. "Then it finally hits me. This is not a ticker-tape parade."

David suggests to his two colleagues in the Oblix offices that they start walking down the stairs, though some around them continue to work. David throws his laptop into a bag and the bag over his shoulder.

It takes them ten minutes to reach the seventy-eighth floor. During the walk, David's mind starts working on him. What could cause all that debris? It has to be worse than anyone knows. He has to get out of the building, by the fastest means possible. At the seventy-eighth floor, they reach a bank of elevators that can take them directly to the lobby. A man's voice on a loudspeaker informs workers that there has been an "accident" at Tower One, but it is completely contained. They should stay calm and remain in their offices. David's boss, Carlos Delatorre, checks the voice mail on his cell phone and suggests they all go back upstairs. "I don't want to waste the morning," Delatorre says. David protests, "Listen, do the math. If it's nothing we're back up here in five minutes. If it's something then we're safe."

David looks at his watch. He calculates that it will take at least an hour to inch down to the ground in the already crowded stairwells. He hits the elevator button. Doors open. People in the lobby around him shake their heads. David doesn't have time to explain: If the "accident" really is contained to Tower One, he figures, the elevators should be fully functional. He and his colleagues (Michael Black, an Oblix systems engineer, in addition to Delatorre) get in with several others. Though they don't know it, a jetliner headed their way is about sixty seconds from impact as their elevator hovers on the seventy-eighth floor. A friend turns down David's request to accompany them. She wants to stay behind to watch over people. "I said, 'Well, good luck to you.' She's like, 'Good luck to you.' That's the last time I saw her. I remember all these faces looking at me as the half-empty elevator closed its doors on them."

The high-speed elevator whisks them to the lobby in less than thirty seconds. David follows a disorganized group of people out some sliding doors. "Immediately outside, I started hearing this roar. It was getting louder and louder. I have a friend and we used to take his boat out into the Boston Harbor and park it at the foot of the Boston-Logan

Airport. I knew it was a jet engine." David's view of the sky is blocked by an awning. As he walks clear of the awning, he looks up, just as the plane hits the building that he's just exited. The next sound dwarfs the sound of the engine. "It was like the world coming to an end."

Pandemonium breaks out. While people around him run for the street to get clear of the building, college football instincts kick in; David and his colleagues run back inside, against the flow of bodies. "It's called running against the grain," he says. He dives over a turnstile headfirst, hands out. As he lands massive debris falls on the streets, where many of the people had fled: steel girders, aluminum, and flames. He runs into the center of the towers where the retail stores are located. "It's amazing what happens when you're that afraid. I didn't stop to see anything. It was like running wind sprints. Don't talk. O.K., go left, go left. Just run, run, run." He runs until he hurts, until he wants to throw up. Amid the confusion, David loses Carlos. He and Michael plunge into a subway station, where a train is waiting with open doors. They jump in. It's packed. The train pulls away. "What is happening, what is happening?" people around him want to know. David tells them, "We are under attack."

Back at his apartment, eleven blocks north of the World Trade Center, at Leonard and Church streets, David looks at the smoldering buildings. As he watches, the first tower starts to collapse, killing, presumably, many of his former office mates. He can't quite register what he's seeing. Even as the building comes down, he turns his head to the left and watches the scene unfold simultaneously on the television, as if to verify his own impressions. The phone rings. From where he's running to safety along the West End Highway, Carlos calls David on his cell phone and thanks him for saving his life. David calls his family. Over the next forty-eight hours, scores of friends call David, many in sheer panic. He listens to their voice mails and eventually changes his outgoing message to tell people he's alive. "It's almost like you're attending your own funeral," David says. "It's touching. Your ex-girlfriend calls, who you haven't talked to in five years, and she calls you 'Baby,' which she hasn't done in five years."

His roommate comes in, hugs him with tears in his eyes, astonished to find him alive. Down on the street, earlier, David's roommate met a dazed and bleeding man. What happened? The man told him he was waiting for an elevator in Tower Two. When the explosion hit, the elevator doors blew inward on the waiting crowds, instantly decapitating people and cutting them to bits. He was lucky that bodies in front of him absorbed that first shock. He hurled himself down the stairs. David's roommate told the man his friend worked on the ninety-third floor. "He's dead," the man said flatly. Right then, one of the towers collapsed and David's roommate didn't wait to finish the conversation.

When I finally spoke with David the day after the attacks, I wanted to tell him that somehow I knew, when I learned he'd been working on the ninety-third floor, that he would have an extraordinary story to tell. That is, as long as he survived to convey it to us. David's parents raised all their four boys with a combination of Italian-Irish bravado that inclines them to think against the grain. It makes them great, if irascible, dinner companions and forceful leaders. I wasn't surprised to hear that somehow David had defied logic and taken an elevator, tried to encourage others to accompany him, talked his boss out of returning to work, and, finally, leaped back into a building when others fled the front door.

But I didn't. When I finally got David on the phone, I

could hear in his voice that his experience was bigger and more searing than anything I might make of it. Inevitably, perhaps, we found ourselves debating the nature and will of God. "The final result is that things lined up in my favor," he told me. "I personally believe God doesn't interfere. If that were the case, I might have more trouble handling this."

A SEASON IN HELL

CHRISTOPHER KETCHAM

SEPT. 19, 2001—Body No. 1 shattered all illusions of finding survivors. He was a curly-haired guy with a paunch and puffed red lips, and he was sleeping on his stomach with his arms over his head, lying very naturally, except he had no buttocks or legs. The firefighters, ten of them, pulled his head up by his hair to show his face, turned him over, a coroner flashbulbed him, and no one said a word.

I was the only reporter there when they dug him up at 1:15 A.M. Wednesday morning, fifteen hours after the towers fell. There was ash and asbestos in the air, and gray drifts of millions of sheaves of paper, and mud in paddies where the tangled hoses had burst or the water had streamed from the ruins. Firefighters lay in makeshift forward triage units set up in buildings named after the Dow Jones Company and American Express, old strange names, inappropriate now. Now this was Zone 1, ground zero, and in the fiery hours of the night of Tuesday, September 11, I slipped past the National Guard perimeter with a Red Cross team, handing out water bottles in the smoke, holding flashlights while medics gave eyewashes to the blinded firefighters. I was stumbling, not knowing how to help, so the medics stuffed my pack with gauze and saline and water and masks, and I tried not to get lost in the unreality and the darkness.

At 10 A.M. that day, attack plus one hour, there was an exodus of ashen New Yorkers on the bridges to Brooklyn, girls in suit pants and heels, and men half-naked in tennis shoes, an orderly flight all in all, but there was fear and awe and silence. I was riding in on a bicycle over the Brooklyn Bridge, against the wave, and cops were saying "Turn back, they might blow the bridge too"—a false rumor, the day was full of them—and F-15 fighter jets pulled long pounding low-altitude arcs over Manhattan. The fallen towers spread soot over the sun, which went out blood orange and then shone in very blue sky, and the day turned hot. Flurries fell, the sun silvered the flakes: ash on every shoulder and every head, whole ash men; men with bloody eyes bandaged; wet towels over mouths; much thirst, and already the asbestos-filled air making throats hurt and skin heat up, and who knew if there wasn't something else in the air, anthrax, radioactivity.

When the towers burned in the moments after the collision and before they fell so impossibly and unthinkably, there were people jumping from seventy and ninety stories up, terrified of the fire, which burnt, the firemen say, at 6,000 degrees. A man and woman held hands and leapt. You could watch the heavy ants falling, and many children stood at the windows of schools nearby. Their teachers, too shocked, did not pull them away.

Trucks full of masked volunteers, a dozen ambulances howling, racing south, and in the plaza of the federal courts, scores of men and women frantically nailing plywood planks over long two-by-fours lined parallel two feet apart.

"They'll need a lot more stretchers than this," a dusty man said, walking up. He tells me there are gangs stealing bicycles in Zone 1, busting open FedEx trucks, taking advantage of the chaos. Another man saw what was being built. "Oh, God!" he cried and put his hands to his head and leapt backwards.

Rumors of twenty thousand dead.

At 7:45 P.M. Tuesday, all power gone from lower Manhattan, twenty blocks of darkness and men running, and the fires stirred winds through the canyons of the buildings, kicking up poisonous dust storms of glass and lime and concrete; four inches of ash on cars abandoned with doors open. We wore goggles and facemasks and everyone was in shadow, with flashlights, watching the ground, and the streets looked white as deserts; "the longest night," the firefighters had said, and we had no idea what they meant or how many they'd lost until the first ruins of the towers rose before us like bombed churches in mist, little red fires at its heart, and we could hear the cries for surgeons among the rubble, someone needed an amputation. And all around were burnt hulks of ambulances, cars, dump trucks, fire trucks—crushed when the towers fell.

"Eyewashes! Eyewashes!" the medics cried out, fanning out in teams of two, and the firemen thanked them. And then, into a wall of smoke and out, we entered the very bottom of ground zero, and for a moment the medics did not cry "Eyewashes!" This was Hiroshima in miniature: rubble and girders and twisted metal stretching into haze and dust, framed in Roman ruins of delicate charred lattice walls six and ten stories high, white-pale in arc lights or disappearing in purple plumes—and over the rubble of 200,000 tons of steel and 425,000 cubic yards of concrete and 43,000 windows and 23,000 fluorescent lightbulbs, the firemen trawling, stumbling, digging, blasting water, thousands of men among the sharpened steaming warped metal that flipped up underfoot, like bear-traps, tore at legs and popped into chests.

And you knew then that this dig would take weeks, and

you'd mention this to a fireman sweating in ash, and he'd say, "Weeks? Fuckin' months. Fucking forever."

Within hours, cigarettes taste like burnt plaster and asbestos and sometimes, oddly, human flesh; "real flavor," someone joked. The hounds and German shepherds are loosed, slipping over the dust on girders, sniffing. You watched the fleet-footed dogs nearly lose their balance over voids twenty feet deep in the rubble; they descended into holes, and then you watched the slimmer of the men do the same thing, hole-crawls with a flashlight and a crowbar.

Volunteer Vinnie Dolan, a young father from Brooklyn, did this again and again, raw and dazed and blank-eyed, spitting green and black phlegm. He brought up three police officers, and at the end of it, the muscles in his cheeks were slackening and tightening involuntarily, his voice was mucusey. At any time the rubble could come down, the smoke could kill you in there. A dog came out asphyxiated, and died.

Relief at the smashed-open supermarkets where the meat was already rotting. In these early hours when the volunteers were few, the food supplies random, cops and firemen and EMTs looted cigarettes, candy, water, chips, big boxes of aspirin—terrible headaches that night, it was the asbestos—and Albuterol and inhalers for the asthma attacks. You took what you needed: It was a zone of mud and rubble and men in fatigues and gas masks, and no refrigeration or electricity or running water; you thought to yourself that much of the planet lives like this, and you had no idea what city or country this was. Then you saw cops in the abandoned Starbucks trying to make Frappuccinos.

I was given black body bags and Civil Defense body tags and was told to hand them out to the firemen as the dead were brought out, but the bodies were a long time coming.

The men dug in groups of two and three, throwing up dust and investment receipts and printer paper and pieces of pipe and wire, and the bucket brigades were just forming. The diggers find flesh; they finger it, hold it up to flashlights; it looks like shredded rope, but "That's skin," they say matter-of-factly, then louder, "Think we got a body!" and a dozen men converge. New clues unearthed with hands and shovels: A white knit sweater shredded on tin shrapnel, and a pair of glasses, fully intact—incredible in this mess—and a Nike shoe. "Got a shoe, Chief. Whaddaya think?"

"People get blasted right outta their shoes in shit like this," replies Chief. "Body could be here. Body could be a hundred feet away."

A hundred feet where? When the dogs roamed the rubble, they nosed and loitered every three or four feet—everywhere the sick smell of it, parts of bodies, parts of parts, entrails in dust—even the men began to hunt by scent. "I can smell it," said a fireman, wrinkling his nose. "Right here." But he found no body. And when the bags went out, they were slumping at the middle, sloshing like water balloons. By the end of the day on September 18, Mayor Rudolph Giuliani announced that only 218 remains had been removed.

A fireman in a Brooklyn bar shook his head at the news. He had done a twenty-four-hour shift. "You have ten-story buildings that leave more debris than these two one hundred-story towers," he said. He was awed. "Where the fuck is everything? A serious weeklong search and we've found two hundred in a pile of five thousand? What's going on? Where is everyone? Why aren't we finding more bodies? 'Cause it's all vaporized—turned to dust. We're breathing people in that dust."

Brian McGuire of Rescue 5 from Staten Island told me

three hundred of his brothers died on Tuesday morning, the worst disaster ever for the firemen of New York City. McGuire hunkered thin-lipped in the bed of a truck tumbled with supplies; the truck was pulling out, fleeing the shadow of a building that was ready to collapse. Vinnie Dolan and I had just been up in that building, ran twenty stories to get the last unwilling residents out; an old woman hunting her parakeet, she wouldn't leave without the bird.

So I was trembling when I climbed in the truck with McGuire, and he was looking away. "I lost ten buddies tonight," he said at last.

There would be firemen marching in the darkness in single file, looking like medieval warriors, carrying awls, pikes, shovels, hoes, and you looked at them differently now, their processions almost holy, because you saw how big their grief was. They'd worked ten and twenty and forty hours in the rubble to forget it, to make something good of it, to find a man, a whole man, give him a decent burial, and perhaps find a survivor. You saw them planted in sleep on brown couches pulled from the smashed windows of ground-floor offices, with signs saying "Dave's Café. Le Menu: 1) water 2) water 3) cold water." You saw them sitting on curbs, in rows of stunned silence, soot-faced, white-eyed, or on benches in ash-scummed restaurants alone in front of candles, and when you saw them you gave them water. And some wept quietly, then quit it suddenly, like hanging up a phone.

And some, just a very few, were saying evil things, crying vengeance, "Nuke 'em"; "Kill Allah" written in ash on walls. Stories, seeping in from outside, of jingoist reaction, feral and blind, pig's blood thrown on mosques, veiled women cursed in supermarkets—war on the Middle East, world war.

There were signs on the inside of madness too: Midday

on September 14, a woman arrived screeching, her husband was alive in a void, he had just called on a cell phone from beneath, and the world of the rubble stopped, turned, wrapped itself around her; they dug faster now, doubling their forces. And then it turned out she was a cruel fraud, the story a hoax, and the woman was arrested and was said to be insane.

At the candlelit vigils in the days afterward, there were little cities of lights on the streets. Vinnie Dolan and I watched them in exhaustion.

A candle flared, I nearly jumped; bad nerves. "Can't sleep," said Vinnie. "Three hours last night. Hard to sleep."

The candle had been glued in a Styrofoam cup and the cup had caught fire, hissing. Finally, the candle toppled over in the blaze.

THE DIG

JAMES CROAK

SEPT. 19, 2001—I went back to the remains of the World Trade Center to dig for bodies.

There is a staging area at Chelsea Piers where city staff determine if one has useful knowledge or experience to help with the rescue. If so, they tape a sign reading "S&R" on you, for Search and Rescue, and send you to the Javits Center for dispersal. They send you uptown, not down. Except for ironworkers, they want no one else there, and have placed the military at all entrances to prevent anyone getting close. It is a polite runaround.

Some ironworkers who had just put in an eighteen-hour shift dropped by my loft at 6 A.M. Thursday and asked if I wanted to go in next time. They weren't sure, because they thought that I might have had enough after having witnessed it all go down. Of course I wanted to go.

We leave Friday in mid-afternoon. In Queens, eleven of us pile into a van and head for the Brooklyn Bridge to the uncanny sight of an altered skyline. We pull up to a commercial equipment store and help ourselves to everything we could carry: cases of gloves, masks, crowbars, pails, and respirators, without a thought of paying for it. The shop owner helps us load it and proudly waves as we drive off.

We have an ex-cop drive the van, and stick a police

parking placard in the window. That gets us by the first four security checks. Then we approach two humvees parked across the road at Park Row and Broadway, with many young men in battle fatigues standing about. National Guard, I think. Then they surround the van. Regular army, I think. And then all six doors are jerked open at once. Marines. Welcome to Not America. I am in the middle of Manhattan in a private car and armed marines are ripping open my doors. I feel better already. They snap our IDs from our hands as fast as we can pull them out. The two in back talk very loud to hold our attention while the others move in among us. Satisfied, they tell us to park and motion us into the site.

We collect our shoplifted gear and walk a quarter mile to the site. The tension in the air is frightening: military vehicles, M-60 machine guns. Hundreds of angry cops. Everybody looking us over. A couple of more checks and we walk into Guernica.

I saw the towers go down, so I thought that I would be prepared for the spectacle, but the immensity of the debris field dwarfs my expectations. It stretches about a quarter mile in any direction. There is no level area: the height varies from 15 feet to over 120 feet. Smoke still rises from all areas. Three of the tower facades still stand up to ten floors but nothing is behind them, just the standing steel front. The field is lower in the center so it appears one has walked into a vast coliseum, the smoking ruins of Pompeii. The exterior of the former towers was twelve-inch steel columns spaced four feet apart. As they fell these shafts speared everything in sight. A dozen of them protrude from the West Side Highway, sticking up like some mad confection. Four of them shot Zeus-style into the side of the American Express Building thirty floors up, knocking off a corner. The debris washed across the highway, smashing into the World Financial Center, blasting all of the glass from its walls.

Looking downward through the wracks of steel beams you realize they are sitting upon a sea of emergency vehicles.

How to Kill Firemen
  1) Make an explosion.
  2) Wait fifteen minutes.
  3) Make another explosion.

Spread out across the debris field are bucket brigades, serpentine chains of two hundred people each—firemen, cops, military—lines meandering up and down to where the dig is taking place. The entire site is being excavated into five-gallon pails that are hand-passed to dump trucks. Not a finger will be lost. Each dig has a cadaver dog: the dog shows us where to dig and then a small hole is made.

In goes a TV camera with a listening device and everybody yells to be quiet. Generators go off and everyone stands still. It's three days later and there is no more sound, so the digging and cutting begins. When they find a body they yell "Body coming" and an adjacent brigade climbs across the wreckage to form an opposing line. The body is then passed in a stretcher between the lines. If it is a fireman (over three hundred of them were lost) his hat is placed atop him and the stretcher is carried, not passed.

My first body is a fireman. His hat tells me what happened to him. Crushed, burned, shattered, it looks to have been brought up from the sea, a Civil War relic. My second body is a young girl, petite, in shape. I can't take this, I think, and consider running away. Thankfully we don't have another for an hour or so. Periodically the line calls "We need paint," meaning they've found a body too deep to dig for immediately. When this happens the area is sprayed red so we can find him later. Several times we pass a body bag the size of a basketball. If the wreckage shifts a Klaxon blows twice telling everyone to run, which we do. A minute later they all run back, me still shaking.

The next body is in a fetal position. She must have been scared beyond understanding, I think, before a billion tons of mess fell on top of her.

All total, we found twenty-seven bodies and carried out nine.

It would be a good idea to bring small groups of the relatives of the victims into the site so they see for themselves why we are not finding survivors. Survivors? We aren't finding *concrete*. We pulled out tangled messes of rebar without a spec of concrete on it; except for being twisted it could have come off the shelf, and it was *inside* the slabs. In twelve hours I did not see a piece of glass, nor office equipment, nor a book, just steel and powder.

You think there are no heroes in America? I see a lanky blonde who could model Chanel tie a rope around her ankle, grab a stethoscope, and dive headfirst down a debris hole that would have shredded a raccoon. I see firemen so deep into the rubble their flashlights are mistaken for fire. The firemen are fearless, shrugging their shoulders at the obvious danger of it all.

But missing from the scene is any talk of how it got like this, why it came down, what should be done about it. Nothing, not a peep.

After twelve hours the accumulated stress and fear get the best of me and I walk home. But I'll be back in tomorrow.

EMOTIONAL RESCUE

WILLIAM HARVEY

SEPT. 25, 2001, NEW YORK—Yesterday, September 15, I had probably the most incredible and moving experience of my life. Juilliard organized a quartet to go play at the Armory. The Armory is a huge military building where families of people missing from Tuesday's disaster go to wait for news of their loved ones.

Entering the building was very difficult emotionally, because the entire building (the size of a city block) was covered with missing persons posters. Thousands of posters, spread out up to eight feet above the ground, each featuring a different, smiling, face.

I made my way into the huge central room and found my Juilliard buddies. For two hours we sight-read quartets (with only three people!), and I don't think I will forget the grief counselor from the Connecticut State Police who listened the entire time, or the woman who listened only to "Memory" from the play *Cats*, crying the whole time.

At 7 P.M., the other two players had to leave; they had been playing at the Armory for six hours and simply couldn't play any more. I volunteered to stay and play solo, since I had just gotten there.

I soon realized that the evening had just begun for me. A man in fatigues who introduced himself as Sergeant Major asked me if I'd mind playing for his soldiers as they came back from digging through the rubble at ground zero. Masseuses had volunteered to give his men massages, he said, and he didn't think anything would be more soothing than getting a massage and listening to violin music at the same time.

So at 9 P.M., I headed up to the second floor as the first men were arriving. From then until 11:30, I played everything I could do from memory: Bach B Minor Partita, Tchaikovsky's violin concerto, the Dvorak concerto, Paganini Caprices 1 and 17, Vivaldi's "Winter" and "Spring," the theme from *Schindler's List,* Tchaikovsky's "Melodie," "Meditation" from *Thaïs,* "Amazing Grace," "My Country 'Tis of Thee," "Turkey in the Straw," "Bile Them Cabbages Down."

Never have I played for a more grateful audience. Somehow it didn't matter that by the end, my intonation was shot and I had no bow control. I would have lost any competition I was playing in, but it didn't matter. The men would come up the stairs in full gear, remove their helmets, look at me, and smile. At 11:20, I was introduced to Colonel Slack, head of the division. After thanking me, he said to his friends, "Boy, today was the toughest day yet. I made the mistake of going back into the pit, and I'll never do that again."

Eager to hear a firsthand account, I asked, "What did you see?" He stopped, swallowed hard, and said, "What you'd expect to see." The colonel stood there as I played a lengthy rendition of "Amazing Grace," which he claimed was the best he'd ever heard. By this time it was 11:30, and I didn't think I could play anymore. I asked Sergeant Major if it would be appropriate if I played the national anthem. He shouted above the chaos of the milling soldiers to call them to attention, and I played the "Star-Spangled Banner" as the three hundred men of the Sixty-ninth Division saluted an invisible flag.

After shaking a few hands and packing up, I was prepared to leave when one of the privates accosted me and told me the colonel wanted to see me again. He took me down to the War Room, but we couldn't find the colonel, so he gave me a tour of the War Room. It turns out that the division I played for is the famous Fighting Sixty-ninth, the most decorated division in the U.S. Army. He pointed out a letter from Abraham Lincoln offering his condolences after the Battle of Antietam—the Sixty-ninth suffered the most casualties of any division at that historic battle.

Finally, we located the colonel. After thanking me again, he presented me with the coin of the regiment. "We only give these to someone who's done something special for the Sixty-ninth," he informed me. He called over the division's historian to tell me the significance of all the symbols on the coin.

As I rode the taxi back to Juilliard—free, of course, since taxi service is free in New York right now—I was numb. Not only was this evening the proudest I've ever felt to be an American, it was my most meaningful as a musician and a person as well. At Juilliard, kids are hypercritical of each other and very competitive. The teachers expect, and in most cases get, technical perfection. But this wasn't about that. The soldiers didn't care that I had so many memory slips I lost count. They didn't care that when I forgot how the second movement of the Tchaikovsky went, I had to come up with my own insipid improvisation until I somehow (and I still don't know how) got to a cadence.

I've never seen a more appreciative audience, and I've never understood so fully what it means to communicate music to other people. So how did it change me as a person?

Let's just say that, next time I want to get into a petty

argument about whether Richter or Horowitz was better, I'll remember that when I asked the colonel to describe the pit formed by the tumbling of the towers, he couldn't. Words only go so far, and even music can only go a little further from there.

THE DEVIL'S SMOKE

CHRISTOPHER KETCHAM

OCT. 4, 2001—I have a friend who when he snorts too much cocaine reverts to a kind of acute paranoia bordering on psychosis. He gets to the point where he hides in corners of his room, with his shirt off, sweating with a wet towel wrapped tightly around his neck; his arms bunch up against his chest, as if he's cold or about to pray. He has the quiet mad belief that squirrels are going to bite the arteries in his neck, and when I see him like this I say, "There are no squirrels, dude, come on, calm down." "Yo—yo—yo," he says, very slowly like a chant, "squirrels—squirrels?" and that's all he can say for some time: "Squirrels?"

Much of the city has become like my friend, though people don't like to show it. The city has been hit with information it cannot process, at least not yet, not for a long time, and surely not if this happens again, which is what everyone expects.

I called a therapist at the New York City Mental Health Association, a calm-voiced man of forty-two named Dr. John Draper, who is the director of the association. I called him for two reasons: to find out the symptoms of those who are calling his hotlines for help, and to ask him for help myself.

"Well, first of all, what's going on with you, Christopher?"

No sleep, Doc, but a lot of pacing; hearing voices and chattering; silly songs that repeat until I have to hit my head to get them out, literally give myself a smack like a jukebox; petty details of tomorrow: where fax that, whom call—enough stamps?; godawful insomnia turning my throat ragged, got the flu now, weak, yet still can't sleep, two, three hours a night, and there are bad dreams:

I'm walking through an abandoned hall of tall white palm trees under an atrium of glass, and there are shadows, and echoes and mumbling, voices I don't understand, and in one place, which was a bakery, there are fat yeasty dough-piles that were being kneaded just hours ago, that still have handprints; and other uncooked loaves lie on trays abandoned; the yeast grew in them, fattened them, and they drooped over the sides of the trays. Neutron bombs took the cooks away.

Or I'm sitting in a Japanese garden cleaning para-trooper boots, I wipe hard but the dried slurry of the ash of the towers won't come off, and in fact as I wipe harder the white residue turns heavy and bluish and soaks into my rag, soaking back into the boot, so as the boot dries the film of white ash seems to grow thicker. "It won't come off," I say, getting desperate, and then a voice, my father's, who comes into the garden where there are wind chimes; he wets a finger with spittle and wipes it across the leather of the steel toe, and where he streaks with his finger the ash goes away . . . for a moment.

Or I'm walking down a long hall in apartment rooms where I can hear trucks hauling rubbish at night through the industrial streets, and there's a view over warehouse buildings where the towers once distantly stood: all plume now, glowing like blue dragon breath in the arc-lights of the Zone. I walk down the hall, open a door, there is some-one in the bed, I go to her, she awakes, she shouts as I approach, looks right through me, "Nononono," she cries, "this isn't happening, this isn't happening," she beats at the covers, backs up in the bed into the corner and swats at my head. I say "Shhh" twice, slowly, and she rocks back and forth until she sleeps once more. She was never awake.

But this is happening. That was the Wintergarden at ground zero, the palms covered in ash, the galleries of abandoned cafés near the towers. That was real. That was my father's home in Brooklyn. This is my home where my girlfriend sleeps.

That's what's going on with me, Doc.

"Your reaction is very normal," Dr. Draper said. "We're seeing a lot of sleeping problems, people who are having nightmares. Many people can't stop visualizing what they saw that day. Have you talked with someone about what you saw?"

"Yes," I said.

"Have you talked about it in excruciating detail?"

No. I remember this from ground zero, though: The body discovered was not a man, it was not a thing, it was a man, it was meat: They turned it over, they examined it, they prodded it, they poked lights at it—all I remember of that place, of the forty hours I spent there, was that it was dark, that there was no sunlight. Slab of meat, he flopped, he coughed dust, you saw it falling out of his nose, and he was already starting to rot. Like a curious child, I touched his bowels with gloved fingers as the dark rot fell on the ground as they picked him up. There are people now I'm talking to who've been digging on and off fourteen hours a day for nearly three weeks. This is all real, and no one wants to believe it; the city, for all the crime and chaos attached to its name, was still much too innocent to believe it. Bear with us, people of Gaza, Tel Aviv, Afghanistan, the Balkans, Rwanda, Colombia—we're just learning. As Dr. Draper told me, "We're really in uncharted territory here."

At the end of a very sunny day just a few days ago, my girlfriend came home green-faced, dizzy, sat in a chair. "I just," she said, and then didn't say anything. "I just . . . saw a woman jump from a building. At Twenty-second and Fifth. They're still washing away her blood."

Dr. Draper said, "At this point, it's too early to say about suicides, whether the rate is going up, because we don't have complete statistics. In the first week, we received very few calls about mental health difficulties, because people were still in shock. Now we're getting two hundred calls a day and we expect that number to go up. As we move further away from the event, people are trying to put it behind them but they find they simply cannot. The problems will only grow now as the reality settles in."

That's when it started, in the second week; the fear came over the city and hunkered and no one knew what to make of it, this new neighbor who seemed more manly than the rest of us: the kind of neighbor who'd take away wives and children and no one would say a word. I saw it arrive first in Bob, old friend, tall unshaven Greek expat, unemployed writer.

I had stopped by his apartment randomly on the bicycle to find his door wide open to the street in a dangerous neighborhood. I walked in, he stood on a tottering chair to set his cuckoo clock; he fell, picked the chair up over his head, waved it around—running from room to room in his underwear turning up radios, drunk. "Can't take it anymore, Ketcham, I can't take looking at that plume, I'm leaving tomorrow by train." His eyes black-rimmed, communicating from the rat brain. And the plume still rising from the rubble and over the city, even a week and a half after, coursing south-southwest in the wind. My friend, thoroughly spooked, thought it came right over his house in Brooklyn. Bob said the plume was the souls of the men and women in the towers, "the Devil's Milky Way, Ketcham!" and that's how it looked, pale-milky and then yellow-brown and sometimes lit with sunlight.

He was right. Three thousand people and only a few hundred bodies recovered? That was a funeral pyre, a crematorium. The ash had men in it. That's human remains you can't get off your boots.

And there was Bob packing bags to rock 'n' roll and banging hands on a table, like bongos, in a frenzied end-of-the-world drunk. When the music stopped for thirty seconds, there were crows at 1 A.M. in the gardens behind his home. The crows said "eeyaaaarrkkh."

"You know what I watched today?" Bob is yelling, every word is panicked and his eyes are bugging; too much drink; he hasn't slept more than three hours in the last three days. Drinking vodka. "You know what I watched? *Barney & Friends!* A whole hour. The big purple dinosaur, Ketcham! You know why? Because Barney wasn't telling me any lies, Ketcham! Barney wasn't lying to me, Ketcham!"

Man, I wanted to take him in my arms, and tell him to calm down, but I couldn't because I wasn't calm and I knew what he was talking about. Like the lie, the biggest of them all, that now we'd have to make war and kill lots and lots of people to secure peace—Orwellian language.

"And the fucking CEOs of the airline companies with their zillion dollar salaries and bonuses and stock options," Bob is saying, "and in the hour of need for their people, the hour of need, they take a piss in a bathroom and on their cell phones order the layoff of a hundred thousand people. It's rot! And then they demand a welfare check of $15 billion? Pigs! Pigs!"

"Yeah, well, that's the American way. When's Barney on?"

"Sunday mornings." And Bob's still yelling, not top-of-the-lungs anymore, because his mouth is getting parched; he takes a long wild suck at a beer. His cuckoo clock started going.

"I'm leaving, first to Boston, then Montreal, then Greece. See my family."

"You're leaving? You're really leaving?"

"I'm fleeing. I can't take it, I can't sleep, I can't cry anymore, I'm at the end."

Newsflash: 71 percent of Americans depressed, according to a recent poll. The pollsters didn't interview any New Yorkers; they thought it inappropriate. I did a poll of my own.

Eighteen-year-old girl, freshman from New York University, who watched the towers fall: "Afterward, I just sat in bed and felt so utterly . . . doomed. Then I understood, for just a few minutes, why people commit suicide."

My neighbor, a thirty-four-year-old musician, who was numb in a dentist's chair getting a root canal, in a high office building in Brooklyn with a view of the towers. "Loog at dat pwaingh," he said to the dentist, who ignored him. "Yes, yes, we're going to finish up that root today." "No! Loog!" And they watched the plane slap into the side of the first tower and explode. "I had sex with three different women in three days that week. Jesus. I haven't done that since I was in my early twenties."

He's depressed at the thought of it; everyone I know is depressed, anxious, confused, waiting. "Everyone's waiting for the other shoe to drop," my sister tells me. She's heard rumors there'll be another attack on the sixteenth of October—more lies. She says a woman who lost her husband in the towers, a woman who is a friend of a friend, went insane afterward.

"I've got this thing now in my leg," a Brooklyn barfly tells me. "This . . . thing. It's like a . . . lump. And when I lie down in bed, I feel like no matter which side of the bed I'm on, it's always the wrong side. It's this thing, this lump. And it's driving me crazy, 'cause I don't know what it is."

"In these early stages, it's called critical incident stress and symptoms are quite varied," explained Dr. Draper. "After a month has passed, on October 11, we can officially classify it as post-traumatic stress disorder. There are physiological, cognitive, and emotional symptoms. You've noticed that just about everyone is exhausted, feeling very tired? This is because the body is hormonally shifting down from a hyperalert state of adrenalized preparedness. That's what we saw in the first week: The body was ready for action, and in many cases people felt good, they felt high. Full of adrenalin. Ready for war, geared up for survival.

"Now we're seeing the crash from that hyperalert state, the comedown into numbness, a state of nonalertness, and this is when the real trouble starts, when the routine of daily life becomes harder and harder to accept because of this wailing inside your mind. Physiologically, people are having stomachaches, headaches, twitches, tics, muscle spasms—ailments they never had before. Some people have memory impairments, to block what they saw, and word loss, because they absolutely cannot find words to describe what they saw.

"Emotionally, there are people who are scared to death. Others suffer from a free-floating anxiety that something worse is going to happen—not an ideal atmosphere in which to heal. For some, there is hopelessness. Feelings of caring and joy, those things that make each day easier to live—people are being cut off from that. There's a lot of irritability too, people quick to temper—people's patience is now running counter to that sense of unity that defined the first week or two."

Bob and I nearly came to fisticuffs that night. It started simply enough. He said he was giving up his apartment to a stranger he'd met in a bar, some guy from out of town who needed a place, and that was that: They signed the lease by buying each other drinks.

Waitaminit, I told Bob, you're just giving the joint up to some random traveler, leaving all your possessions, not even taking a deposit—Bob said he trusted the man, enough that he, Bob, would in fact be paying the rent in advance for however long he was out of the country, and his tenant would simply leave the checks for him on his kitchen table.

"Bob, you're fucking nuts, man," I told him. "You're gonna just trust some dude you got drunk with the other night?"

"Ketcham, I know this guy, I mean I don't know him, but I know him, I trust him—"

"All right, bro, it's just you can't trust people, especially not now—"

And then Bob flipped.

"And all this is evil? All this is evil?" he swept an arm across the room, presumably across the city, across the country. Then I understood why he was angry. Because in his caustic pessimism and fury at the world, Bob nonetheless really believed that people were essentially good, and the terror of the falling towers had nearly broken his faith. That's why he left his door wide open in a dangerous neighborhood, that's why he was giving his apartment up to a stranger. It was a last act of faith, a clinging to hope. So when I rebuked him, he cursed me, rushed at me purple-eyed, his hair dark with sweat, he balled his fists, he stood an inch from my face—

"Fuck you, Ketcham! Fuck you fuck you fuck you! You're telling me I'm going to be robbed if I leave my door open, you're telling me this man is going to rob me—You think we're all evil? Go to hell, Ketcham."

"Listen—"

"Maybe you should get out of here."

When we finally shook hands after a long long silence, we decided to go to a bar and drink, we got on our bikes and rode, but somewhere along the way we lost each other. I doubled back, looking for him; I couldn't find him and he never showed up at the bar. He had said to me at the last minute, "I'll be back by New Year's. Promise." But we never had a proper parting, and I had a sick feeling that I'd never see him again.

And when I went home, I had this nightmare—with the terror of nightmare, the stunned waking: It is of an auction in a room full of dust and blank-eyed people on broken chairs. "Human. Sunday," the auctioneer cries out, pointing to a man in a display case, a living man, lying on his side on a bed with his back to the audience. He is not sleeping; resting quietly. "Human. Sunday," cries the auctioneer. "Human. Sunday." No one is bidding. They should be bidding, especially now in these dark days, why aren't they bidding?

Nothing Will Be
the Same

WRITING IN THE DARK

RICK MOODY

SEPT. 18, 2001—It's stupid to say so now, but I had a really hard time flying out of La Guardia on Monday. The shuttle was snarled up. Thunderstorms, mechanical problems.

The Attack—what else can I call it?—is a web of narratives that buckles at the World Trade Center and the Pentagon, and this is just my piece. I was going to D.C. to serve as a judge for the National Endowment for the Arts fellowships, and also to have dinner with the first girl I ever kissed. She lives in Charlottesville, Virginia, and agreed to meet me halfway. The dinner with this childhood acquaintance was heavy with the ravages of time, full of sadness, and I woke Tuesday wobbly from it, and headed down to the NEA offices, in the Old Post Office of D.C. Like any other morning, of course, guys hosing off the sidewalks, others on benches devouring bagels with coffee before work.

Up in the Endowment offices, we convened, and we amounted to twelve or so novelists, including some people I have long admired. We were just getting organized, when a deputy director of the Endowment, charged briefly with making a speech about our mission, mentioned that there was trouble in New York.

Everybody knew someone who was hurt in the last

WTC bombing, in 1993, and I guess I didn't think the Attack could be much more than that. A slap on the wrist, though outrageous and horrible. But Amy Osborn, my partner, my lover, works on Water and Wall, due east of the World Trade Center towers. I had trouble concentrating, therefore, while the director of the literature program was attempting to galvanize us with the sanctity of our mission. So I missed the sound of the Pentagon being struck by a jet. We were inside on the seventh floor. Immediately, though, the deputy director came back in to announce that the agency had been closed by executive order, like all government offices that morning. We rushed to the windows of the Old Post Office, where we could already see the plumes rising from the Pentagon.

I can't say I felt tremendous anxiety about Washington, unfortunately, though I was apparently here for the duration, since the airports were about to be closed. Instead, I felt awful about *not* being in New York, where so much difficulty was unfolding, awful about powerlessness, awful about estrangement. My cell phone was worthless, as were the land lines. We gathered up our manuscripts and applications and notes, because what else was there to do? Literature, if no better than a flower stuck in the barrel of a submachine gun, shouldn't be thwarted by brutality. Because it is one of the invaluable records of what came before and what came after. On foot, on Eleventh Street, heading for our hotel with another panelist, I heard an unmistakable explosion. It's not a sound like other sounds. And we're still debating it. Pentagon collapsing? The bomb in front of the State Department? Then the fighter planes began scrambling.

About the same time, the first girl I ever kissed, with her true gift for bad luck, was being evacuated from Reagan National, and *watching* the Pentagon explode. Airport security people were herding the last few unlucky passengers out into the parking lot, shouting anxious remarks about another plane apparently on its way toward the airport, the one that would soon crash outside of Pittsburgh.

In New York, my girlfriend, evacuated from her office building, attempted to catch a cab. Her driver was Middle Eastern; it was just one of those New York things. She made it only four blocks, abandoned the car because of gridlock and started across the Brooklyn Bridge on foot. When the first tower of the WTC began to collapse, and when the debris cloud billowed toward the east, people on the bridge began *to run*. Only a few calm heads managed to forestall the stampede.

I was in a room full of writers, too, during the night when the Iraqis began raining Scud missiles on Tel Aviv, and I learned then that writers react to calamity just like everyone else, except that they are a little quieter. On Tuesday, during the Attack, it took a while for the writers to begin to inquire into these webs of narrative that are our diagram of calamity, our strategy for survival: How did the hijackers get the *knives* onto the plane? Did they use Travelocity.com or other online services in order to select the flights they'd use? If this was such a large-scale operation, why did it require no more than knives and watches? Was the plane in Pennsylvania *shot down?* What's the insurance angle on all this? What were the exact contents of the white clouds of the WTC building collapses: sheet rock? Plaster? Asbestos? Paper? *Who were the lost and how did they live?*

Then we shut off the television and got to work. To make sure that the voices of Americans would ring out in this next darkness.

NO MORE HIGH HEELS

JANET FITCH

SEPT. 21, 2001—I guess what keeps hitting me most profoundly is that there were more than three thousand people in those two buildings and four planes, alive, setting out on their everyday business, and then they were gone. There you are, getting on your flight, checking your watch, your bottle of water in one hand and a fashion magazine in the other, or getting out of the subway and going up to work, thinking of the calls you need to make, the fight you had this morning with your kid . . . and then, you find out that you've had it. I kept putting myself in the position of those people on the planes, the ones trapped on the 101st floor of World Trade Center Tower One. That's it, I think. That's the end of it. Calling my husband, saying I love you, over and out. On a piece of paper, I wrote "Today is the last day of your life." Just to look at it. That's what I've been thinking about.

I have a hard time with abstractions. I always go to the personal. If that was me . . . What it would have been like to have been one of those numbers. If I were under the rubble, pinned under a girder, fifty feet below the surface, what would keep me going, what would sustain me in my despair? I realize I don't know enough poems by heart, I don't know enough songs, enough prayers. I don't hold enough of the world inside myself to sustain me through something like that. My thoughts about God are vague and abstract. My connection with the energy of the universe is shaky. That is what I think about.

Last night for a little relief, some friends came over. We had dinner and they brought a movie, *Men in Black*. A bit of a comedy, a bit of a thriller—safe, we thought. But there, behind Tommy Lee and Will, was the New York skyline, and there, the twin towers. Nobody said anything about it, nobody commented—nobody had to. I hear they're talking about airbrushing the twin towers out of backdrops and TV and movies. I can understand why Letterman would get it off the backdrop of his show, watched every night by so many millions; it would just be too heartbreaking.

On the other hand, I think that it's right and fitting that every so often, we do see those towers, rising there on the skyline, in a movie or an old TV show, and have that moment of grief. If you've lost a family member, you don't put her photograph away. You allow yourself that pang, because it is not bad to remember. We are accused of being a nation of amnesiacs, moving from one shocking news event to the next and not remembering what happened ten years ago. We don't remember, for instance, that we were the ones who built up the Taliban regime as a way of fighting against the Soviets—that was way back ten years ago. I want to remember the twin towers, I want to see them every so often, I want to feel that hurt, diminished with time but still present.

There are other ways I know this is going to affect me. I'll be damned if I'm going to be caught in high heels during any emergency. I won't be caught on the sixty-seventh floor because I'm a vain broad and I've got these stupid fashion items on my feet. I'll probably get a cell phone, something I've never wanted before. I am flying a flag in front of my house. I don't even know where it came from; I remember my daughter playing with it in nursery school. Maybe we gave money to disabled veterans or something. I think it'll come out every September 11. I know I will rupture into sobs whenever I sing "America the Beautiful"; it was always my favorite patriotic song, because it was never about bombs bursting in air, but rather a plea for God to help us be what we're trying to be.

I went to a memorial service at one of the big synagogues here in Los Angeles, and I found myself profoundly upset that they didn't search my purse, that there were no metal detectors, that there was no taking of license plate numbers in the parking lot. Not that I was really afraid a terrorist was going to blow up the Wilshire Boulevard Temple that night, but it seemed to negate the new seriousness that life has taken on for me after September 11. It's a new world, everybody knows it, why are they pretending it's not? I want to see its visible impact. I want them to rip apart my luggage, I want to be stopped because the steel shanks in my shoes set off the metal detectors. Is it masochistic that I want to feel this?

I only hope that as a nation, we can rally our determination to defend the very freedoms and ideals that distinguish our country from Taliban Afghanistan. We too had begun to step aside from the U.N. and the world community, allowing religious fundamentalists in this country to dominate our own national policy. Most specifically there was our refusal to pay our U.N. dues or to sign the U.N. initiative regarding the fate of the world's children because it might help women around the world achieve a degree of determination over their own bodies. I think many of Bush's supporters would love to see Taliban-style restrictions in our own country. I'm afraid that we project enemies and fail to see the enemy within ourselves; we project evil and fail to see the evil we ourselves harbor.

I'm left praying that the spiritual evolution many of us have struggled for in this country doesn't fly out the window in the face of "The Battle Hymn of the Republic," that we can retain what we know and temper what we feel in light of it. Can we, finally, distinguish the perpetrators from the innocent, justice from blind vengeance? The next months should tell it all.

CONSCIOUSNESS ON OVERLOAD

CAROLINE KNAPP

SEPT. 20, 2001—The sense of purposeless exhaustion set in around Day 4, Friday night, a fatigue that seemed both bone-deep and unjustified. Like me, most everyone I saw and spoke to that day was safe, insulated from the disaster, mere spectators. We hadn't lost loved ones, we'd only seen the devastation on TV and in pictures, we weren't involved in rescue efforts and so our weariness felt out of proportion and strange. I walked my dog that afternoon; the people I ran into looked uniformly shell-shocked and felt uniformly guilty about it, as though we hadn't quite earned our despair. Fear and horror—the dominant sensations earlier in the week—had given way to a vague heavy-hearted despondency by then. The stories of individual tragedy were beginning, cruelly, to blur. Even language had failed us, leaving most people I know with a single empty fallback word: "stunned." *I'm stunned. I don't know what to do with myself, I'm just stunned.* I went home that night, watched TV in a teeth-clenched, blank-faced way, and then fell into the darkest sleep.

I am not used to harboring such a wide variety of conflicting emotions at one time. Usually, it's one feeling at a time, maybe two. Anxiety here, contentment there. A dash of melancholy on a bad day; a flash of joy on a good one. By

Friday, and persisting well into this week, that simple synaptic system was all out of whack, consciousness on overload. This may be normal, but it's also deeply disorienting. The magnitude of the physical devastation; the fear about what it may unleash; the sense of sudden vulnerability; the reach of the grief, each life lost touching an incalculable number of other lives: This is more than an ordinary brain can process, and so the mind is left to flit from one sensation to another. It cannot land on just one, it cannot absorb them all.

Which is why the neurons seem to be firing from all directions. I feel enveloped in safety, insulated within my own little house and also deeply jittery. A plane flies overhead and I freeze: What is it? Who's on it? Is it about to crash? I feel compelled to watch footage of the towers collapsing over and over and over and then compelled to look away, not sure what's voyeurism and what's an attempt to grasp the ungraspable. One emotion surges only to be supplanted by its opposite.

A blind man tells a CNN reporter how his guide dog, a yellow Labrador retriever with the most noble gaze, led him to safety down eighty-seven flights of stairs, and the heart melts at the miracle, man and his brave attendant. Moments later, an executive breaks down in sobs on camera, seven hundred of his employees unaccounted for, among them his own brother, and the heart tightens and sinks, a stab of pure sorrow. The most heartening pride at human kindness mixes with despair at human hatred, often in the same instant. A woman I run into tells me she started to weep without warning on a subway train in downtown Boston and that a total stranger, a man sitting beside her, took her hand and held it, simply and firmly, for the duration of the ride. She felt so touched by this display of compassion she cried even harder, but then, when she left the subway station, she saw fresh graffiti on a wall: NUKE ISLAM.

How to reconcile all of this? I, a woman who's never responded to an American flag with anything more stirring than benign indifference, feel deeply, surprisingly, wholly patriotic and also, perhaps less surprisingly, deeply skeptical, mistrustful that our political and military response will be anything but rash, expensive, and short-sighted. I feel protective and defensive about the depth of hatred toward America, a mama bear guarding her cub, and I feel humbled, aware that we've played no small part in earning and fomenting that animosity. And I also feel ashamed, embarrassed by the self-constructed cocoon of ignorance and complacency I've been living in: Until last week, I could not have spelled the name Osama bin Laden, let alone told you what degree of threat his organization represented.

Our culture thrives on black-and-white narratives, clearly defined emotions, easy endings, and so this thrust into complexity exhausts. Too many feelings competing for head space, no happy ending in sight, no tacit belief that our minuscule attention spans will protect us this time, and little solace from our ordinary opiates—movies and sports and computer solitaire. The people I talk to feel an odd, almost adolescent yearning for leadership, craving and mistrusting it in the same breath.

Some of us feel compelled to reach out—give blood, light candles, sign petitions, anything!—and simultaneously compelled to retreat, edges of paranoia leaking in, talk of terrorists in the backyard. I feel catapulted from one extreme to another: protected one minute and vulnerable the next, heartsick and then detached, connected and then estranged, so full of goodwill one moment I'd like to hug the guy at Starbucks who pours me my coffee, so irritable the next I'd like to slap the man who cuts in front of me while I'm trying to pour milk. Mostly I feel unmoored, some rock of permanence and safety having given way to shifting sands, the familiar now eerily unfamiliar. Sirens sound different, scary and consoling at the same time. Work feels irrelevant. Normalcy as yet undefined.

I suppose this is what people mean when they talk about being stunned—this gamut of feeling, which overwhelms the psychic system, leaves you feeling exhausted and powerless and unable to tease out one emotion from the next—and I think the response is both human and frightening. Surely, it's one of terrorism's intended effects, to literally stun our morale, to blow up strength and will along with buildings, and the reaction is hard to counter.

On Saturday, still feeling blank and enervated, I spent part of the afternoon at a gathering of people who met to talk about caring for a mutual friend, a man who's dying of cancer at the age of forty-nine. The lens shifted suddenly, the unfathomably wide panorama of disaster yielding to a much more personal and individual close-up of tragedy, and it suggested something to me about the numbing effect of emotional overload, which can so easily mutate into a kind of hopeless despair. I did not particularly want to go to this meeting; I drove there feeling fragile and depressed, but I showed up anyway, and sat in a room with twenty other people, and faced a loss in a communal and reflective way. We talked about how we felt about watching our friend die, what we were scared of. We talked about practical things we could do: cooking meals, doing laundry, spending time with him.

Unlike the thousands of lives so hideously obliterated without warning, this man and the people who love him have an opportunity to approach death consciously and with foresight, to say things that need saying, to help one another without the mobilizing impetus of disaster. This, too, is exhausting work, but it's important work, its value immediate and tangible, and it reminded me that the line between feeling stunned and being passive can be very thin. I can give blood. I can send money to relief organizations, I can write letters and sign petitions. I can also be present and active in my own small world, which is a gift that cries out for recognition, even from this stunning roar of mixed emotion.

SEX IN A TIME OF TERROR

COLE KAZDIN

Editor's note: Some names have been changed.

SEPT. 21, 2001, NEW YORK—My sex-kitten friend Ruby met a cute man in a bar Saturday night and he walked her home. "I don't mean to be presumptuous," she said to him as they stood in an awkward moment in front of her building, "but do you want to come up?" Pause. He hesitated, so she jumped in to reassure: "No, no, no, not for terror sex—just to see my apartment."

Ruby didn't want him to get the wrong idea. And she had been noticing a new phenomenon among her close friends since Tuesday. The world had changed; so had relationships. Now, just about everyone she knew was having what she and her friends call "terror sex."

It sounded so inappropriate. We are experiencing horror and disbelief at what happened. We are grieving for friends, family, and even strangers, who were alive just last week. Thinking about sex in a time of crisis seemed cheap. It reeked of bad-movie cliché: Cue the majestic music. The sounds of war outside as the barrel-chested man comforts the weeping woman. She tells him she doesn't want to sleep alone tonight. "Hold me," she cries. And he does. A fighter plane zooms overhead.

Wait.

A fighter planed zoomed overhead. Really. They are flying over my house even as I write this, so nothing seems far-fetched. Anything can happen.

Sonia doesn't know exactly how it happened with her. Exhausted after a nearly ten-mile walk last Tuesday, she watched the news at a bar with friends, and one of them came home with her. The two went to her roof to watch the incomplete Manhattan skyline, still burning. The next thing she knew, they were making out.

"I didn't think about it at all," she said. "When you walk home from Manhattan to Brooklyn with people covered in dust and blood you don't care." She didn't want to be alone. She was in a daze, traumatized.

And the sex was incredible.

"We thought it was the end of the world." She paused and grinned. "Whoops." Still, the sex felt as if their lives depended on it. "We had sex like it was the end of the world, and if I could do it over again, I still would."

How can we make emotional room—amid the fear and confusion and personal loss—for any thread of sexuality? People are talking about their deepest emotions with total strangers; message boards are popping up all over the Web. We feel we need to connect with others more than ever before.

Connecting with others is almost an understatement in this case, says Dr. Peter Salovey, professor and chair of the department of psychology at Yale University. We have never faced anything like this before. People are questioning everything and reassessing their priorities. We are feeling that "life is precious and civilization is precarious," he says. In the anxiety and uncertainty, people are reattaching their bonds.

But why not just hug?

"You want some kind of homage to a life force," says Pepper Schwartz, professor of sociology at the University of Washington and author of numerous relationship books. "I'm alive, I'm functioning, I'm real. There's a euphoria, a triumph in sexuality that you can see why someone would want to do it as a very profound act." It is the deepest physical closeness, of course. Sex is basic in the most biological sense, she says. It is about flesh, tissue, heart.

Symbolically, it is profound as well. "It's not so much sexual arousal as it is wanting the security and the closeness that it represents," says Salovey. In trauma and tragedy, he said, it comes to represent closeness and commitment, rather than passion.

Schwartz says this connection can be particularly profound for men and that physical intimacy is often a direct line to the emotional equivalent for them.

Julie doesn't know how long she and her boyfriend, Martin, were just holding each other, terrified on the day after the attack, when he turned to her and said, "I want to make love to you."

"He's at his most vulnerable in that state," Julie said. "For him, it was a real need to connect on that level." It was different from the sex they had in everyday life. It was Important. There was urgency to it. She felt like he was going off to war and this could be the last time.

My grandmother felt the same way about fifty years ago. "Boys were going away and you didn't know if you were going to see them again," she told me. She was a teenager—gorgeous, brash—and she definitely liked to have a good time. Already, in her native Canada, the military boys that she danced with until long past her curfew had suddenly gone away.

She arrived in the U.S. around 1940. Then, Pearl Harbor left her and the rest of the country speechless. "Everything seemed irrelevant and unimportant," she remembered. War changed everything. It intensified relationships. And though what we now refer to as the baby boom officially erupted when the troops came home in 1946, my grandmother saw the beginnings of it in December 1941.

Today, many are predicting a new baby boom. Sara and her husband, like many New York couples, spent the entire day Tuesday frantically trying to find each other, each trying to get home, frustrated by the busy signals, emergency recordings and disabled cell phones. She foresees a lot of new babies nine months from now. "It's not like my husband and I have been having a lot of sex," she said. "But now I have this heightened awareness of how much I love him." After they were both safe and at home that night, "I kept saying to myself, 'I'm so grateful I have my husband, I'm so grateful I have my husband.'"

This kind of intensity leading to a new baby boom makes sense to Schwartz. "During crises, birthrates go up," Schwartz said. "People want to connect. It's life-affirming to feel your body attached to your head."

Back in the early 1940s, family friends introduced my grandmother to the man who was to become my grandfather. They married quickly. All her friends were doing the same. "We were 'war brides,' " she said. "It was a scary time. We used to talk about how the world was going to end."

This carpe diem attitude that many of us are feeling today inspires throwing caution to the wind. All of our emotions—not only passion—are heightened. And sometimes there are consequences. "People make promises," says Schwartz, "and then once their heightened sense of emotion is gone they say the emotional equivalent of 'just kidding.' That can be devastating."

But for many, being able to drop their guard, to be close and to live in the moment is a relief. Alberto and Jonathan recently started dating, and they weren't feeling very sexy last week. At home, the dust and smell of the burning buildings was unbearable. They sat on opposite ends of the couch, legs intertwined, and they talked, telling stories of their childhoods, getting to know each other.

"And that's weird for gay people," Alberto said. "I think gay people engage in hot sex first and intimate sex second. This was a beeline to intimate sex." He felt a connection that otherwise probably would not have developed until much later. Now, they are talking nonstop, calling to check in on each other; and when they do have sex, Alberto said, he feels something more intense about it. "The way we were touching felt more intimate."

Stephen found that same kind of intimacy in a sexual encounter with a virtual stranger, days after the attack. "We talked afterward," he said, almost incredulously. "Which I never do." Stephen was traumatized and almost speechless from witnessing both planes crash into both towers. He had been rushing to get to the World Trade Center for a temp job. He was running late, and watched the entire tragedy unfold, sitting on his bicycle on the Brooklyn Bridge.

"I was watching thousands of people die. Thousands more get maimed. And I felt like I had died." That night and the next day, he went to vigils, online to chat rooms, almost looking for love—or at least sex. "I wasn't horny," he said. But he wanted to be with someone. "I don't remember his name," he said. "But I will always remember him. We had sex as if it was our last time to have sex." Stephen said that for many gay men sex feels so readily available that, after a while, it almost becomes deadening. Now, that's all changed, he said. He almost laughed at himself when he called it "making love," but he was earnest.

"Whether you have sex with your husband of twenty years or a stranger on the street, it never feels like the last time," he said. But since the tragedy, it does. "Three thousand people had sex for the last time sometime last week."

For married couples who already feel that kind of intimacy that comes from being together for years, it's less about the sex act itself, and more about reconnecting.

"After twenty-seven years of marriage, you want your own space," said James. "But we've slept spooning lately." James received a hysterical cell phone call from his wife as she watched the World Trade Center explode from across the street. After spending what seemed like the longest day apart from each other, they gently hugged in reunion. "I said to her, 'I believe you are here'—not 'I don't believe you are here' but 'Yes, I believe you are here.' It was the only thing that felt real."

"Relationships are real," said Salovey. "Most gratification isn't from work, material things or routines, but from relationships."

And trauma makes that all the more salient. "Love is more potent than death," James said of his personal experience. "I believe in this moment right now more than I believed in any other moment up until now."

So perhaps it is not terror sex so much as it is a breed of love that touches strangers and longtime lovers across the board. Roberta and her husband would have been in Manhattan were it not for an appointment with her obstetrician in Long Island for a sonogram. She is four months pregnant. When she heard the news of the terrorist attack, she said it felt "not so much like the end of the world, but the end of our world if something had happened to the other one."

My grandmother thinks the whole idea of terror sex or terror love, though crass in phrasing, was inspiring in spirit. "It is possible," she says, "not only to fill the need to be close to another human being, but a belief in the future, that our children and grandchildren will continue to keep this beautiful country alive."

REQUIEM FOR A STRANGER

JENNIFER FOOTE SWEENEY

OCT. 12, 2001—I wait to read the page until I am on the subway, when I am surrounded but completely alone. I wait to read it until I've read everything else, except I don't read everything else, I read the headlines. It's like what manic-depressive author Kay Redfield Jamison said it was like to be taking too much lithium—at the moment I can't read anything that requires academic engagement, linear thought, or understanding. Not unless I have to.

But I can read these. And I do. All of them. I go in order of how the pictures hit me. I might start with a strapping trader who is shining—he's glistening—in a photo obviously taken at his wedding. ("He loved telling jokes, and he was not above stealing other people's anecdotes and improving them.") Then I might move on to the mother of four whose snap was taken on the fly, maybe at a special occasion in a restaurant, maybe by her eldest son. ("The boys knew that malingering in bed beyond that signal, unless you were really, truly sick, would not be wise.")

The obituaries in the Nation Challenged section of the *New York Times* used to be called "The Missing and the Dead." Now they are "Portraits of Grief." But this isn't what they are, or at least it isn't the only thing they are. They are the little baby books of grown-ups, paragraphs that remind me of the disparate facts, figures, and hanks of hair that parents place in silk-covered journals to get a handle on the giddiness of new life, and the fear of the unknown. It is an exercise in getting it down on paper: the first word, weight at birth, the first smile that wasn't gas. But these entries—produced in column inches by a battalion of eloquent journalists—hold the details of adults, some barely out of youth, and they mean to diffuse the terrific sadness of new death, the fear of forgetting:

"At home in Danbury, Connecticut, where he was born and raised, he was rebuilding a Volkswagen bug and learning to play the bagpipes."

"Their favorite food, Mr. Klein said, is salmon—the same as their mother's."

"Mr. McGinley was known for singing at every party, which he attended or gave, with 'Danny Boy' his most requested number."

"His wife said he had a distinct relationship with each of his children but a single message for all: 'Stop fighting.' "

" 'All his cousins wanted to be as cool as he was,' Mrs. Gazzini said."

It doesn't matter how dry, how seemingly absent of sentiment these details might be; they constitute, like the facts and figures of the baby book, information that is adorable, intimate, or hilarious. This is the found poetry of tiny non sequiturs gathered in haste. There is little for the record books, but volumes for aching strangers:

"She was the defiant one who returned from a Cancun vacation with a tattoo on her lower back."

"At Mr. Broghammer's fortieth birthday party, he allowed himself to be dressed in alpine shorts and lederhosen, as fifteen couples roasted him to the strains of 'The Sound of Music.' "

" 'Steve could not be quiet,' said Jim Hughes, his brother-in-law."

"As a boy of nine or ten, young Ramzi dug a hole in the backyard for a terrible report card and put a stone on top. 'He said it was dead and buried,' said his sister, Dina Doany Azzam."

"At family dinners he always sat at the head of the table."

It all adds up. The big story is sadness, as it would have to be, but the subplots are myriad: the secret lives of people in their twenties ("There was a little romance, on New Year's Eve 2000, with a scuba diving instructor at Club Med Martinique, but Ms. Hague was thinking she would like to meet a Southern guy, move back home to Parkersburg, West Virginia, and have a dog."); the truth about firefighters ("Off duty, he went to art museums, and watched Sister Wendy's art lectures on TV."); the enduring myth of New York ("It was the life he dreamed of—no need for a car, a party on every corner, and a job with overnight hours that came with one irresistible perk: He could work and watch the 11 P.M. edition of SportsCenter without interruption."); the cruelty of happenstance ("They had an appointment with a fertility doctor for this week.").

There is too much sweetness to mention, especially in the discovery by survivors that the people they loved were not entirely what they seemed. They were better. "Every time someone calls, I say, 'I didn't know that,'" said Mary Mercado, mother of Steve, a thirty-eight-year-old firefighter. Said Joyce Boland of son Vincent, "His friends are telling me that he was funny. I didn't know that."

These are the stories behind the homemade missing posters, the captions of hastily Xeroxed snapshots that gave us early hints about our losses and telegraphed the enormity of grief. But now there is more to know and there is so much more to worry about, so much more to mourn. With knowledge of who they were, with clues about what they planned to do, with evidence of their plans for later, we begin to imagine the scary resonance of these people's sudden disappearances. It feels important and unfathomable: Scott Hazelcorn is not going to buy an ice cream truck. Yvette Anderson will not open her dream restaurant. Charles Henry Karczewski will not be hiking in the Grand Canyon. Soccer coaches, football coaches, family chefs, a guy who was going to have a summer camp for needy kids—they are gone.

It is not hard to think about this as you might think about the extinction of a certain frog or a tree or a flower. Karen Joyce Klitzman once lived in Macao in a house wedged between a pig farm and a brothel. She escaped to Hong Kong on the weekends and then she taught English in Beijing, where she lived in a hovel with a suspicious landlady. She was an energy specialist. She played a crackerjack tennis game. Michael Asher kissed his wife, Diana, good-bye every morning while she was still asleep. Andrew Fisher, on his way to Kennedy Airport, pulled over and made his family get out of the car because his newly married sister was still holding her bridal bouquet and he wanted some photos of her tossing it. They are gone, so are thousands of others, their ghosts drifting from the twisted heap as welders do their business. There are huge holes in our atmosphere, now stuffed with fresh spirits. What will we do without them?

Maybe this is the reason that it is tempting to cut these stories out of the paper or at least circle words, underline phrases, keep a tidy stack that will never be recycled. These are beautifully written, vivid documents, not bland farewells. They are not obits meant for us to scan in an attempt to feel safe or young or immortal. Instead there is easy recognition and no fear in finding ourselves in these stories. Perhaps the reason is more grim than we imagined. Our new vulnerability tells us that these people—happy, interrupted, not close to done—represent the vanguard of an open-ended tragedy. The only difference between us and them is that they went first.

U2 ELEVATE NEW YORK

DAVID TALBOT

OCT. 29, 2001—The Irish are experts at grieving—and no band is more blessed at putting grief into song than U2. Last week Ireland's greatest contribution to music (along with Van Morrison) brought its "Elevation" tour to New York's Madison Square Garden; with its towers turned to dust and its people brought low, no city was in more need of elevation.

It was my first visit to New York since September 11 and the sorrow that hangs over this supremely self-confident city made it seem strangely unfamiliar. I bumped into an old acquaintance on the street one evening; he was hurrying to a counseling session for his two young children. They go to a school, he told me, that is near the World Trade Center and they saw too much that morning. He is a big man, from an established New York family, and I had remembered the way he seemed to plow through life. But now he seemed bent-shouldered in mourning.

He urged me to visit a SoHo gallery on Prince Street that had been turned into a photo archive of the city's calamity—hundreds of professional and amateur pictures of war-torn lower Manhattan, the sale of which is benefiting the orphans of September 11. When I went the next day, a line of somber people stretched down the street and around the corner. Inside the gallery, the crowd shuffled quietly and respectfully from one haunting image to the next, a crushed fire helmet, a man collapsed in tears on the shoulder of a policeman. The photo exhibit, titled *Here Is New York*, has become one more wake where the city bids farewell not only to its dead but to its sense of invulnerability.

But it's the wound known as "ground zero" that attracts the most people. They come by the thousands each day, the suffering and the morbidly curious, like the crowds drawn to the statues of bleeding saints. The morning I visited, a blaring headline in the New York *Daily News* warned that the monumental pile of rubble is a toxic dump. As soon as I got out of my cab at a National Guard roadblock near the site, the stench announced itself, as alarmingly wrong as the smell of an electrical fire. I walked past Trinity Church, ghostly in its coating of dust, its wall covered with flowers and posters with condolences from mourners who have trekked from London and Bali and Tel Aviv. We filed past a police barricade, one block from the wreckage. On the corner, a street vendor wearing a gas mask sold red, white, and blue scarves. There were hundreds of people on the streets, but it was as quiet as a funeral procession.

The noise level at Madison Square Garden on Thursday night, the second of U2's three sold-out New York shows, was a lot higher, but there was a similar seriousness of purpose. One of the most frequent criticisms of U2 over the years—aimed mainly at lead singer and lyricist Bono—is that they take themselves too seriously. They clearly see their mission as spiritual as well as musical, although this is leavened by occasional self-mockery. ("Have you come here to play Jesus / To the lepers in your head?") But the audience on Thursday night was on the exact same wavelength—they had come to party hard and to cry, and U2 delivered the Irish wake they were looking for.

No rock band's body of work seemed more appropriate for the occasion. U2's songs have often ached with suffering and loss, from "One Tree Hill" to "Peace on Earth" ("They're reading names out over the radio / All the folks the rest of us won't get to know / . . . Their lives are bigger than any big idea.") And some of their music is a direct rebuttal to the cycle of terror and revenge that has wracked their own land ever since they were boys. When, in the middle of "Sunday Bloody Sunday," Bono screamed, "I'm so sick of it," his anguish seemed to resonate throughout the arena, although New York's suffering has decades to go before it matches Belfast's.

When Bono sang "wipe your tears away," he touched his face with an American flag someone had handed to him from the front rows. "How long must we sing this song?" asks Bono in "Sunday," and the answer might come soon, at least as it relates to Northern Ireland's homegrown terror. The week U2 came to New York, among the only hopeful international news was the report that the IRA had finally decided to dismantle its arsenal, in part because of the revulsion against terrorism even among key Irish-American supporters in cities like New York and Boston after September 11.

There was a chord of nationalism in the air at Madison Square Garden—people waving the Irish flag ran around the upper aisles and more than once a loud round of "U.S.A., U.S.A.!" erupted from the crowd. But Bono's comments on the war were more elliptical. Between songs, he spoke of the need to "destroy their weapons" and he vowed, "We're not going back."

Yet much of the band's song selection was pro-peace. If war was unavoidable, Bono seemed to be communicating, it was not an occasion for celebrating. The band under-scored the costs of war with their version of Marvin Gaye's "What's Going On," which Bono and a host of other stars recently recorded to aid the victims of September 11. And they used "Pride (In the Name of Love)" to pay tribute to America's great apostle of nonviolent struggle, Martin Luther King Jr., punctuating the song with a video clip of his "I've Been to the Mountaintop" speech delivered the day before he was shot, which always brings a catch to the throat: "I may not get there with you . . ."

U2's main mission that evening was to bind New York's wounds, a role that musical concerts and TV benefits have played very effectively in recent weeks. The crowd was eager to celebrate its besieged city, and the band gave them the perfect opportunity when they broke into the opening chords of their metropolitan homage, "New York," from their most recent album, which was quickly greeted by a collective roar and thousands of fists pumping the air. Bono introduced the song by praising the city's "tolerance, atti-tude, courage, and heart." But the lyrics about New York's global diversity now carried a bitter irony: "Irish, Italian, Jews and Hispanics / Religious nuts, political fanatics . . . Living happily."

The concert often verged on becoming a religious cere-mony, with the Edge's distinctive chiming guitar never sounding more celestial. For secular baby boomers like me, raised on the idea that music can save your soul, emotion-ally charged shows like this have provided the only oppor-tunities for catharsis during the past few weeks.

The evening's emotional peak came when the band played "One." As Bono sang, "We're one / But we're not the same / We get to carry each other," a massive white screen behind him was suddenly filled with the names of the flight crew and passengers from United Flight 175 and

American Flight 11, as well as the firefighters and police officers who had lost their lives on September 11.

The names scrolled up the screen and then kept slowly ascending toward the ceiling, ghosts of white light against the vast darkness of the arena's cathedral heights. Next to me, a woman with tears in her eyes held up her cell phone so, she said, a friend who could not be there could hear the song.

Toward the end of the show, Bono urged New Yorkers to lay down their sorrows and launched into "Walk On" ("And I know it aches / And your heart it breaks / And you can only take so much, walk on"). The song's closing stanza urges us to leave behind "all that you fashion / All that you make / All that you build / All that you break." I know the blessing the band meant to give, that you can find solace in transcending worldly cares. But for me, someone who lacks this Buddhist sense of clarity, it was too hard to let go of the physical symbols of what we have lost.

The next day, I bought a beautiful black-and-white print of the lower Manhattan skyline as it once was, dominated by the gleaming World Trade Center towers. I had forgotten how soaring they were. A Russian street vendor was selling these eerie portraits of the past and he said he was doing a brisk business. I wanted something to help my seven-year-old son to remember.

He is dazzled by skyscrapers and mountain peaks and is forever asking questions like how many Empire State Buildings, piled end on end, it would take to reach the top of Mount Everest. Last fall, we took him to New York for his first visit. After eating dinner in an Italian restaurant in TriBeCa, he and I stood outside on the sidewalk, staring up at the impossibly tall towers, bathed in moonlight and mist. We tried to count every floor. It was the last time I really gave them a good look.

KING KONG'S HOME
AWAY FROM HOME

STEPHANIE ZACHAREK

SEPT. 21, 2001—Suddenly, here in New York, everyone is missing a building no one ever much cared for before.

In the days after September 11, people riding over the Manhattan Bridge from Brooklyn on the subway would, almost to a person, gaze out the window at that incomprehensible mass of smoke, an inadequate placeholder for the glossy dual monoliths that by all rights should still be there. More than a week later, people still look out—not everyone, or at least not all at once. But it's a given that everyone's feelings about the World Trade Center have changed: Its absence is a presence in itself. The hole it's left is much bigger than the building ever was.

New Yorkers are used to seeing their city reflected back at them from movie screens: We see familiar streets dotted with restaurants or shops we've visited, and public parks where we've walked our dogs. Most of all, we're used to seeing our buildings, particularly our skyline. Every city's skyline has its own memorable contours, but New York's—perhaps for no better reason than as moviegoers we've seen it so often—is the most iconic.

The view from a subway window isn't much like a movie screen. But in a pinch, it will do. The subway ride in that first week was something of a trial run—a way of adjusting to the new skyline, but also of getting ready for the weirdness of having it reflected back at us in its new state. The New York of the movies, specifically the buildings that make up its skyline, belongs to everybody, not just to New Yorkers. Better to reckon with it in the harshness of broad daylight than in the darkness of a movie theater, a place that we all prefer to think of as a source of pleasure.

Getting ready to adjust to a world of movies with no World Trade Center means coming to terms with what the building meant when it was still standing. Before September 11, it was almost a full-time job for many New Yorkers to pretend the World Trade Center didn't exist. Unless you worked in or near it, it was pretty much a "tourist thing." In a noisy patchwork of a city with so many incredible little pockets, so many smallish neighborhoods with so many eminently charming buildings, it was just too *obvious*.

But secretly, when no one was looking, we loved it. In the daytime it stood guard over the city, gazing straight up Fifth Avenue, more benevolent than imposing. I know for a fact that tourists weren't the only ones who'd look for it if, emerging from the subterranean bustle of a subway station, they needed to orient themselves quickly.

And lit up at night, its magnificence always pulled you up short. When I look at pictures of the old nighttime skyline now, I see the World Trade Center as a gorgeous, dignified misfit, too tall for all the buildings around it, and just not caring because it was *all that*. It was confident without being arrogant; its size made it glamorous, but its simplicity made it elegant. It was so New York.

This past week, New Yorkers returned to work, putting a brave face on the act of returning to normal—as rough as things have been, we're all happy to have the attempt at normalcy to keep us busy. But I've noticed that no matter what part of the city I'm in, I'm always aware of my location in relation to the ruins, and other New Yorkers have said the same. We desperately need to be in touch with where that building used to be; the space it occupied, no matter what is or isn't built on it in the future, will always mean something to us. It's a new point on our compass, a necessary addition to north, south, east, and west.

People around the country can't feel precisely the same way, of course, but there's no doubt that to almost everyone a New York with no World Trade Center is just plain wrong: They've all seen the pictures of our skyline, with its two front teeth knocked out. People have talked about how strange it will be to fly into the city without the welcome of those towers.

If part of what America does when it feels lousy is go to the movies, this might be a good time to reconsider John Guillermin's 1976 remake of *King Kong*. People laughed at it when it came out (perhaps thinking that it wasn't in on its own jokes—although I'm not sure how that could be, given that it features a giant oil corporation named "Petrox"). But even those who don't care for the movie can't deny now that its producer, Dino De Laurentiis, knew a star when he saw it. And in every one of its scenes, the World Trade Center is a natural.

The building's big entrance doesn't happen until the last half-hour of the movie, but it's foreshadowed at the beginning: In Kong's island habitat there are two large rock formations rising straight up from the horizon like towers. It's only natural that Kong, displaced in nighttime New York, would catch sight of the World Trade Center's brightly lit twin towers and head for them. To him, they look like home.

As cinematographer Richard H. Kline shows them to us, they're incomparably beautiful: They fill up the frame, silent and sparkling. The only decoration worthy of them is the bright disk of moon hanging nearby. Later, as Kong begins to climb, we see the building's ground-level decorative grillwork—grillwork that we've seen countless times on news footage, a bent and mangled tracery of metal standing, cathedral-like, silhouetted against mounds of rubble. In *King Kong*, the sight of it, in its proper place and serving its proper function, is soothing.

The World Trade Center comes to little harm in *King Kong*. Save for a moment when a dazed helicopter crashes against its exterior, which is difficult to watch, the building emerges unscathed. (It is poor Kong, a poetic hero with a leathery chest, who meets his tragic end at the very top.)

Just as the memory of those two tall rocks triggered impulses of longing and joy in Kong, the World Trade Center has made an indelible imprint in ours. It lives on in countless movies, mostly as a supporting player in the skyline, sometimes as a cameo in an establishing shot. There has been plenty of talk, in the press and in casual conversation, about how it will look to us in the movies from now on. Reportedly, its image is already being removed from some completed movies—as if it were remotely possible to erase the memory of something so goddamn big!—and a trailer for the forthcoming film *Spider-Man* that prominently featured the twin towers has been recalled.

Will the sight of the World Trade Center, in either new movies or old ones, bring people down? Will it remind them of a horrible event they desperately wish they could forget?

Something tells me that the answer is no. On Wednesday night, in New York, there was a screening—one populated by both critics and civilians—of a new movie that's set here in the city, partly downtown in SoHo. In one scene, the camera gazed idly down one of those narrow SoHo streets, a corridor of shops and restaurants and pedestrian traffic, a textbook shot that normally wouldn't make you look twice. And there at the end, not the focus of the shot but a clumsy bystander who happened to be in the way, was the World Trade Center.

The sound that swept across the audience in a ripple was a murmur of surprise and delight, the kind of sound that slips out of you before you realize it, a spontaneous "Oh!" I had the sense of a roomful of people leaning forward in their seats just a bit, involuntarily, as if the screen had a kind of pull on them.

A few people, after they'd composed themselves, clapped. But the "Oh!" that rose up from that audience was nothing so obvious as a wince or a shout or a mournful cry. New Yorkers are fond of sighing—it's part of the city's unspoken but not unfriendly language—and this was a sigh that encompassed a universe of things that under normal circumstances, New Yorkers would never say:

"There it is!"

"Gosh, it's big!"

And last, the biggest, most overwhelming rush of feeling: "I never thought it would look so beautiful."

The Enemy

DECIPHERING SUICIDE

JEFFREY EUGENIDES

SEPT. 26, 2001—The president insists that we are dealing with an enemy who strikes from the shadows, an enemy who kills and runs for cover. But the hijackers, terrifyingly, left the shadows and struck in full daylight, with the whole world watching. They didn't kill and run for cover but, in killing, killed themselves.

Had the hijackers survived the attack on the World Trade Center, we would now be reserving a large measure of our retribution for them. Timothy McVeigh fled the scene of the Oklahoma City bombing and, whether or not he acted alone, the person we most wanted to catch was McVeigh himself.

The suicide bombers have short-circuited the cry of an eye for an eye. They are beyond the reach of our vengeance now, and so that vengeance has become distinctly second order: We must catch not the murderers but the planners. Consider how quickly the hijackers are beginning to fade from the scene. At first the papers were full of their photographs. But soon another face replaced them—that of Osama bin Laden. It's as though, by dying, the hijackers have gotten away.

Suicide flows from many sources: despair, anger, mental illness, and sometimes even grandiosity. Much has been said of the celestial rewards reserved for holy warriors. But

what motivated the terrorists to commit this atrocity had
less to do with the next world than with this one. Aside
from the sexual pleasures of paradise, a good part of what
they were after was self-glory. They wanted to emerge
from invisibility, to get even for a hundred slights, to be
remembered back home, and to prove their manhood by
striking against a power that they believe to be a mad ele-
phant loose in the world and trampling it.

I read in the *New York Times* the other day that the con-
cept of suicide bombing goes back to the eleventh century,
having its origins with the Assassins. This keeps it in the
Islamic tradition. My friend Edwin Frank, however, pointed
out to me that such an act is not unknown in the Old
Testament. Samson was an Israelite at a time when the
Philistines held sway over Israel. Blinded and made to perform in a house containing three thousand people, Samson
cried: "'Lord God, remember me and strengthen me only
this once . . . so that with this one act of revenge I may pay
back the Philistines for my two eyes.' And Samson grasped
the two middle pillars on which the house rested. And he
leaned his weight against them, his right hand on one and
his left hand on the other. Then Samson said: 'Let me die
with the Philistines.' "

President Bush wants to frame the argument around the
notion that what is being attacked is our freedom. On
CNN Karen Hughes insisted that the terrorists hated the
fact that she could work outside the home. We don't help
ourselves by oversimplifying the causes of the horror visited on the country on September 11. Was it really an
abstraction like freedom the terrorists were lashing out at?
Would a thirty-three-year-old Egyptian national give his
life to keep American women from working? People do not
generally kill themselves in order to change social customs
on the other side of the globe. The women's suffrage

movement provoked no suicide missions from the Middle East. A number of suffragettes committed suicide themselves, taking no one with them. In their case, as in the self-immolations of Buddhist monks during the Vietnam War, suicide became a heroic act.

With the hijackers it is otherwise. They are seeking no clearly stated political end, only destruction, pain, and revenge. They lacked the heroism of martyrs; all they had was the violence. Nevertheless, that many people in the world feel constrained to commit such atrocities is not something we in the West should take lightly. To resort to biblical formulations, to call them "evil-doers" and leave it at that, is to regress to a fundamentalism of our own. For reasons of security as much as anything else, we can't ignore the social and political conditions that brought about this vicious attack. But neither should we be moved to empathy by an act whose barbarity eliminates all possibility of moral suasion.

President Bush dignifies the attack by calling it an assault on freedom. In reality it was nothing so philosophical as that. The hijackers' suicides inspire no admiration from their enemies, only fear. The terrorists operate out of an impoverished moral imagination and so cannot lay claim to justice. If we are scared now—and we are—we should take comfort from the fact that the suicide bombers do not understand the power of suicide, and so cannot harness it. There is more to martyrdom than merely dying.

THE MARTYR IN WAITING

ASRA Q. NOMANI

OCT. 19, 2001, ISLAMABAD, PAKISTAN—"Seventy-five paisa," the soft-spoken, bespectacled young man says from behind the photocopy machine.

At first he claimed it was a rupee a page, but after I gently raised my eyebrows, he immediately lowered the price. I later confirmed that seventy-five paisa is at the bottom end of what's charged around here for a decent photocopy, using the thinner, Pakistani A4 paper (imported paper starts at one rupee a page).

I'm making photocopies to show my stories to some of my sources and family here. He observes a photo of Mohammad Sohail Shaheen, the Taliban's deputy ambassador in Islamabad, on a story I wrote about a recent visit with Shaheen and his two wives at their house.

To most patrons of this store, he would just be the "photocopy walla," the photocopy guy. But he has another identity. "I trained in Kandahar," he tells me softly, in Urdu. Oh. "I'm ready to go now to become a *shaheed*," he says. He doesn't know, or prefers not to say, who ran the camp he attended—was it al-Qaida?—though when he went, in 1998, the area was firmly under the control of the Taliban, so it surely had its stamp of approval. He says he's ready and wants to go back to fight the U.S.-led coalition. *"Insha'allah,"* he says. God willing.

But for now, the imam at his mosque told the congregation gathered for *jummah*, Friday prayers, that the Taliban didn't need *afraad*—manpower—yet. (They did, however, request blankets.) So he waits. (The Pakistani government has warned mullahs to refrain from rallying *mujahids*.)

Qaiser Nadeem is just twenty, with only the slightest bits of mustache and beard sprouting from his young face. He is wearing a simple monotone-colored cotton *shalwar kameez* when I first meet him at a video store where he works, surrounded by what are likely bootleg copies of *Mulan, Alice in Wonderland, Small Soldiers*, and a whole row of *The Little Mermaid*, along with, of course, the copy machine behind which he stands. He's somewhat difficult to speak with because he averts his eyes from mine. The Quran warns against mixed-gender eye contact with anyone other than a relative, lest it create lustful thoughts. But he does talk to me, this Western Muslim woman journalist, and after a while I let my eyes drift to the copy paper as I speak, hoping to make him comfortable enough to keep talking.

It would be easy to portray Nadeem—an aspiring *mujahid* willing to cross the border and battle the U.S.-led forces in the name of Islam—as the product of the zealotry that sways uneducated youth into a blind hatred for the West. He doesn't hate the West, he says. He doesn't like its culture and doesn't like selling it from the shelves of the store where he works. It's a job, though, he says. He looks down upon what he sees as a decadent lifestyle. Most of all, he hates its foreign policy, particularly its support of Israel.

"If they did the right thing, then nobody would hate America," he said.

The next time we meet, we sit curbside in front of Toy Land 2 at Jinnah Super Market, a toy store with a stack of toy boxes piled outside, including the Just Start Scooter. I have a sense of irony about the place; the last time I was here in 1992, my cousins had arranged a secret meeting with the man I was about to marry on the eve of our wedding. As in other cultures, it's considered unlucky over here for a husband and wife to see each other before their wedding (and in many arranged marriages that's the first time they're meeting), and I guess it turned out to be unlucky. Though this was a "love marriage," it was supposed to follow the same rules as an arranged marriage. But when we both showed up at Jinnah Super Market, escorted, of course, by our battalion of cousins (all of whom have insisted on anonymity in these dispatches), we broke one of the key rules.

Now I sit next to this young man, both of us looking off in other directions to avoid eye contact. He explained that his transformation began after a cousin came back from Kandahar several years ago a more religious man, preaching against music, television, and those who didn't pray the requisite five times a day. Nadeem was living a modern life, watching Bollywood movies, not very religious, mostly a troublemaker, he says. But he was intrigued, and crossed the border around this time of the year in 1998 to train in Kandahar.

What was the training camp like? He broke into a grin.

"*Bahoth acha laga.*" I liked it a lot.

"*Bahoth maza atha tha.*" It was lots of fun.

"*Bahoth suhkoon hoe thah hay.*" There is lots of peace of mind.

In his daily life, he says, he has to squeeze time out of a day in which he works from 10:30 A.M. to midnight in this video store that belies his religious convictions, only to eke out a monthly salary of about two thousand rupees (about $30.76).

At the camp, "*dhimagh saf hoejah thah hay.*" Your mind gets cleansed.

The camp lasted three months, and was attended by about two thousand others, like himself, he said. They woke up around 1 A.M. to 2 A.M. for a special *namaz*, prayer, called "*tahajjud*," which isn't one of the day's five required prayers, but falls between the night's *isha* prayer and the predawn *fajr* prayer, earning special *sawab*, blessings. (I'm familiar with the prayer because my *dadi*, my father's mother, often falls asleep in her chair praying this *namaz*, battling sleep to earn those extra blessings.)

They would go back to sleep and then rise again before dawn at 5 A.M. for *fajr namaz*. Then they had *thalawath*, reading of the Quran and *durs*, lectures about the Quran.

That was followed by light exercise, he said, to get the blood circulating, including jumping jacks. Around 8 A.M., they'd eat breakfast that always included *roti* (bread) and *chai* (tea) (which he considered "first class").

Military training would begin afterward, learning to shoot a firearm—pistols and Russian-made Kalishnikovs— many of which were provided by the CIA to the Afghan *mujahedin* during its war against the Soviet Union. The trainees, for the most part, took aim at a bucket or a rock, making fun of each other when any of them missed the target. Then they broke for lunch, the afternoon's *zoh'r namaz* and a two-hour nap until 4 P.M.

They awoke for the day's third prayer, *as'r namaz*. There would be more *durs*, until around 6 P.M. or 6:30 P.M. They would pray the sunset *magrib* prayer, eat dinner, and gather again for *taleem*, study. And, then, the night's last prayer, *isha*, before going to sleep.

He knows the stereotype about students like himself being the blind followers of Mullah Omar and Osama bin Laden. He says, in Urdu, with a couple of English words parachuting into his thoughts, "*Onkee guidance hay.*" I have their guidance.

"May tho kodh say soch kur kurthah hu." I do it with my own thinking.

And becoming a martyr for Islam is something he has thought about a lot. "My most important thing is my life. If I can give that then I will give my life," he said. What would he accomplish? "If I was successful for Islam, then Taliban will survive."

That's all he has time for, so he gets up and returns to work, where he reluctantly pulls *Little Mermaid* down from the shelf for a customer. But all the while, awaiting orders to move across the border.

AT HOME WITH THE TALIBAN

ASRA Q. NOMANI

OCT. 10, 2001, ISLAMABAD, PAKISTAN—Welcome to the other White House.

It sits here at the intersection of two narrow dirt lanes, pocketed with bumps and jolts, very different from the wide, tarred streets in the posh neighborhoods diplomats call home. There are no *chokidars*, guards, sitting outside the squat attached houses virtually atop each other. There is a tin shack, a *khoka*, at the corner with a sign for Al-Asif Paints on one side, sundries for sale inside, including three-rupee packets of Pantene hair conditioner attached to each other like a necklace from the low ceiling.

The house at the corner has its name carved onto the front wall, much like many houses in this part of the world: White House, in curling Urdu script. Inside lives the No. 2 diplomat representing the Taliban government here in Pakistan. Mohammad Sohail Shaheen, burly, bearded and wearing a turban, has frequently stood at the right hand side of Mullah Abdul Salam Zaeef, the Taliban ambassador in Pakistan, as both have denounced the U.S.-led coalition's attacks on Afghanistan as an act of terrorism. Surely for many Western viewers, after Osama bin Laden, these men have represented the faces of twenty-first-century caveman barbarism.

On Tuesday, word trickles out of confirmed civilian

deaths. The latest: four Afghan United Nations workers. The first day's bombing has the Taliban claiming that as many as twenty civilians have died. The Taliban spokesmen say the death of civilians in Kabul is no different than the murder of thousands in the World Trade Center. "That was terrorism. This war is a terrorist act."

What I am warned in my two visits to the home of this Taliban representative, drinking green tea with his two wives, many of his eight children trickling through, is that America may win Kabul but it won't win the war. "It will be a very long, long war. Bloodshed. Destruction. We have fought the Soviet Union for ten years. We know." It's a grim prediction that more echoes President Bush, with his warnings of a long-fought war on terrorism, than Pakistan's president, General Pervez Musharraf, who has asked for a "short, sharp" attack that will end it all quickly.

Even if the Taliban loses power, Shaheen says, they will fight as rebels against a new leader in Kabul. "They will be like somebody in a cage. We will take over the highways and provinces. They will be in a prison in Kabul. Life will not be normal. Then, one day, they will have to negotiate after destruction."

"We have thousands of caves in the mountains that cannot be destroyed by bombing," Shaheen continues. "If this problem had been solved by talks, it would have been better for America and for Afghanistan. History shows superpowers become micropowers. Look at the British. Once such an empire. The sun never set on the British Empire. Now, its power is limited to an island in Europe."

He uses the kind of American colloquialism you'd expect from a retired three-star U.S. Marine. "We know war is not a picnic."

His mobile rings once while we speak. Maybe 450 civilians have died? He calls the Taliban foreign minister in

Kabul. The report is false. He laughs into the phone. He relates that he has asked the twenty-something foreign minister: "Are you afraid?" The response in Pashto, he says: *"Hitchkulah."* Never.

This is my second visit to Shaheen's house. The first time was before the bombings and I was escorted and expected. This time I arrive only with my cousin, who joins me because she too is curious to see the face of a Taliban. We stand outside, able to hear the crackle of a shortwave radio through the door that leads into the sitting room. This was where Shaheen sat during my first visit—without a turban but rather a simple white cotton *topi*, hat. The room is used for male visitors, and I wonder if a meeting is in process.

I come back wondering if stepping into this private world—under a massive attack seemingly from the entire world—would possibly dismantle the enemy image. I've brought along a few of the souvenirs that I bought before leaving New York: three New York City skyline postcards (one for Shaheen, one for his first wife, one for his second wife), three New York City key chains (one for each of them), and a New York Police Department pen (for the second wife). When I couldn't find my pen during my first visit, she gave me one and said, *"Thofa,"* in Urdu, gift. On the pen were images of foreign currency emblazoned with a simple word, "Euro," and I smiled at this symbol of Western capitalism from a woman literally behind purdah, the rule that separates women from men.

I knock on another door, one through which I can't hear the radio. I know it leads to the very small hall where, during the last visit, the women ran, scampering in bare feet on the terrazzo floor from the sitting room when they thought a stranger, a man, was about to venture inside. I wear my *dupatta* like an aunt taught me to do when I was thirteen, so not a strand of hair tumbles out. It's pulled back a little farther than regulation; the top of my hair at my forehead peeks out. My cousin impresses me; she's a practicing Muslim but wraps her *dupatta* lightly over her head. I bind mine tightly, to keep it from falling off. Or, perhaps, out of fear that it might come off.

I can't remember the name of the second wife, even though I can describe her porcelain face to the slightest detail, from the black liner that frames the inside of her eyes to the faint pink lipstick that brought a gentle color to her face. Shaheen politely asked ("It is my wish. It is our culture") that I not publish her name for the traditional reasons of privacy that keep her inside the house, so I let it slip from my mind, and I suddenly feel terrible about that.

I peek inside and see a little girl on the stairs beside the window. She sees me. She wails in fear and runs away. Whoops.

We stand long enough for me to notice the screen bent from the doorframe like a dog-eared worn novel. The door creaks open. It's the second wife, her *dupatta* draped gently over her head, like my cousin's. She greets me with a long hug. I introduce my cousin, and we enter.

My cousin crosses her legs to sit on the floor upon one of the thin, deep purple cushions that line the edge of the small sitting room. I spot her through the frame of the door. She looks more than a slight bit uncomfortable in this room of only men. I slip off my scruffy black rubber sandals that look perpetually dirty and step into the sitting room, relieved that Shaheen, talking on the phone, greets me with a broad smile. I move to sit down, but then remember the pen I want to give the wife, so I step into the kitchen where she stands at the stove and give it to her.

She smiles and takes the NYPD pen and postcard, with the

Empire State Building and World Trade Center sparkling in the night skyline.

I slip back into the sitting room. There are two kind of scary-looking men opposite my cousin and me. Big, burly, bearded. The blades of the ceiling fan cast dark shadows spinning above them. Shaheen gets off the phone and I apologize for arriving unannounced. "No problem," he says.

Shaheen is a young-looking forty-five, given to smiles and wistful thoughts. I give him one of the postcards of the New York night skyline and a key chain. Perhaps it seems odd that I'm giving this man, a Taliban leader, a picture of the World Trade Center. The postcards, unfortunately, were among the only cheap gifts I stocked up with in New York before I left. Though they're cheap gifts, I knew that, even over here amid anti-American slogans, there is an intrigue about the West, transforming these otherwise tacky souvenirs into sentimental treasures. And the towers were also the topic of a previous conversation I had with Shaheen two days earlier. He had once lived in Flushing, New York, as the Taliban's representative to the United Nations, he said, and had even visited Windows on the World, the restaurant on top of World Trade Center Tower One. He smiles when I hand him a postcard.

I put my finger over the image of the World Trade Center. "Now it's gone," I say, stating the obvious.

"Yes," he says, "very sad."

He says that he, like many from this part of the world, would like to return to America. "We are not against America or Americans," he says. "We are against the arrogance of intimidation.

"We are also human beings. We have not sprouted in the soil, not come down from the skies. We have families, fathers, mothers, like other human beings.

"I like America. I like Americans," he says. "I just don't like American foreign policy."

What is it that he likes about America? I ask. The spirit of rigorous research in all fields, he says. The professional work ethic. The strength of technology. Freedom of speech.

"I like that they can freely criticize," he says.

He used to criticize even the Taliban, Shaheen says, as a journalist covering the mujahedin uprising against the Soviets, and the days afterward when he was editor of the Kabul *Times*. What kind of criticism? Like money laundering, he says. Like the time electricity poured through a Taliban official's house even though the other houses in the neighborhood were dark. He wrote an exposé that prompted the Ministry of Water and Power to yank the electricity from the official's house.

We sit here now as his second wife, about twenty-two years old, maybe twenty-three (I ask him, he's not sure) pours Afghan green tea in clear glass mugs for my cousin and me, her *dupatta* pulled forward so far that it hangs like Little Red Riding Hood's cape, shielding her from the eyes of Big Bad Wolves. When she is finished she sits elegantly between us with her back to the men.

Shaheen's mobile phone rings. I tell the second wife that when she left the room, my cousin had said she had the bearing of a princess. I say it loud enough for her husband to hear. He smiles with mischief on his lips. Off the phone now, he pleads for us not to tell her such things.

"Her power will only increase?" I ask, as his wife leans forward with a smile, mischievous also, and tweaks the top of his right hand.

On my first visit, I noticed that she seemed feisty with her husband, never disrespectful, just alert, like when she admitted freely that she learned Urdu watching Bollywood movies. And like everyone else, I'm deeply interested in the

Taliban, and the stories of their oppression of women. Their relationship intrigues me.

She's both feisty and girlish. She knows all about India's Brad Pitt, an actor named Salman Khan. Her husband knows nothing about Salman Khan.

She has power, her husband answers. "She has power of voice," he says. "Her mouth power is stronger than mine. For every one thing I have to say, she has seven things to say."

He smiles. She smiles. He calls her his student, some-one with whom he discusses politics. She clearly has a strong opinion about many things—including the fact that she is a second wife.

His first wife filters into the room, but I'm not sure she is his wife until later. She is older, perhaps his age, and weak from years of being ill, he explains. And she is very frail-looking, with bluish tattoo tribal markings on her "third eye," between her eyebrows, and a spot on her chin below her lips. He writes into my notebook the province from which she comes: Paktya Province. He explains to me that when she grew sick, she could no longer take care of her household duties. So some six years ago, the marriage proposal went out to another young girl.

"They are happy among themselves," he says, his two wives sitting beside each other on the carpet, each with one knee pulled up, almost like two mismatching bookends, leaning forward to comfort a little girl crying at their feet. "In America you may have one wife, but husbands and wives, they have many relations with others," he says, try-ing to explain. "I have no relation with other women than my wife. In our view, this is better."

Delicately, I ask: Why not just get a maid?

"It is not in Islam to have another lady in your house other than your wife," he says. "Even if you do not have relations, the wife will suspect you."

His second wife says in Pashto, with her husband translating, that he is committed to his wives. It's an arrangement, of course, difficult to understand. But she slips into Urdu to tell me, *"Mujkho bahoth acha lugtha hay."* I like it very much.

"Amrika acha kam nahee kurtha hay." America does not do good work, is the literal translation. Work is deeds. It is about infidelity, adultery and premarital bed-hopping that she is talking about. I'm a single woman of the West exhausted by going in and out of relationships. I've got to say they have a point. Is *Sex in the City* really our model for civilized living?

"The thing I don't like," he says, "is this free sexuality. This indecency. This one-parent families. Women living with men without marriage. Pro-choice. This I don't like." He pauses, remembering one more vice. *Sharab*, alcohol, banned in Islam.

He knows the American dream. A house. A car. A family. A vacation. Does he have the same dream? "It is the same dream. A house. A car. Family. Vacation." He leans forward. "We have something more." To serve one God and to serve others, he says.

He has had long conversations with his wife about watching TV. "I try to convince her," he says, about the strictest mandates of Islam against entertainment. He is proud to say: "She doesn't see TV. She doesn't listen to songs."

"I'm not an imperialist. I'm a husband and a friend. I don't want to bully her." The topic broke off with the sound of shattered glass. His young daughter had dropped a glass in the foyer, shards of glass everywhere. A family relation scoops her up quickly before slivers of glass pierce her bare feet.

There is one type of music he allows in the house.

Patriotic Afghan songs, *"thahrahnah"* in Pashto. He gets up to bring a cassette and presses the "play" button on a little red boom box. Deep incantations fill the room. Crows caw outside. He writes the phonetic translation and literal translation in neat English with curls starting his *m*'s and *n*'s.

"Kari khidmat da waran wijar hewad abad kari. Khapal nikona yad kari." Serve your country. Build this destroyed country. Remember your ancestors' deeds.

He leaves the room for a moment. I ask the first wife her thoughts. She speaks quietly and plainly in Pashto without much expression. The younger wife translates into Urdu. I don't understand it all.

When he slips again to the floor, I ask their husband to translate. He resists. "She doesn't know much about politics." Indelicately, I persist. It was a long thought.

The first wife repeats her thought in Pashto. He translates into English: "She said that America will resort to killing innocent people. They will have the same experience as the Soviets. They will not achieve anything. They will not achieve what they want."

He cannot suppress a smile. "Even I am surprised. I did not know she knew so much about politics." Before I can ponder the thought too long this is the moment when the women jump up to escape into the foyer where they huddle after hearing the footsteps of a stranger, a visitor for Shaheen, nearing the screen door. They remain out of sight until the visitor leaves.

During my first visit to Shaheen's house, I asked my escort, an intermediary, "Would it make him more comfortable if I cover up completely?"

My escort was quick with his response from the front seat. "You should not do what makes other people comfortable. You should do what makes you comfortable."

Excellent. I kept my *dupatta* on as I learned to wear it as a child. When I entered the sitting room the first time, I knew not to sit too close to the men, nor to try and shake their hands. I faced the Taliban representative and sat cross-legged on the floor a pillow away from my escort. They talked to each other in Urdu about the latest developments in tensions. It was a day before the bombings. They discussed the merits of any diplomacy from the Reverend Jesse Jackson, who had approached them with an offer to mediate—not the other way around, Shaheen said. He said that he figured that Jackson was acting with the knowledge of the Bush administration, even while President Bush laid out a "no negotiations" policy.

During a quiet moment, I ask the second wife what she thinks of my defying, for my work, the Muslim values she embraces to stay behind purdah. She looks at me seriously. *"Bahoth achah kahm hay. Bahoth naik kahm hay."* It is good work. It is pious work.

I thank her. When I tell her husband her response, he smiles, cocks his head, and says, "We don't agree on everything," but continues to spend hours talking with me. Journalism knows no gender, a cousin of mine later says.

His phone rings. It is someone asking about British journalist Yvonne Ridley, who was caught trying to sneak into Afghanistan wearing a *burkha*, but without a visa. He says he called the British Embassy to tell an official to pick up the journalist at 5 P.M. at Torkham Gate at the Pakistani border. "He said, 'The counselor is not available. We'll call you back.' I said, 'Don't call me back. Pick her up, otherwise we'll have to take her back to Kabul." He has a good laugh. (And isn't shy to spread the account of Kabul police, whom he says were horrified at how much the journalist cursed at them. "She wasn't behaving with us like a lady.")

The second wife eagerly leads me through the narrow circular stairs that lead upstairs. Her bedroom door is next to the top of the stairs. The bedroom of the first wife faces the stairs. Bright pink fabric hangs over the windows. A stack of suitcases is covered with the fancy fabric from her *jah-hayz*, the trousseau of new outfits and linens a new bride takes to her new life. There is also a narrow shelf stuffed with books. It was her husband's collection. Many in Farsi, Pashto, and Urdu, like the poetry of Allama Iqbal, a Pakistani philosopher and national poet. Tucked with them are others: *Effective Business Communications, English Grammar and Composition, Fundamentals of English Grammar, HTML 4.0, Word Power* by the editors of *Reader's Digest,* and *Dictionary of Synonyms.*

When Shaheen last came back from America he brought shampoo among his gifts. A little plastic fly sits on the ledge about the books, another gift. Somebody brings in a plastic rat from the first wife's room. Another gift from America for the children.

Pakistan is this family's adopted country. Shaheen curls his body over his five-month-old son, born here, with a tiny shirt that reads PAKISTAN. His family lives in Peshawar. But he was born into a Kabul shopkeeper's family. He says that he wasn't much of a practicing Muslim until he reached about twenty. He fought early against the Soviets and then started covering the war as a journalist.

"When the Taliban came I joined them because they were the saviors of the nation. They were fighting raping of women, killing." He says he sided with the Taliban when he heard the tale of a man whose eighteen-year-old daughter had been abducted by rebels fighting for control of Kabul after the Soviets had withdrawn. His friend interceded to help the man, going to the commander of the rebels, who told him there were many women in a basement.

"Go to the basement," he was told. The friend called the man's daughter's name in a basement filled with some seventy women, Shaheen says, who had been repeatedly raped by soldiers. No answer came. The commander instructed him to go to another basement. Again, no answer. Then a meek voice said, "Tell him you are here." The girl answered but told the man to bring back clothes because she and the other women were naked. The friend bundled her into a jeep in which she wept. The friend tried to console her: "It was not your sin that they raped you. It is their sin." Shaheen says when the friend looked over at the girl again, taking his eye off the road, she had died from shock.

"I heard many such incidents," says Shaheen, his lips pressed together grimly. "This is why we want to protect women. The respect I have for women is so great. It's the nature of the Afghan culture to protect the oppressed, the weak."

I can't confirm this story, of course. And it is a similar story that journalists have repeated as the explanation for why Mullah Omar rallied men from Muslim schools, *madrassa*, to create the Taliban to stop abuses by certain factions of rebel soldiers. Shaheen insists that it was the brutal treatment of Afghan women during the country's civil war that led the Taliban to impose the purdah, or curtain, for women. He says the Taliban—contrary to many reports from journalists and human rights organizations—wants girls to study and women to work; they just haven't had the money to establish schools and hospitals for girls and women only. Unspoken, of course, is that these services are provided to men first.

I ask what he thinks about bin Laden, and his alleged involvement in the September 11 attacks. "If he is involved, then many of the Taliban will not accept him," he says.

He is analytical about why the tensions led to war. "The reason the problem was not solved was the lack of confidence" by both sides for the other. Within the Taliban government, "there was suspicion that America would have resorted to more allegations: 'There is no human rights. There is no women's rights. They are anti-democracy.'" Then, there was worry about the response from common Muslims, not necessarily Muslim governments. "If Osama was delivered to America, then the Muslim world would say this Taliban government handed over a good Muslim, a *mujahid*, to America. They betrayed a *mujahid* and a Muslim."

But did arrogance lead to this clash? He accepts the point. "This is Afghan culture," he says.

He wonders aloud about the "Yahudhi" conspiracy, the Jewish conspiracy, that underlies the doubts of many Muslims about bin Laden's guilt. In Urdu, he says he prays to find the *aslee mujrim*, the culprit behind the September 11 transformation of reality. He rattles off as fact a rumor, since debunked, that has taken strong hold over here: that four thousand Jews didn't report to work at the World Trade Center on September 11.

The clincher, to him: reports that some of the hijackers were drinking alcohol and spotted at strip clubs. That's no sign of a Muslim motivated by rabid faith, let alone a bin Laden disciple.

"Even if you give me $1 million I won't drink." He pauses. "I doubt they were Muslims."

This is a house much like any other. A child slams the screen door. The second wife winces. *"Ch!"*

Her husband continues his thoughts.

"We love our independence more than anything else."

More than life?

"More than life."

"If America wants to snatch our culture we will not accept it."

He quotes American political philosophy. "The government of the people . . ." He pauses to remember the rest. ". . . for the people, by the people."

He asks his second wife to get a book. The one with the Statue of Liberty picture, she asks, putting her hand up as if she is holding a torch. She brings the wrong book. He doesn't get irritated. He goes upstairs with her and brings down *The Brief History of America*, a gift from the U.S. Embassy written in Farsi, the fourth language in which he is fluent besides Urdu, English, and Pashto.

"Would the American people like it if their president will be chosen in London or Moscow or Rome?" He paused. "This, I think, is a global dictatorship."

BIN LADEN'S CREEPY CHARISMA

JOAN WALSH

OCT. 12, 2001—"He looks like Jesus," my friend said about Osama bin Laden the week after the September 11 massacre, and the Catholic girl in me recoiled in horror. "He *does*," she said patiently—"the Middle Eastern version, not the blue-eyed one you grew up with."

And I realized she was right—the reviled Saudi terrorist does sort of look like the vaguely Semitic, post–Folk Mass, "after all, Jesus was from somewhere in the Middle East so he was probably a little bit swarthy," Jesus we began seeing, at least in liberal Christian churches, in the 1970s.

It was at that point I realized I'd never really looked at Osama bin Laden, didn't know who or what he looked like, never met his eyes in the various mug shots, never sized him up for charisma or charm. Even on Sunday, when he appeared Phil Donahue–like in a prerecorded video, cordless mike in hand, and with his two closest colleagues laid out the case for jihad against the U.S., I paid attention to the translation of the menacing Arabic words and hardly watched the screen. To the extent I did, I thought the tableau silly: three middle-aged men in turbans and combat fatigues, hosting a talk show in a cave, live from Afghanistan! Fidel Castro crossed with Jesus Christ, with a little bit of Oprah thrown in. What a weirdo.

That impulse to ridicule, to diminish an enemy, is self-protection, but also self-delusion. *Osama: The Movie* went over big in the Muslim world. The next day, Palestinian Authority police fired on their own people for the first time, killing three, to try to halt the politically unacceptable spectacle of pro–bin Laden riots in Gaza, at a time when the Bush administration is making noises about a Palestinian state. Mothers in Muslim countries were already naming babies Osama before September 11; now it's supposedly second only to Mohammed in popularity in the Islamic world.

"Messrs. Bush and Blair may tell the world they are going to win the 'war against terrorism' but in the Middle East, where Osama bin Laden is acquiring almost mythic status among Arabs, they have already lost," the British *Independent*'s Robert Fisk wrote Wednesday. "Mr. bin Laden's voice, repeatedly beamed into millions of homes, articulates the demands and grievances—and fury—of Middle East Muslims."

But as many Muslims thrill to the sight and sound of bin Laden, Americans are having their access to him limited. In an unprecedented and stunning move, five American network executives agreed, at the behest of national security advisor Condoleezza Rice, to limit the rebroadcast of the Sunday video. The Bush administration has mostly abandoned the pretext it gave on Wednesday for censoring bin Laden: that his message contained secret codes to his followers to begin or delay new terrorist actions. (Will Ari Fleischer never tire of being pushed out on the front lines to mislead reporters?) Instead, Rice urged the TV execs not to let bin Laden use their networks to agitate against Americans.

"Her biggest point," said NBC News president Neal Shapiro, "was that here was a charismatic speaker who could arouse anti-American sentiment getting twenty minutes of air time to spew hatred and urge his followers to kill Americans." Incredibly, Shapiro and his patriotic peers were convinced—as though the American TV viewers would somehow be in danger of following bin Laden's orders to slaughter one another. Meanwhile, overseas audiences, including the entire Arab world, are going to see and hear him no matter what Rice says.

On one level I had to enjoy the spectacle of our female national security advisor telling TV's alpha males what to do, a picture-perfect inversion of gender relationships under the Taliban. Only in America! But the networks' cave-in is cowardly and scary, too. It's the U.S. failure to really look at bin Laden, see him and hear him, take in his appeal, that makes me worry about whether we're equipped to win this war.

Forbidden by Condi Rice, I had to take another look at what I could find of Sunday's video, this time to try to understand bin Laden's appeal, rather than ridicule him. America's worst nightmare is charismatic and gentle in affect, not Hitler nor Ayatollah Khomeini either. Rather than hector or scold, he mostly soothes and seduces, although he works himself up to a sterner, more forbidding pitch in the end. Long, elegant fingers grasped the microphone. I had to admit, he's even striking in a non-Western way: long-faced, strong-featured, with soulful, deep-set eyes, high cheekbones. Of course Americans are not supposed to see any male appeal: One favorite story—broken by the tabloid the *Globe*, chuckled about by journalists, repeated Wednesday by the *New York Times*' Maureen Dowd, mistress of the most humiliating putdown possible—is that he is under-endowed, anatomically speaking, and his hatred of the U.S. arises from being ridiculed for his inadequacy by an American woman. We *love* this story! If only it were true.

It's his eyes, more than anything else, that call up Jesus, I think—the sad, sick, soulful eyes. But it's the Jesus of the cross, of the crown of thorns, of the long walk toward Calvary; the martyred, dying Jesus. Bin Laden is a wounded leader, with a mysterious range of health problems—we know about his enlarged heart, we know he often uses a cane. The leader who seems strangely like a loner: Though one of fifty-four children, he was in some ways an only child, since he was the only issue of his father's marriage to his mother, an exotic Syrian, in a family where the children of each wife banded together as mini-tribes for protection. Now his siblings enjoy their wealth in Western style while he makes war upon them, in the name of Mohammed, peace be upon him.

Yes, he talked of peace on Sunday, while waging war, in his soothing, gentle voice. And his message, too, had perfect pitch. "What America is tasting now is only a copy of what we have tasted. Our Islamic nation has been tasting the same for more than eighty years, of humiliation and disgrace, its sons killed and their blood spilled, its sanctities desecrated." Eighty years—this didn't start with the Gulf War or even the founding of Israel, he made clear. He wants to return to the days before the end of the Muslim Caliphate in 1924, which had ruled the Islamic empire, once stretching Spain to Syria to Turkey, for centuries; back before Britain's Balfour declaration, which committed the West to a homeland for Jews in Palestine and advanced the cause of Zionism.

And of course he embraced the Palestinians' cause, never before his top grievance against the U.S., with new fervor. "I swear to God that America will not live in peace before peace reigns in Palestine," he said, "and before all the army of infidels depart the land of Mohammed, peace be upon him."

Of course we want to look away from the sad-eyed killer, the soft-voiced assassin; we do not want to have to understand him. It has long been lamented that the Palestinians have not produced a Gandhi, that there's no Martin Luther King Jr. of the Muslim world. But a cruel interplay of colonialism, poverty, Western indifference, and Muslim culture—mixed with his singular family history and his own cruel choices—has given us bin Laden, instead. He's what we have to deal with, and we look away at our peril.

Instead of censoring bin Laden, Bush should refute him. Instead of caving to Condi Rice, the networks should have redoubled their efforts to help Americans understand this worldwide enemy, and his malevolent but complex appeal. Robert Fisk is right: America has lost the first round of what he calls "the talking war." Let's hope our intellectual cowardice doesn't hurt us on the battlefield as well.

BIN LADEN'S DIARY

TOM McNICHOL

OCT. 12, 2001—

September 9

All praise and glory to the Most Holy One from whom all mercy flows. Last night I reach my mother on the heretic satellite phone to say that I will be out of touch for a while. The woman tells me I'm never in touch anyway, so what's the difference. Be gone, you bitch, I say. That makes you a son of a bitch, she replies. May God in His Infinite Mercy subject this woman to everlasting torment in the next world, all praise be to Him.

September 11

Praise be to God, the Cherisher and Sustainer. On the evening of this fateful day in which America has been filled with horror from north to south and east to west, I have a strange dream. I am piloting an airplane into the infidels' tallest building. As I approach, I see an imposing figure standing in one of the windows. It is my long dead father, Muhammad bin-'Awad bin Laden. "Why, Osama, why?" he implores just as I strike the building. Then I remember: He was a building contractor.

September 15

Peace and blessings be upon the prophet, his companions
and his kin. Following the righteous attack on the
unbelievers, I journey under the cover of darkness to the
town of Mazar-e-Sharif. The villagers are curiously
subdued upon my arrival. The men mutter under their
breaths, the women hide their eyes beneath their veils, and
the children burst into tears when I approach. I have
befriended a dog with scabies and adopted him as my pet,
praise be to the Most Righteous One.

September 16

All glory to the Most Exalted One from whom all honor
flows. The dog with scabies has run away. May pestilence
rain down on this depraved and unworthy creature.

September 18

By the grace of God, Praise and Glory be to Him who
delivers us from our enemies. A message from my apostate
broker in al-Riyadh: American Airlines down 6 percent.
United Airlines down 11 percent. By selling short, I have
gained back most of the money lost by investing in the
corrupt technology sector. May the Most Powerful One
heap Yahoo, Webvan, and Pets.com together and cast
them into the bottomless pit of torment.

September 19

By the Grace of God, Praise and Glory be to Him. My
mother leaves an insulting message on the heathen voice
mail that is an affront to all Islam. A plague of locusts be
upon her.

September 20

A thousand praises be unto Him from whom all
compassion derives. The degenerate satellite dish
transmits that most popular program of the infidels, the
so-called *Friends.* Truly, this is a frightful assemblage of
all that is unclean and corrupt in the heretics' debased
culture. These vile characters discuss their vulgar
personal lives while sitting in an establishment that
dispenses artificial stimulants expressly forbidden by the
Quran. The woman named Rachel is a particularly
unchaste She-Devil. She not only brazenly refuses to
wear a veil, but this evening has been revealed to be with
child, though unmarried. Against my will, I find myself
longing to stroke her depraved cheek. May God cast the
temptress into the pillar of fire for infecting me with
such thoughts.

September 21

All honor to the Most Blessed One from whom all
kindness flows. Word comes that brother Cat Stevens
refuses to lend his support to our virtuous jihad. May this
turncoat's Peace Train be laden with explosives and
rammed into the Mountain of Mohammed, peace be upon
him.

September 22

Praise and glory be unto Him who provides sustenance in
our righteous struggle. The latest publications produced
by the infidel are late in coming, due to the difficulty in
getting a messenger to journey from Kabul to the remote
caves of the Baghlan province. *Time* and *Newsweek*
naturally refuse to put me on their covers, but their

biological weapons package supplies some interesting
ideas that had not occurred to me. The Zionist *New York
Times* pretends to be objective but cannot resist running
an unflattering photo of me on Page 1. Had I known
there was food in my beard, I would not have granted the
unworthy photographer an audience. The repulsive *Sun*
tabloid dares to question my manhood, stating that the
length and breadth of my sword of Allah compares
unfavorably to those of other men. Even if this were
technically true, I condemn these blasphemies as unjust
and tyrannical. May God strike down all who repeat
them, particularly those in possession of so-called
photographic evidence.

October 2

By the grace of God, praise and glory be to Him who
delivers us from the evil one. Based on the information
supplied by tonight's sinful satellite feed, the father of
Rachel's baby is Ross. May God smote this wretched
infidel and cast him into the unquenchable fire, leaving
Rachel for me.

October 8

All honor and power to Him from whom all favor flows.
The pagan air strikes have begun. The cave that I now
inhabit reeks with a most fearsome odor, another hardship
for this faithful solider of Allah. I cannot fathom from
whence this stench emanates, for I am alone in this barren
cave. My Taliban guide assures me that the odor was not
present before my arrival, and then he hastily takes his
leave. May he who creates this foul stench be cast into the
River of Woe.

October 12

By the Grace of God, Praise and Glory be to Him. The constant air attacks by the infidels have not broken my spirit, although the explosions have caused me to befoul my loincloth repeatedly. My Taliban guides now refer to me as "Osama Big-Load-in"—may the most gracious God infect their bodies with running sores. Many in the village have defected, and those who remain are frightful to behold. While drawing water at the stream today, I see the face of a hideous man, his loathsome visage twisted by centuries of hatred, his eyes those of a hunted animal. I fear he intends to harm me, but praise be to God there was no cause for alarm. It was only my reflection in the water.

Afghanistan

ALL CRAZY ON THE KUNDUZ FRONT

PHILLIP ROBERTSON

NOV. 26, 2001, TALOQAN, AFGHANISTAN—I had no idea when I arrived in Afghanistan how much of my time would be spent waiting. I based myself in Taloqan, and I was in luck: Almost immediately I watched that city fall to the Northern Alliance. Kunduz, just fifty miles west, would be the next to go, I was told, and I had a seat at the front. But for almost two weeks, I watched and waited for the fall of Kunduz, in vain.

On Monday, the city finally fell, but actually witnessing peace will require more waiting. Northern Alliance commanders are now fighting among themselves, and there's no way to tell which side will prevail. Meanwhile, fighting continues in Mazar-e-Sharif, where Taliban prisoners revolted, and hundreds are reported dead. Farther south, U.S. Marines have landed at Kandahar. A string of quick Northern Alliance victories—Mazar-e-Sharif, Kabul, Taloqan—was supposed to mean the end of the Taliban, but didn't. All of this could go on for a while.

I have no idea how to get out of here.

The war began for me, for real, almost three weeks ago. I woke up at 7 A.M. November 8 in a hotel in Dushanbe,

Tajikistan, deathly ill after being poisoned by the notori-
ously foul water. My local fixer was waiting for me outside
the Hotel Tajikistan in his lime green Zhiguli sedan. I
almost couldn't make it downstairs, and Azam, my elfin,
bald protector, wanted to know if I'd been drinking.

"Mr. Phillip, I am very fond of you," he said. "Have you
been at the bar?" Azam, this shrewd man in his fifties, looked
like the Mongolian version of the great American physicist
Robert Oppenheimer in his later years. Completely unable to
speak, I piled into the car and we drove to the Foreign
Ministry building where a convoy of journalists was getting
ready to drive to the Afghan border. Breakfast was a handful
of Cipro and a malaria pill.

After the obligatory mumbling and checking of names
on a special list, the cops gave the OK, and a Tajik police
car with wailing sirens and squawking bullhorn led our
convoy of six cars up into the dust-colored hills, past the
ruins of Soviet agricultural collectives. Soon the road
degenerated into a rutted track, and in the small villages,
everyone came out to wave at us as we passed. Tajiks stood
by the road by the hundreds. The women with their hair
covered by bright scarves, decked out in velvet dresses
and looking very much like Hollywood fortune-tellers,
raised their hands and tried to peek in the windows of the
passing cars.

At one of the last checkpoints before the ferry crossing
to Afghanistan, Graham Day, a freelance cameraman from
London, got out of his car and fed Jelly Belly candy to the
tribal elders. One bearded and turbaned ancient was unsure
whether he should take one when Graham said, "Go on,
don't be daft. Now pop it in." The old man ate the ruby-col-
ored nubbin and moved on, after a puzzled grunt of thanks.

It took us another three spine-jolting hours to get to the
border. By that time the light was failing, turning the Amu

Darya River the color of motor oil. At the ferry, all was chaos as we handed over our magic safe-passage letters to the Russian troops, without which we were utterly screwed. Buses full of Afghans, journalists with expensive television equipment, and mujahedin all piled onto a rusted platform on which we tried to arrange the weight so it wouldn't sink. Then, midway across the river, just as I noticed that the ferry was powered by a tractor engine, the shelling started, and all of us shut up. Taliban positions were just a few kilometers away, and when the shells hit, every twenty seconds or so, I felt the concussions in my chest.

On the other side, we cleared customs and lied to the Northern Alliance fighters about how much money we were carrying. Afghanistan is fundamentally a feudal society, awash in cheap Soviet weapons, where the most reliable form of transportation is a donkey. Next on the list of desirable transportation choices is the tricked-out pickup truck, a vehicle that has a monster suspension rendering it capable of fording rivers and driving up the sides of mountains. Afghans reverently call these "Datsuns," no matter who the manufacturer happens to be.

The familiar features of the West were beginning to disappear for me. The Hindu Kush Mountains take the place of the Rockies, reducing them to foothills. Cars turn into horse-drawn carriages. Dust storms beat out rain. Women disappear. Men grow Kalashnikovs on their backs, and children become rocket bearers. After a long journey, I'd finally reached my destination, in the tenth century A.D.

I was in time to witness the quick fall of Taloqan to the Northern Alliance on November 11, but the very next day, on the road to Kunduz, I saw the Alliance's limits. Probably the most dramatic clash I witnessed was at Bangi Pol on November 12, the scene of a horrifying Northern Alliance retreat in which twelve fighters and one commander were killed, as the column hurtled down the road in a blind panic. After that, there was little action for more than a week.

I began to feel like I was waiting for the Northern Alliance to reach the end of its patience, gather up its nerve, and finally invade Kunduz. Though they encircle the city quickly, they seem reluctant to capture it.

Instead, the benighted city becomes the subject of endless peace negotiations, international intrigue, and infighting among Northern Alliance commanders. The one constant is wave after wave of bombing runs by American B-52s. I make a morning pilgrimage to the front lines to watch the airstrikes, which are biblical in their intensity. After the B-52s release their payloads, whole mountains seem to dissolve into dust, and mushroom clouds rise a thousand feet in the air.

The Northern Alliance fighters, or mujahedin as they are called here, love the show and practically dance up and down when they spot an explosion. But it isn't a happy situation. The bombs and a Taliban ethnic-cleansing policy have created a massive flow of refugees out of the area around Kunduz. The journey from Kunduz to Taloqan runs the length of the Bangi River Valley, a green ribbon surrounded by the barren Ambarku Mountains. Mud-brick villages line the river, but the settlements near the front at Bangi have been abandoned, the residents having fled for safer ground. Beyond the safety of the Bangi bridge, where all the television reporters congregate, the villages on the way to Kunduz are named Choga, Kaleh Surhakh, and Choge Nawabad, and they're in a no-man's land, controlled by neither the Alliance nor the Taliban. Behind Taliban lines, there is Amirabad, Khanabad, and, finally, Kunduz, which lies just over a mountain ridge, and that's the war zone in a nutshell. The remaining territory in this part of the country has fallen to the Northern Alliance.

After a walk that can easily take days, mostly Tajik and Uzbek refugees from Khanabad, Amirabad, and Kunduz arrive in Taloqan, without food or a place to stay. This stately march of tribesmen with their donkeys and children is part of an equation in which misery increases geometrically with time. For each day of airstrikes, and each day that Kunduz isn't taken by the Northern Alliance, there is a day of ethnic cleansing, and hundreds of fleeing people on the road. Refugees have also brought with them stories of massacres—of Tajiks and Uzbeks killed by ethnic Pashtun Taliban; and of Pashtun Taliban killed by the fearsome foreign Muslim Taliban, who've come from Saudi Arabia, Pakistan, Chechnya, even China to join this jihad.

At around seven every morning, I climb into a jeep driven by Amin, a former fighter who is a devout Muslim; my translator Nazar; and my friend Sion Touhig, a Welsh photojournalist. After a breakfast of tea and bread, we drive off to Bangi Pol, the lunar place that was the scene of the horrifying November 12 Northern Alliance retreat. Vehicle tracks are still visible in the river, where half the column jumped the bank and plowed through the water to relative safety.

In northern Afghanistan, the war follows the road. Columns of mujahedin typically race down what's left of the Russian blacktop until they capture an abandoned city or run directly into an ambush, and the war at Bangi, where the Alliance has been stopped for close to two weeks now, is no exception. The ambush, the game where one side doesn't know it's playing until it's too late, has been elevated to a national pastime in this country.

But the truth is that I prefer being out there with the fighters, and at Bangi the filth and intrigue of Taloqan— squabbling Northern Alliance forces, increasingly thuggish mafia elements in the foreign ministry—all recede into distant hassles. The mujahedin are mostly friendly and eager to help a foreign journalist cover the war, even if they have no idea what's really going on, either. After twenty years of war, and a complete collapse of the education system, many are illiterate, and when they see a notebook and a pen, it's not unusual to attract a crowd: hip cats with their Kalashnikovs, rocket-propelled grenades, and tripod-mounted machine guns. Plus, at Bangi, the fighters and their commanders have spent the last week bored out of their minds waiting for orders that never come. When they see a stranger, it's a big show—and the visitor is the entertainment.

The standard Afghan technique for greeting someone from another country is to stand uncomfortably close and stare, which unnerves Westerners who haven't figured out how to cope with it. Many members of the international press scuttle away, hoping the fighters will fuck off and leave them alone. What the journalists rarely understand is that the mujahedin are just waiting to shake hands and say hello—have a bit of human contact in its pure, primate sense. They want to know what sort of alien being would come here dressed so strangely, what it sounds like when it talks, which country it comes from.

Of course, the situation isn't quite so benign for female journalists. At Bangi, bored young Tajik and Uzbek muja-hedin like to check out the women in the international press corps. The women have to keep moving around, because if they stand too long in a single spot, or make the mistake of chatting with a Western man, a crowd of heavily armed gawkers will instantly materialize. Mobs of fighters surrounding female journalists are commonplace. A photographer from the *Dallas Morning News*, who kept getting pokes in the ass, had started to punch her assailants back.

But mostly the mujahedin protect me. Out at Bangi and

on the other front lines, they follow me everywhere, sometimes taking me around, showing me what's going on and
making sure to never let me out of their sight, until I arrive
at a secure place. The secret deal between me and the
fighters seems to be this: I write down their names and
ages, and they save my life.

I am also on the lookout for actual news, which, despite
the many stories about Kunduz on the cable networks and
newspapers, is scarce. On November 19, there are reports
that a U.S. bombing raid accidentally hit a village, Choge
Nawabad, killing whole families. But the place has been
impossible to visit, despite the fact that it was very close to
Northern Alliance lines. Every commander I spoke to gave
me the same answer: No, you can't go, it's in Taliban-
controlled territory—even though technically, it was in the
no-man's land controlled by neither the Taliban nor the
Alliance.

But Wednesday, November 21, was my lucky day, or
seemed like it. I made my daily pilgrimage to the front
lines, where nothing much was happening, as usual. After
some milling around, I walked down through the nearest
abandoned village, Choga, with my translator Nazar, who
spends most of his time begging me to turn back. "Phillip,
this is a very bad place. Very dangerous." I tried to be
patient with Nazar, whose blood sugar was perilously low
due to Ramadan fasting.

We were heading down to the stone bridge, a favorite
spot, well away from the pack of bored mujahedin and TV
people, to where we could see the American airstrikes. It's
at the bridge where I had my stroke of good luck, and ran
into an Afghan friend, Nazir Mohammed, a twenty-six-
year-old commander from the Panjshir Valley. He's a beautiful man who takes care of his beard, and sports seventies
amber aviator glasses along with a traditional Tajik Pakula

wool cap, which many of the fighters wear. Mohammed is also very levelheaded, one of the few people I trust.

We touch cheeks and talk about the American bombs that fell on Choge Nawabad, which reportedly killed at least twelve civilians and created waves of refugees. I asked Nazir if we could go, despite having been rebuffed by so many other commanders. He simply said yes, knowing that he was giving me a gift. Nazir collected seven of his men, which included his younger brother, and without saying anything about it, they formed a circle around me, and we walked west, in the direction of ever increasing weirdness, down the road toward Kunduz. Foreigners aren't allowed this far into the lines, and it made me feel like a king.

At the point on the road where Northern Alliance control essentially stopped, and no-man's land started, Nazir Mohammed turned south, cutting across the rice fields, where we walked single file, watching the ground for mines. Above us, tanks firing down on Amirabad from the mountains created deafening explosions that echoed off the opposite ridge. The shells, traveling on invisible arcs, sailed over our heads on the way to their targets.

We kept going for another half-mile or so. Then, at Kaleh Surhakh, a village elder from Choge Nawabad came out to greet us. I explained through the translator that I was here to see the place where the bomb landed, and he nodded and fell in with us. Commander Nazir, who didn't want to stay out in the open for very long, led us to a two-story house filled with rotting onions. On the roof, he showed me the craters from other bombs that had fallen in the wrong place. Then the old man carefully recounted the names of those who were killed, adding their ages when he had them. He watches as I write them down. First the adults: Boi Malang, 35; Shiringol Malang, 40; Emam Gul, 30; Gul Bibi, 60; Khoda Gul; Said Bibi; Kamela Malang.

And then the children: Gul Khan, 8; Amit Khan, 12; Sher Khan, 13; Ismail Khan, 12; Zar Khan, 11.

My friend Nazir wouldn't let me go any farther, and so we headed back toward Bangi Pol. I'd spent my day protected by Northern Alliance soldiers, but that night, one almost killed me. It reminded me that the country's supposed liberators are also, many of them, thugs and bandits, and there are very few Nazir Mohammeds, to say the least.

I made a mistake, one that began with an attempted phone call. The pathetic and unreliable gadget I use to talk to the world is an Iridium satellite phone, the poor man's version of a proper communication setup for this country. Iridium, the Motorola project that went spectacularly bankrupt and has been recently rescued by the Defense Department, is a frightening way to have a conversation with someone back home. Static, freakish sound effects, and dropped calls are totally normal, reminiscent of early cell phone days. The Iridium network is also far too slow to receive e-mail, though I can send it, very slowly.

To get the Motorola to work at all, I have to step outside in the cold, survey the immediate area for obstacles that will prevent it from seeing the sky, and watch the display until the signal strength seems sufficient to make the call. The window of opportunity lasts about four minutes. It is a ridiculous dance, one that usually takes place in the dead of night, on the roof of wherever I'm staying.

But the night after my Choge Nowabad expedition, the owner of the house where I stay had squirreled away his ladder, and the only place I could get a decent signal at midnight, when it was time to send a message, was the street. Like many Afghan houses, his place has a courtyard surrounded by high mud walls and a steel door with a bolt. I put on a coat, gathered up the phone and cables, and stepped outside into a pitch-black street, which smelled of wood smoke and dust. Everything in Taloqan is coated in this lunar, powdery substance—the roses in the garden, the leaves on the trees—and the street is made out of it, a tan ribbon of dust. During the day, old men scoop water from the irrigation ditches and throw it over the road, so that when horse-drawn carriages and donkeys go down the street, the visibility doesn't drop to zero. Walking on it feels like new-fallen snow.

Once I'm outside, I boot my computer, turn on the phone, and get ready to send a message. Nothing seems out of the ordinary; it's another quiet night in this quiet neighborhood. A few minutes later, while the phone is still trying to make a proper connection to the network, I notice that about 100 feet down the road there is a soldier, who is standing very still. This one isn't dressed like a mujahedin, who usually wear traditional blankets and Tajik caps, but is instead wearing a new Chinese military uniform.

The soldier yells at me in Persian, wanting to know who I am. I tell him I'm an American, and he steps away from the building into the road where he can get a better look. He heard me just fine, but he's starting to act like there's a serious problem, and in one sickening instant, he pulls back the bolt on the Kalashnikov and raises the gun to take his shot. The sound of the gun is a horrible promise. Here it comes, I think, alone in this empty place with the dark pounding in my ears, and I turn away and run down the street. I'm thinking, maybe the sonofabitch will miss me in the dark, and that's when I hear him fire.

In the complete blackness, I run halfway down the block, listen for footsteps, don't hear any, and keep going until I see a single electric bulb. I stop there; my plan was simply to beg whoever owned the light to let me in, until the soldier gave up on the idea of killing a foreigner.

Under the bulb, I see figures moving around, tending a mud oven. Little kids with shaved heads are peering at me, this strange man who has shown up out of breath, and who keeps saying *"Salaam Aleikum,"* over and over like it's some kind of prayer. One man then steps out from behind the oven and motions me to sit down, and I fall to my knees right there, sick with fear for the first time since arriving in Afghanistan. His name is Nangulee, and he's a baker, working through the night to make cookies, which he sells in the bazaar the next day. The little kids are his trainee assistants at his Old Tonga Til bakery, this haven adorned with the magic fifty-watt bulb. Nangulee says to me, in near-perfect English, "Please tell me what happened to you." I tell him everything.

He sits me down near the fire, and tells me that he won't let the soldiers in, because I'm now part of his family. He tells me that if the soldiers come he'll fight with them and tell them to go away. He tells me not to worry. I believe it all, every word. After a few minutes, Nangulee's father comes out and tells me to relax, in Persian, and asks me if I need something to eat. I say no, thanks. We go into Nangulee's house, where his cousin Hassan brings out a sleeping mat. They wedge me in between the father and Hassan, in a warm room filled with cooling sweets. After an hour of racing thoughts, I sleep and feel safe.

Which I was, but only thanks to Nangulee. While I was in the back room sleeping, the soldier who had shot at me came back with seventeen friends to finish the job. They collared the trainee assistants out front and asked them if they knew anything about the foreigner. The kids ran inside and asked Nangulee what they should tell them. "Tell them you are only students and don't know anything about a foreigner." Nangulee went out after a few minutes and told them to go screw themselves. Eventually they went away. When I asked Nangulee why they wanted to find me so badly, he said they wanted my money and telephone. Northern Alliance soldiers are not paid a regular salary, and most of them cannot read or write. "Most of these soldiers are crazy," Nangulee said. "Never go out at night."

I'd been here two weeks, and Northern Alliance soldiers had both protected me and tried to kill me. I knew it was even possible that some who were my protectors by day turned into thugs and bandits at night. In the morning, I walked back down the street to the guest house, very much aware it was Thanksgiving Day. I was intensely grateful to Nangulee and his family, but I was hoping Kunduz would fall soon and this war might be over, so I could go home. And now it's fallen, and peace seems as elusive as ever.

PANIC AT THE BANGI BRIDGE

PHILLIP ROBERTSON

DEC. 21, 2001—In an unheated apartment in Dushanbe, Tajikistan, a few days before crossing the border into Afghanistan, I had a nightmare in which I was making terrible mistakes. It was one of those quick, bad turns your head sometimes takes when you arrive in an unfamiliar place and the dreams are unnaturally vivid. There was a fake tank at a fake checkpoint in a fake war-torn country, and then something happened that couldn't be undone. In the sequence, I had given the wrong answer to a soldier's question.

A bad dream, no big deal, hatched by anxiety and anti-malaria pills, but I remember it now because of what would happen ten days later, at the bridge over the Bangi River on November 12, the day after the Northern Alliance took Taloqan in a nearly bloodless victory. It was a victory that made us feel all warm and happy inside because we had the good fortune to witness the column of fighters glide into the city, where the population came out to greet them by throwing coins and banknotes onto the hoods of tanks and jeeps as they passed while some even held out pieces of bread to the fighters, which they took and ate as part communion, part welcome.

The crew of journalists I'd fallen in with, five writers and photographers from the United States, Canada, the

U.K., and Portugal, had witnessed the fall of Taloqan from the back of a Toyota pickup.

After the town fell, we spent a cold night on the second floor of a shop in Taloqan, without blankets, crashed out on piles of luggage and coats. In the morning, we found some female doctors at the clinic who told us what life was like under the Taliban, and we were so excited at the prospect of speaking to unveiled women, we fell upon them with a hail of inane questions. The interview went longer than we had expected, and by the time it was over, Daoud Khan's soldiers had already left for the front, now moving west. He had offered to take us with him, but we were stranded, left to find a place to stay in Taloqan.

Our driver, whose name was Kandahar, stopped the Toyota in front of a place on the main street, a house owned by a rich man who claimed that he had rented it to Arabs before the Northern Alliance had arrived. We were welcome for $20 a night, but there would be no food, no running water, no electricity, and rent was to be collected in the morning before we were out of bed. In one long room, the room we would stay in, there were sleeping mats and pillows; covering the windows were sheets of milky plastic. All in all, it was a terrible deal, but we needed shelter from the relentless cold and dust, which would make everyone sick as dogs.

Like our new pad, every house in Taloqan has a garden surrounded by high mud walls. More often than not, the garden will have roses, which are fed by delicate irrigation channels dug into the packed earth, which, if followed to their source, go through the walls, out to the street, finally threading back to the river. The city is a maze of these channels. Old men wash in them, rub their teeth with the water, using it to prepare themselves for prayer. On the street, the trees line the irrigation channels, their leaves covered with the dust from passing trucks.

The correspondents milled around the guest house garden wondering what to do next, whether they had enough to file for the day or whether they would have to pile into a car and drive through the rice fields to find the mujahedin column. The consensus was "bad idea," and most of them stuck around to file the hospital story.

I kept talking about driving up to the front toward Kunduz to find the mujahedin, but Kevin Donovan from the *Toronto Star* told me to forget it, saying it wasn't a good plan since we didn't know what was going on up there. He was a good reporter and swaggered a bit, an act that went well with his Marlboro Man looks. As we debated what to do, the Afghans, a knot of translators and drivers, squatted near some young trees waiting for us to make a decision. Kevin chose to stay, which meant that I was without a ride and a driver.

A minute later, Sion Touhig, a Welsh photographer, came up and said to me casually, "So how about we go up there and just have a look?" He said it like there were girls having a pillow fight in the next house, and maybe we should take a peek before their brothers get there. I agreed.

Donovan said to me, "You're going. Are you going?"

"Yes."

"You understand that I can't let you have Kandahar take you up there?"

Donovan didn't need Kandahar, but he wasn't happy about lending him out.

"No problem," I said.

It was a huge problem.

We still had to find a driver, but the owner of the house, always eager to get in on the flow of dollars, said that he would find us a reliable man, a relative of his, to take us to the front.

I agreed to it and suddenly thought it might be a good

idea to shave first, overwhelmed by the urge to be clean after three solid days of muck and sweat gathered by traveling over mountain ranges and down rivers. Abdullah, the water bearer, brought a bucket of hot water to the washroom, a concrete cell with a drain in the center of the floor, and poured it slowly over my head, making the dust come off in muddy rivulets. Abdullah then carefully washed my back with a rag, while I knelt and prayed to a reproachful God of strip malls, fast-food chains, low-interest financing, and trout fishing to watch over me, just this once. The prayer was a long apology.

When I was done, Sion was ready to go and pointed out that the driver was outside waiting, the gear was packed, and we were late and wasting time. It was the middle of the afternoon; the sun was out. We were ready to go, even though we didn't have a translator. There wasn't time to find anyone on such short notice who could speak English. When we got outside, the driver of the cab told the owner of the house he wanted $600 to take us to the column. We haggled. Sion snorted in disgust at the unreasonable price. The driver came down to $200 and we got in. In Afghanistan, going anywhere by car meant paying extortionate rates, usually an amount set by the Foreign Ministry as a kind of wealth redistribution scheme. If the driver smelled desperation, the price instantly doubled or tripled. We were not allowed to bring drivers, cars, or translators from neighboring countries, which made matters much worse.

After all the negotiations were over, the cab's owner, a young man with a thin beard named Sabur Ghalfoor, looked as though he could not believe his good fortune. Ferrying a couple of foreigners up to a front where he thought nothing was happening was a perfect piece of cake. He grinned and pointed out places of interest. Ghalfoor told me the names of the mountains. "Ambarku, Ambarku," he said. They looked like ideal hiding places for snipers.

We drove in silence on the Soviet-built highway toward Kunduz. In the first four miles, where the asphalt runs down the center of the valley, we watched rice paddies roll by. Uzbek peasants were out on the road where they had spread their harvest, scuffing their feet in the grain to turn it over every so often so it would dry in the sun. Their children made small furrows in the rice with their toes. To the north and south, dust-colored mountains without a single tree formed the river valley's boundaries. After fifteen minutes, driving at a remarkably swift eighteen miles per hour, we passed through a market town with an iron arch, and as the valley narrowed as we went farther west, we climbed into a desolate landscape of dead villages. Rock shards covered the road, thrown out of the cliffs from bombs or rockets. We drove past a dead Taliban fighter left to rot in a field, then a burned-out tank.

The village of Qabil Qazi went by, a set of broken teeth.

Finally we found the mujahedin column parked at a place called Bangi. The town was just south of the river, situated on a hill where Daoud Khan's commanders had positioned three tanks and a rocket launcher, their guns facing west. Most of the column was getting ready to move, and since it was roughly a mile long with at least a thousand fighters, in trucks and jeeps, there was a sound that rose up from it, transmissions grinding, engines pulling overweight loads.

Sion and I got out of the cab, poked around, and decided to keep moving forward with the fighters, so we told Ghalfoor to keep going. He didn't give us any problems, he just put the car in gear and drove down the hill, over the concrete bridge, over the Bangi River, and then up the opposite side, where he pulled over and parked.

Once we arrived, Sion hopped out and disappeared up a trail mooching around for a shot, while I walked around taking notes, counting trucks, and watching for mines. Then Ghalfoor had a bright idea and turned his cab around so it faced back toward Taloqan on the opposite side of the road. He waved to let me know what he was doing, since we couldn't understand each other. I waved back and walked to the west side of the hill, to the farthest extent of the front, watching the hillside for problems and listening.

Then the gunfire started.

It was a well-coordinated Taliban ambush. At least one Talib opened up on the Northern Alliance convoy with a machine gun just on the west side of the cut in the road, about thirty feet away. It wasn't short bursts either but long stuttering paragraphs, like he was cleaning up. This was soon followed by rocket-propelled grenades. I skirted the road, avoiding the soft earth on the shoulder, and made my way back toward Ghalfoor's cab, ducking behind jeeps and trucks for cover. Through the spaces between the vehicles, I saw a friend from the *New York Times* running in slow motion back toward his pickup, and knew it was time to split for real. But it didn't seem like there was all that much to run from, that the fighters would go up into the hills and take control. We just needed a little more distance while they worked.

Sion was nowhere to be found, and the entire mass of fighters was starting to panic, swallowed whole by their terror of the other side of the hill. Jeeps rode up on the hillsides, nearly tipping over, while mujahedin abandoned their weapons, getting into anything that would move. The entire column, more than a thousand fighters, was turning around thinking that there was an entrenched Taliban force waiting to slaughter them all, and they moved as fast as

they could to get out of there, without so much as returning fire. By the time I found Ghalfoor in his yellow station
wagon, he was ready to go, gunning his engine, and I made
him wait until Sion returned.

"OK? OK?" he kept asking, his only English word,
wanting desperately to floor it and take off.

I shook my head and put my hand on him to calm him
and make him wait for Sion. The column roared past us
back toward Taloqan, the machine-gun fire coming over
the hill. It seemed to be coming closer. I got out of the car
and looked for Sion, and shouted for him at the top of my
lungs, a shout that went nowhere and immediately disappeared into the roar and the engine noise. I got back in the
cab. More of the column went by, truck after truck, as the
cab sat on the gravel turnout on the hill.

Looking at Ghalfoor sitting behind the wheel with his
eyes as wide as saucers made me start to feel what the fighters were feeling, the horse-in-a-burning-barn fear of certain and inevitable doom, but I didn't feel it for very long.
He chose that very moment to put the cab in gear and join
the stream of panicking fighters. He just took off and that
was that, we were moving. Sion had been left behind.

Ghalfoor now had the cab in the column but it wasn't
moving fast enough for him and he laid on the horn, coming down hard on the accelerator, unthinking, and we
weren't even at the bridge over the Bangi, and he laid on
the horn again, but we couldn't hear it, and the fighters
running in the road ahead of us couldn't hear it either.

So he ran them down.

The first man Ghalfoor hit was on my side of the car,
his knees snapping where the fender impacted. There was a
look of disbelief on his face as he turned toward the road
and collapsed in the powdery dust. Ghalfoor found a clear
section of road and accelerated. He wasn't making the

slightest effort to avoid them, he drove in a straight line, a man possessed.

The next fighter he ran down went up on the hood, coming all the way up to the windshield while the metal buckled under him and made a sound like tympani. When he rolled off the car and hit the ground, I saw his rifle sail through the air and land on the shoulder thirty feet away.

And so it went, man after man. I lost count at eight. It's strange how I can see it now, this nightmare instant, overlaid like a hallucination on the rest of the normal world, an image that can't be discarded because it has a soundtrack of sickening crashes, bones breaking on the fender, and clattering weapons.

One fighter who wasn't in front of the car as it cut a path through the mujahedin shouted bitter curses at us as Ghalfoor shot past, while I yelled for him to stop, even punching him to get his attention. But he just kept looking straight ahead at the road and when he finally made the decision to drive off the shoulder and into the river, I gave up. Ghalfoor just didn't have time for the bridge, so he steered the cab toward the steep bank.

There was a rocky edge to the river—which was low this time of year, running in a few fast and shallow streams in the middle of its stony bed—and Ghalfoor threw the wheel of the station wagon to the right and just took us down the side and into it. He hit the water at twenty miles an hour and I was sure the engine would stall and we would be stuck there, forced to get out and walk the distance back to Taloqan under fire. But he kept us moving, keeping us out of the deepest part of the river. As we reached the center of the stream, a fighter who was running away from the battle jumped into the passenger window so his head was in my lap, his legs dangling out of the cab. We carried him like that, up onto the opposite bank.

The fighter was crying.

We let him off somewhere on the road back to Taloqan, and just east of Chun Zai, one of the dead villages, I found the car carrying Lois, a writer from the *Washington Post*, and explained that I lost Sion up at Bangi. I wanted to know if she'd seen him. She hadn't because she was ahead of us in the column, but she was sure he would be OK, and told me not to worry. She didn't know anything definite, it was just something to say. There were only a few correspondents on the hill when the fighting started, perhaps four or five, most of them photographers, so there weren't many people who would know what happened to Sion, and I was sure that he was the last one to leave. We talked for another minute about what happened, and then I got back in the cab and we drove on to the market town with the iron arch.

Ghalfoor drove and I said quietly, "I'm going to tell the world what a sick fuck you are."

Ghalfoor shrugged. We kept going.

When we pulled over at the farmer's market, a crowd formed around the cab, mostly Uzbek peasants who worked the fields who wanted to say hello, and ask about the war situation. An elder with a white beard and a black turban greeted me and I explained to him what had happened, making a fist with one hand and running fighters with the fingers of another, I showed the old man how Ghalfoor had run down the mujahedin by moving the cab-fist over the fighter-fingers and he understood the gesture instantly. When I explained in Dari that Ghalfoor was being paid $200, the elder took him by the coat and shouted at him, admonishing Ghalfoor for his cowardice and his greed. Ghalfoor freed himself from the old man, got back in the car, and we drove back to Taloqan.

When we pulled up in front of the guesthouse, I noticed

that the cab was beat to hell. It had started out fine but now sported enough dents and scratches to made it look a hundred years old. There was a long gouge on the right-hand side; the left-hand door wouldn't shut properly; both mirrors were gone. Ghalfoor probed at the cab and bent to look at the damage, and I left him there and went inside the guesthouse, thinking that if I had to look at him another second, I would beat him to death.

"Where's Sion?" Kevin Donovan wanted to know.

"I lost him."

"You lost him?" He couldn't believe it. When I told him how Ghalfoor panicked when the column turned around, how we left Sion behind in the chaos, how the driver ran down the fleeing fighters, Donovon recoiled and let me have it, saying at the end of a hackneyed older brother monologue, "I'm through with you."

That was fine. If Sion and I had been among the first journalists in a fallen Kunduz, we would have had a heroic scoop on our hands. Sion would have taken his historic pictures, and we would have been so happy at getting there first while everybody else had decided to cool their heels and file the clinic story. But I didn't say it, because I was now living in the parallel universe where everything had gone wrong, and I was sick with dread about what could be coming next.

Kandahar, who had driven us up the sides of mountains and down fast rivers, got the story of what had happened from some of the men who were hanging around the courtyard, and told me through one of the interpreters that it was a mistake to trust a cab driver to go up to the front. I told him it was all we could get at the time and he pinched my cheek and smiled. Then Afghans, many men whom I'd never met, stopped by to say that they knew that Sion was going to be fine, that he would walk out or hitch a ride on a truck back into town, and they would pat me on the shoulder, to let me know it was not a totally fucked situation. They offered their consoling words right up until Donovan, unnerved by the ten Afghans wandering around the courtyard, threw them out of our compound. "There are too many Afghans in here. Get them out," he said.

After about twenty minutes, I went outside and found Ghalfoor shooting the breeze with a bunch of friends waiting to get paid. I threw the $200 in the dirt at his feet, spat, and went back inside, and then waited another hour for Sion to appear. It was now nearly five, and getting dark, and I was left to mull over worst-case scenarios. I thought Sion had been injured at Bangi or captured by the Taliban, both preludes to an instantaneous execution. There was nothing I could do about the fighters Ghalfoor ran down, except believe that they'd been picked up once the panic subsided. It was impossible to think clearly.

Another hour went by with no sign of him, so I went back outside to get away from the others. I couldn't bear to talk about it anymore, and leaned against the wall and looked down the street into the blue dust until Sion came walking out of it, a retouched image from a Hieronymus Bosch painting—Man Emerges from the Gloom and Desperation of War.

During the battle, Sion had walked across the Bangi River and back down the road toward Taloqan, getting into a jeep that immediately broke down. He was picked up again by another group of fighters with a truck who took him the rest of the way back to town. He hitched his way out, just as Kandahar had said.

"It's OK," he said, like it was no big deal. "I figured the driver legged it when he heard the shots."

A friend wrote in the *New York Times* the following day that a Northern Alliance soldier had turned the column of fighters back by threatening to shoot anyone who continued to retreat, which made sense, in the logic of Afghanistan, as the only way to stop the panic, the only way to keep the front from collapsing in on itself.

When we returned to Bangi the next day, there was the burned-out shell of a jeep at the crest of the hill, black and pocked with bullets, marking the spot where we had parked the car.

Later, when I heard that twelve mujahedin had died in the ambush, I wondered how many of them had died after being run down.

THE FIRST CASUALTIES

SEAN KENNY

OCT. 9, 2001, PESHAWAR, PAKISTAN—There was no electricity in Hayathabad Hospital, Peshawar, and Assadullah's ward was pitch-black and very hot. By the light of a cigarette lighter, I saw bloody bandages wrapped around the boy's arms and legs, and there was a large round bandaged stump where his left foot should have been.

According to Assadullah, sixteen, he is apparently one of the first victims of the raids on Afghanistan Sunday night. At the time, he had just taken a break from working at his French fries stand in Jalalabad when the town was hit by cruise missiles. "I was thrown fifty feet by the blast. When I woke up I was in Jalalabad Hospital," he said. "My father had found me and taken me there."

Assadullah is apparently one of just a few casualties to make it over to the Pakistan side, and to Hayathabad Hospital, though reports of civilian injuries dominated the day's news from the region. Four workers at a United Nations–funded mine-clearing operation just east of Kabul were killed, according to the U.N., the first independent confirmation of civilian deaths inside Afghanistan. Taliban representatives were claiming that civilian deaths from the first day of bombings ranged from eight to twenty.

According to Assadullah, the explosion ripped off his

left foot and two fingers on his left hand. His right knee and foot were also badly wounded. He bit his lower lip as he described waking up in Jalalabad Hospital on Monday. "In the morning I felt extremely lonely and scared. There were no doctors or nurses in the hospital. I felt totally alone."

By Monday afternoon his family had found a taxi willing to take Assadullah to the border, where, he said, his father had to plead with soldiers to let them enter Pakistan. Finally, Assadullah and his father were allowed through and made it to the hospital in Hayathabad, thirty-five miles from the border.

"My father is here with me but my mother and sisters are still in Afghanistan," he said. "I lay here and worry about them."

Hayathabad Hospital is a decrepit and depressing place. Tonight the electricity was down, despite the fact that just half a mile away the neon signs were flashing outside the burger joints and boutiques frequented by Peshawar's middle classes. Some wards were lit with candles; in other wards—like Assadullah's—men lay in the dark as relatives fanned them with newspapers. There was little medical equipment and few doctors or nurses attended to the patients.

In the emergency ward, eight policemen surrounded a man with blood-caked bandages on his head and patches of dried blood on his face. Heavy chains shackled him onto the hospital trolley.

"Islam *zinderbad!* America *murtzabad!*"—long live Islam, death to America—he cried, thrashing his head from side to side.

The policemen said that the man had been found wandering Peshawar carrying a hand grenade. He escaped once, but the police recaptured him and beat him with their batons.

"Then we put the grenade in his mouth and asked him if we could pull out the pin," said one of the policemen.

In another stuffy hospital ward Mohammad Raza, thirty-five, lay on his back with his shirt open, panting heavily and staring at the ceiling. His cousin, who had brought him to Pakistan on Monday, said that Raza had been getting out of his car at his farm near Jalalabad Airport on the first night of the attacks when a bomb landed nearby. Some kind of debris or shrapnel had hit him in the neck.

"Now he is a full paraplegic, paralyzed from the neck down," his cousin said. "There's no chance of him ever walking or using his hands again. He doesn't want to speak to you himself because he is afraid he is dying."

Israralik Khan, a hospital dispensing chemist, said: "We don't know if more people will come, but we are prepared."

The Home Front

GET A GRIP, AMERICA!

LAURA MILLER

OCT. 20, 2001, NEW YORK—I'm not the type to love a place just because I happened to have been born there, but I've always wanted, at the very least, to respect America, and mostly I have. If our nation hasn't always lived up to the ideals it trumpets, I believe that we get closer every year because the majority of us are committed to making this experiment work. What I've never questioned is America's know-how, resilience, and fortitude—our *gumption*—even when I've had my doubts about how we use it.

That is, I hadn't questioned our gumption, until about two weeks ago.

In the days following the body blow of September 11, my faith in our nation's ability to behave with grace under pressure seemed to be borne out. It wasn't just the firefighters and police officers; it was the volunteer rescue workers, the people standing in line for four hours to give blood at the hospital on my block, the citizens from other states who got in their cars and drove day and night to reach us here in New York so they could offer their help in any way. The corresponding slogans—"United We Stand," etc.—were cheesy, but they didn't seem outright delusional.

All it took to explode that dream were a couple dozen contaminated letters. Now, doctors are besieged with requests for Cipro prescriptions by patients who have no reason to think they've been exposed to anthrax. The government is planning to blow a huge chunk of the public health budget on this probably unnecessary drug. The House of Representatives closed up shop in a paroxysm of what the media politely called "jitters"—the *New York Post* was alone in calling them "wimps"—after Senate Majority Leader Tom Daschle's office received an anthrax-laced letter.

Columnists like the *New York Times*' Maureen Dowd and the *Washington Post*'s Sally Quinn write of frenzy among the chattering classes (make that the teeth-chattering classes), leading to runs on gas masks, canned goods, and of course, more Cipro. Paranoid Americans who think they've been exposed to bioterror are threatening to cripple the healthcare infrastructure that would be our first line of defense in the event of a serious attack. The thin, high whine of panic is in the air.

It's worth reiterating right now that exactly one person—the first person diagnosed, before we even realized his infection was intentional—has died of anthrax so far. A mere seven more have contracted the illness, and all are expected to make a full recovery. The remainder of people who "tested positive for exposure" aren't even sick and don't amount to more than forty victims. Salmonella has probably killed more people in the past two weeks than anthrax has, and I'm sure that more have died in automobile accidents. So why don't we all stop eating, and resolve to walk everywhere we go?

It's depressing and demoralizing to see a nation that two weeks ago was congratulating itself on its "unity" dissolve into a collection of gibbering hypochondriacs. On the big screen of our collective imagination, in that movie where a handful of mismatched strangers is trapped in an imperiled high rise or ocean liner or spaceship, we Americans want to believe that we're the Bruce Willis character, the cool-headed, competent, wisecracking, fast-thinking man with a plan. In reality, we're the incoherently screaming lady who has to be slapped until she comes to her senses—and even then turns out to be little more than dead weight.

Oh, and by the way, there's a war on, a tricky, demanding conflict with the potential to set off a worldwide cross-cultural military conflagration. That merits a bit of our attention, I'd say. Yet stories about it are being driven off the front page by articles in which public officials and so-called experts make vague, inflammatory statements about the anthrax menace that later have to be semi-retracted or otherwise qualified by other officials and experts and unnamed sources. (Just what is "weapons grade" anthrax and exactly how sophisticated does a lab have to be to produce the powder that failed to gravely afflict anyone in Daschle's office? Your guess is as good as mine.)

Of course there is a real danger, even if it's a small one, and it's true that we can't predict where this not very lethal terrorism will hit next. People need to take some precautions, to be observant. But the quality that's called for is prudence, not hysteria, which is the flip side of the empty, ignorant bluster other Americans have indulged in since September 11. In a perverse way, Osama bin Laden's al-Qaida paid us the compliment of believing that it would take coordinated, massive attacks and hideous carnage to shake America to the core. Yes, bin Laden called us "soft" for pulling out of Somalia after losing only eighteen sol-diers in the disastrous 1993 raid on Mogadishu, but little did he realize how spineless we really are. Mohammed Atta and company might have saved themselves a lot of trouble by staying safe and snug in a Florida suburb, and just firing off a couple of tainted letters every week.

The genius of targeting the media—no shortage of high-strung neurotics there—is a testimony to the perpetrators' savvy. Yet I can't help but think that postal terrorism lacks the flourish, the opportunity for glorious martyrdom typical of the mujahedin. We still don't know who's responsible for the anthrax scare, but in my darkest hours, I wonder if the sneaky, craven tactic of sending poisoned anonymous letters mostly to *celebrities* isn't in its own way quintessentially American.

It's especially painful now to think of the way the British behaved during the Blitz, when they were subjected to the kind of punishing bombardment that Americans have dished out but never actually taken. They huddled in cellars with candles, singing songs together, and when the bombs stopped falling, they dusted themselves off, changed their clothes, and went out to the theater.

To be fair to the public, the government has utterly fallen down on the job for the past two weeks, doling out announcements that range from unconvincingly blithe reassurances to scary tidbits that resemble nothing so much as the rumors passed around on elementary school playgrounds. Without leaders who demonstrate a responsible, adult response to the domestic situation, people who are so inclined have been encouraged to run around like chickens with their heads cut off.

It's not just that the Bush administration has been logistically unprepared for this sort of crisis, it's that they're conceptually unprepared. Here in New York, as Michael Bloomberg launches into the last leg of his mayoral campaign, pointing to his success as a businessman as proof of his qualifications, what I keep thinking is, "Yeah, but New York is a city, not a corporation." We need a mayor, a civic leader, not a CEO. Likewise, the Bush administration approaches governance as if it were the equivalent of running a big company, with no instinct for the skills of reassurance, motivation, and inspiration that leadership through dark times requires.

I'd like to believe that Americans want to be brave, want to pitch in, want to find a meaningful way to respond to this crisis, this titanic shift in our perceived role in the world. We've just forgotten how. Maybe when our leaders can't come up with a better recommendation than "Go shopping," when their vision of citizenship is so impoverished that consumerism is how they suggest we exercise it, it's not that surprising that our civic culture degenerates into every-man-for-himself drug hoarding.

But America's government is more than a service provider, and all of us are citizens, not customers or clients. The current crisis is about more than just the fear of disease and hijackers and car bombs; it's about remembering what, beyond mutual self-interest, holds us together, what it feels like to care about something bigger than ourselves. We sure could use some help getting back to where we once belonged.

I LOVE OLD GLORY—BUT NOT THE CREEPS WHO'VE WAVED IT ALL MY LIFE

KING KAUFMAN

SEPT. 18, 2001—I'm wrestling with the American flag.

It's everywhere now: tiny ones riffling on car antennas, medium ones waving from porches, giant ones yawning from cranes. People are wearing them. Every Old Navy flag shirt ever bought has been pulled out of the drawer this week, and Stars and Stripes 'do rags are all the rage.

There's no flag flying on my porch. I don't have a flag, and they're hard to come by these days anyway—not that I've tried to get one. And if I had one, I can't figure out if I'd fly it or not.

See, Old Glory and I, we go way back, and we've had our problems.

For most of my life, the American flag has been the cultural property of people I can't stand: right-wingers, jingoists, know-nothing zealots. It's something that hypocritical politicians wrap themselves in. It's something that certain legislators would make it a crime to burn—a position that's an assault on the very freedom that the flag represents. It's something brandished at times like these by idiots who say things like, "Let's go over there and burn those rag-heads!"

During the Gulf War, I hated the American flag. It was everywhere then, too, on porches and car antennas and

140

over the left breast of every uniformed athlete, all in support of a war I and many others thought to be immoral.

But I also love the flag. Seeing it stirs something in me, even when I'm mad at it, or disagree with those who wave it. I am, after all, an American, and despite being opposed to every single military adventure this nation has undertaken in my lifetime, I'm a patriotic one at that.

For me, though, patriotism is more about the freedom to criticize the government than it is about waving a piece of red, white, and blue laundry around and singing "God Bless America." It's about loving our shared national personality—aggressive, impulsive, and open, unimpressed with such Old World nonsense as royalty. It's about feeling at home in a country where the first question asked of new acquaintances is not "Where are you from?" but "What do you do?"; where a loutish baseball star can sit next to a president and say, "Hot as hell, ain't it, Prez?" and be loved all the more for it. It's about loving this country's crazy cultural stew—that "melting pot" that we give ourselves more credit for than we should, but that really does exist.

For me, statements like "America right or wrong" or "America: Love it or leave it," a chestnut from my childhood, are the antithesis of what this country is all about. And those are the sentiments that the flag has come, over many years, to represent for me.

So you'll be surprised to hear that I have an American flag shirt, and maybe surprised to hear that I sometimes wear it—without irony!—on occasions such as the Fourth of July. First of all, it's a hell of a shirt since, after all, it's a Grand Old Flag. But I also like what it says. It says I'm an American. Not for me the pretentious Europhile weenieness that sometimes plagues my fellow middle-class American white boys. I'm a proud son of the country that's produced Bart Simpson and Ambrose Bierce, Robert

Johnson and Abe Lincoln, Michael Jordan and Doc Holliday. Bruce Springsteen said something in his "Born in the U.S.A." days that stayed with me: "That's my flag too." How did the right-wingers and the gun nuts and the xenophobes co-opt it?

There are two kinds of patriots: The "God Bless America" kind and the "This Land Is Your Land" kind. I'm the latter.

On the surface, the songs sound similar: simple melodies with lyrics about America's natural beauty, the mountains and deserts and "oceans white with foam" in one; the redwood forests, Gulf Stream waters, and "sparkling sands of her diamond deserts" in the other.

But that's only because we don't sing all the verses that Woody Guthrie wrote in his song, an answer to "God Bless America," which he hated for its sentimentality and dumb, blind devotion. Here's one of the verses school kids don't sing: "As I was walking, I saw a sign there / And that sign said 'No trespassing' / But on the other side, it didn't say nothing / Now that side was made for you and me." Another verse has "my people" at the relief office, "wondering if this land was made for you and me."

That song's political and social criticism, its questioning, are also part of what make this country great. These things, as much as our culture, our national personality, our country's physical magnificence, are what the flag represents to me.

But when I see that flag flying from a neighbor's porch, my first thought is, "Oh boy, right-wing nut," even when I know better. And I'm not hearing people singing "This Land Is Your Land" over the last week, though "God Bless America" is everywhere.

While I'm not quite a pacifist, I have a pretty simple, even simplistic view of war: You don't fight unless you've been attacked. So now that this country has been attacked,

I agree with the vast majority that some sort of military response is warranted. This is a new feeling for me, this feeling that we're the good guys and we're fighting the bad guys. It makes sense that I'd want to fly the good guys' flag, but that flag comes wrapped around a lot of baggage.

There's the bell. The wrestling match continues.

ISLAM'S FLAWED SPOKESMEN

JAKE TAPPER

SEPT. 26, 2001, WASHINGTON—Less than a week after the September 11 terrorist attacks, President Bush appeared at the Islamic Center in Washington, standing with various leaders of Muslim groups like the Council on American-Islamic Relations (CAIR) and the American Muslim Council (AMC) to make a public show of support for American Muslims, as ugly acts of violence and intimidation were made against Muslims and Arab-Americans.

"It's a great country because we share the same values of respect and dignity and human worth," Bush said. "And it is my honor to be meeting with leaders who feel just the same way I do. They're outraged, they're sad. They love America just as much as I do."

CAIR and AMC have emerged as possibly the two most outspoken U.S. Muslim organizations in the wake of the tragedy, protesting "hate crimes" against Muslims and Arab-Americans, explaining why increased security need not preclude civil liberties for those from the Middle East and Near East, and trying to put a moderate face on a religion Americans only seem to hear about when it rears up in its most extreme incarnations.

USA Today, the *Washington Post*, the *New York Times*, Fox News Channel, and *Salon*—as well as hundreds of media outlets throughout America in search of expertise, information, and a moderate face for Islam—have sought out CAIR and AMC executives in recent weeks. When CNN's Bill Hemmer tackled the question "What do we really know about Islam?" it was Al-Haaj Ghazi Khankan, executive director of CAIR, to whom he turned. And it was Aly Abu Zaakouk, executive director of the AMC, who explained to the *San Francisco Chronicle* how the term "Infinite Justice," the Pentagon's initial name for a U.S. military strategy overseas, would be "offensive to some in the Muslim community."

But reporters are learning it's not easy to find leaders who can authentically speak for Muslim Americans, who represent a wide variety of ethnicities and languages, sects and political views ranging from completely secular to Islamic fundamentalist. CAIR and AMC in particular would not be chosen as representatives by many Muslims. In fact, there are those in American Muslim communities as well as law enforcement who consider CAIR and the AMC to be part of the problem, because both have been seen as tacitly—if not explicitly—supportive of extremist groups guilty of terrorism.

Ibrahim Hooper, communications director of CAIR, refuses to outright condemn Osama bin Laden. "We condemn terrorism, we condemn the attack on the buildings," Hooper said. But why not condemn bin Laden by name, especially after President Bush has now stated that he was clearly responsible for the September 11 attacks?

"If Osama bin Laden was behind it, we condemn him by name," Hooper said. But why the "if"—why qualify the response? Hooper said he resented the question. And what about prior acts of terror linked to bin Laden? Or that bin Laden has urged Muslims to kill Americans?

Again, Hooper demurred, saying only that he condemns acts of terror.

Both groups also refuse to outright condemn Islamic terrorist groups Hamas and Hezbollah. In fact, leaders from both groups have, in recent years, been quoted defending or exhorting organizations that the U.S. State Department classifies as "foreign terrorist." Steven Pomerantz, former FBI assistant director and chief of the FBI's counterterrorism section, once charged that CAIR's activities "effectively give aid to international terrorist groups." Other American Muslim leaders have raised questions about their possible alliances with radical groups, and many academics are disturbed by the groups' prominence.

But CAIR and the AMC strongly disagree with such criticisms, blaming an anti-Muslim bias—or a pro-Israel one. When asked Friday about accusations from other Muslims that his group may be extremist, Aly Abu Zaakouk, the executive director of the AMC, said, "You are trying to blemish our reputation. Get the heck out of here," and hung up the phone. "This kind of thing has been going on for years," said CAIR's Hooper. Asked about Muslim clerics who have complained that his organization is extremist, Hooper said, "The pro-Israel lobby hooks up these guys to be their Muslim front men."

An even more basic problem for many Muslim academics and some clerics is the presumption that these organizations represent their views. "There is general concern among Muslim intellectuals about how not only CAIR but some of these other organizations are claiming to speak in the name of the Muslim community, and how they're coming to be recognized by the government as spokespeople for the Muslim community in the U.S.," says Ali Asani, professor of Islamic studies at Harvard University. "That troubles people."

Neither CAIR nor the AMC divulge their membership numbers, though both seem to be, as AMC executive director Aly Abu Zaakouk says, "working to be the voice of American Muslims in Washington, D.C., in state capitals and local governments, from PTAs to Pennsylvania Avenue."

But unlike, say, the Catholic Church, Islam in the U.S. doesn't have an organized hierarchy. That is, Asani says, "something the American Muslim community has been struggling with." There are moderate-seeming groups like the Islamic Institute and others that will likely gain greater visibility as this crisis continues. But with Muslims coming from so many different countries, with so many different sects within those countries, often the loudest group—or the ones who lobby Congress—are the ones the U.S. government turns to as representative of the estimated 6 million to 8 million American Muslims.

When leaders of these groups speak to the media, Asani says, "Very often whoever's speaking for them represents a very homogenized global form of Islam that refuses to recognize diversity of opinion.

"One of the things I have noticed as a result of this crisis is that there are so many people—this imam and that imam—and everybody is claiming they represent the Muslim community," he says.

Particularly problematic is the attitude of CAIR and AMC toward Islamic terrorist groups. CAIR was critical of the prosecution of Sheik Omar Abdul-Rahman, whom U.S. authorities deemed the ringleader of the 1993 bombing of the World Trade Center, and who was convicted with nine followers in October 1995 of conspiring to blow up the Lincoln Tunnel along with other New York City landmarks.

CAIR went so far as to list Abdul-Rahman's lawyers' criticisms of the trial as "far from free and fair" on a 1996 list of "incidents of anti-Muslim bias and violence" in a book called *The Price of Ignorance* that dealt with the "status of Muslim civil rights in the United States." And CAIR's founder, Nihad Awad, wrote in the *Muslim World Monitor* that the World Trade Center trial, which ended in the conviction in 1994 of four Islamic fundamentalist terrorists, was "a travesty of justice." According to Awad—and despite the confessions of the terrorists from the 1993 attack— "there is ample evidence indicating that both the Mossad and the Egyptian Intelligence played a role in the explosion." (Awad—who met with President Bush last week— has been more circumspect in his comments after this World Trade Center bombing.)

Leaders of the AMC also have expressed concern for the 1993 World Trade Center terrorists who, it should be remembered, differ only from the September 11 bombers in efficiency. "I believe that the judge went out of his way to punish the defendants harshly and with vengeance, and to a large extent, because they were Muslim," Abdurahman Alamoudi, then the executive director of AMC, wrote to his members on August 20, 1994.

Last year, questions about Alamoudi and the actual moderation of the AMC came to light when both Governor George W. Bush and Hillary Clinton returned $1,000 given to their respective campaigns by Alamoudi, no longer the executive director but still a board member of the organization, according to the AMC. Last year, however, Clinton and Bush expressed concern not with Alamoudi's claim that the 1993 World Trade Center bombers were the victims of anti-Muslim bias, but because of his support for other terrorist organizations.

At a November 2000 rally against Israel in Lafayette Park, across from the White House, Alamoudi said to the crowd, "Hear that, Bill Clinton! We are all supporters of Hamas. I wish they add that I am also a supporter of

Hezbollah. Anybody support Hezbollah here?" The crowd cheered.

According to the State Department, Hamas engages in "large-scale suicide bombings—against Israeli civilian and military targets, suspected Palestinian collaborators, and Fatah rivals." A pro-Hamas Web site proudly lists the organization's various acts of violence, against both Israeli military and civilians. Hezbollah, the State Department says, is "known or suspected to have been involved in numerous anti-U.S. terrorist attacks, including the suicide truck bombing of the U.S. Embassy and U.S. Marine barracks in Beirut in October 1983 and the U.S. Embassy annex in Beirut in September 1984. Elements of the group were responsible for the kidnapping and detention of U.S. and other Western hostages in Lebanon. The group also attacked the Israeli Embassy in Argentina in 1992."

But neither CAIR nor the AMC or other Muslim American organizations—much like several of the Arab nations Bush is trying to bring into the anti-terrorism coalition—appear to consider Hamas or Hezbollah terrorist organizations. Nor does it mean that Israeli civilians—especially those who live on settlements in disputed territories—are necessarily considered "innocent civilians" to these groups, either.

But Azar Nafisi, a culture and politics professor at Johns Hopkins University's School of Advanced International Studies, says the support of certain terrorist groups poses a fundamental problem for any organization that hopes to speak for American Muslims. Even if they condemn bin Laden, "Different Muslim organizations in the United States support Hamas," she says. "Are some acts of terrorism valid and some not?"

CAIR's Hooper repudiates the charge wholeheartedly, arguing that no one can point to any example of the major

American Muslim organizations supporting Islamic extremism. He says that they are faulted for "sins of omission, not sins of commission," and that criticism comes their way from other Muslims for not speaking out against terrorist organizations or human rights abuses in Muslim countries, not for necessarily voicing support.

Hooper's comments about Hamas and Hezbollah are even more qualified than they were about bin Laden. "If someone carries out terrorist acts, they should be labeled as a terrorist," he says. "If they don't, they shouldn't." Pressed to address these two terrorist groups by name, Hooper said, "If Hamas kills innocent civilians we condemn them. But I'm not going to condemn legitimate resistance to Israeli occupation."

CAIR, Hooper continues, has never even mentioned the word "Hamas" as an organization, so why should they start now? But that, of course, doesn't include all the mentions of Hamas that CAIR's leaders have made—including CAIR founder Awad's 1994 declaration that before the peace talks between Israel and the Palestinian Authority he "used to support the PLO," but that now he was "in support of the Hamas movement more than the PLO."

Hamas, meanwhile, has claimed credit for the murders of countless Israeli civilians. Middle East scholars believe that Islamic fundamentalists don't consider many victims of terrorist attacks "innocent," which is how they can defend Hamas as not killing innocent people. Hooper, however, refused to answer questions exploring that theory.

"What you're trying to get me to say is the Palestinians don't deserve to live in peace and freedom," Hooper says—though neither the Palestinians nor Israel had been mentioned. Questions about whether CAIR would condemn organizations by name unequivocally, instead of qualifying the condemnations, were just "word games from the pro-

Israel lobby," Hooper said. Instead, Hooper said that the very questions were the problem, and part of a Zionist conspiracy. "This is a game they play," Hooper said, referring to the pro-Israel lobby. "They give me a long list of people to condemn and if you don't give sufficient condemnation you're a terrorist. We would condemn any person or any group that kills innocent civilians. But it's not my duty that when the pro-Israel lobby says 'Jump' I say 'How high?' "

Hooper says that his attitude about whoever is behind the attacks is "go get 'em," but his job is to preserve the rights of Muslims in this country and be vigilant in that task. He criticizes the investigation into the September 11 attacks, saying that when law enforcement refers to "associates" of the terrorists, they're stretching the term. Law enforcement is using the term "associates" too loosely, he says, in a way to target Muslims. "It's like the 'Six degrees of Kevin Bacon' game," he says. "No Muslim is more than six degrees away from Osama bin Laden."

Hooper then ended the interview, and refused to discuss questions about a series of 1994 meetings that CAIR coordinated for Bassam Alamoush, a Jordanian Islamic militant who told a Chicago audience in December of that year that killing Jews was "a good deed." Nor could he be asked about CAIR board member Siraj Wahaj. Wahaj, the imam of the Taqwa Mosque in Brooklyn, decried on TV the September 11 attacks as "criminal" and "wrong." But Wahaj also had invited convicted terrorist Sheikh Omar Abdul Rahman to speak at his mosque, and even testified on his behalf. Before then, in 1991, speaking to the Islamic Association of North Texas, Wahaj called Operation Desert Storm "one of the most diabolical plots ever in the annals of history," and that the war was "part of a larger plan, to destroy the greatest challenge to the Western world, and that's Islam." Just as the U.S.S.R. fell, so too will the U.S., Wahaj said, "unless America changes its course from the new world order and accepts the Islamic agenda."

Long before the September 11 horror, one of the most bold critiques of Muslim American organizations came on January 7, 1999, in a speech to the U.S. State Department by Shaykh Muhammad Hisham Kabbani of the Islamic Supreme Council of America, another nonprofit organization for American Muslims. Kabbani spoke critically about the ideology of the major Muslim American organizations. Warning that too many Muslims in America were supporting terrorist leader Osama bin Laden in a variety of ways, and that too many mosques in the United States were becoming havens for Islamic extremists, Kabbani said that some Muslim American organizations were a big part of the problem.

"There are many Muslim organizations that claim to speak on behalf of the Muslim community but that in reality are not moderate, but extremist," Kabbani said. While Kabbani made no direct references to any group in his speech, it is with AMC and CAIR that he has publicly feuded.

Muslim extremism is dangerous, Kabbani cautioned, and the media needs to learn the difference between Islam and extremism. "What I am seeing, unfortunately, are those that are advising the media, or advising the government are not the moderate Muslims," Kabbani said. "Those whose opinion the government asks are the extremist themselves."

And in a January 1997 letter to a Muslim Web site, Seif Ashmawy, an Egyptian Muslim and peace activist who published the *Voice of Peace* newsletter about Muslim affairs, slammed both CAIR and the AMC for defending Islamic extremism. "It is a known fact that both the AMC and CAIR have defended, apologized for, and rationalized the actions of extremist groups," Ashmawy, who died in a 1998 car accident, wrote. "The real challenge for moderates like myself is to prevent my Muslim brethren from [being] deceived by extremist groups that pretend to represent their interests." The groups' defenders argue that groups like CAIR and the AMC are naturally and rightly critical of the Israeli policy in the West Bank and Gaza. And they make no apologies for vigorously defending the civil rights and civil liberties of Arab-Americans and Muslims, which sometimes leads them to butt heads with U.S. law enforcement. CAIR's Hooper says Kabbani represents just a small group of Muslims. Law enforcement officials who make charges such as Pomerantz's are "anti-Muslim bigots."

But the views of the more radical American Muslims will continue to face increased scrutiny, and in some cases, condemnation from the American public. Until early last week, for instance, the Islamic Center of Boca Raton, Florida, posted on its Web site an openly anti-Semitic essay that referred to Jews as being "known for their treachery and corruption" and quoted from a Muslim text that read, "O Muslim! There is Jew behind me, kill him!"

Dan McBride, spokesman for the Boca Raton mosque, said the essay, titled, "Why can't the Jews and Muslims live together in peace?" generated three e-mail complaints, so they took it down.

"As fellow Americans, we're all a little sensitive right now and we don't want to increase any tensions," McBride said. "So we're trying to be a little politically correct right now."

Which is not to say McBride disagrees with anything in the essay. In fact, he defends it word for word, including passages that Art Teitelbaum, the southern area director of the Anti-Defamation League, calls "filled with poisonous anti-Semitic bigotry." McBride defends the assertion, for instance, that Jews are "usurpers and aggressors, who have oppressed and persecuted others, and who are known for their treachery and corruption throughout the world, historically and in the present age." And that Jews have "carried out chemical and radiational [*sic*] experiments on their prisoners, and taken organs from them for transplant into Jewish patients." McBride says "that's all documented," though he could not provide any documentation.

"This is the kind of ranting and ravings that you get out of—I would like to say fanatics, but it's not just fanatics, it's people who are ignorant," says Johns Hopkins' Nafisi, who was raised Muslim in Iran. "It's one interpretation of Islam, an interpretation that has been encouraged by many Muslim leaders around the world. But it's not the Islam I was raised on."

Ultimately, as the American public requires more knowledge of Islam, the challenge will be in finding leaders who can explain the faith, while being free of their own ties to the religion's fundamentalist sects. But for any American Muslim leader, in trying to appeal to a wide variety of people, there may easily be examples of, or acceptance of, Islamic extremism in their past.

During the national day of prayer and remembrance September 14 at the National Cathedral, attended by Bush and other U.S. dignitaries, Muzammil Siddiqi, imam for the Islamic Society of North America, read from the Quran, saying that "Those that lay the plots of evil, for them is a terrible penalty; and the plotting of such will be not abided."

But, as columnist Charles Krauthammer wondered in the *Washington Post*, one has to ask "who are the layers of plots of evil" to whom Siddiqi refers? "Those who perpetrated the World Trade Center attack? Or America, as thousands of Muslims in the street claim? The imam might have made that clear. He did not." It was not the first time

Siddiqi was disturbingly noncommittal. In 1989, after the *fatwa* death sentence issued against author Salman Rushdie for his book *The Satanic Verses*, Siddiqi's view on whether Rushdie should be killed was difficult to assess. "Asked whether he personally thinks capital punishment would be appropriate in Rushdie's case," wrote the *Los Angeles Times*, "Siddiqi was non-committal, saying that would have to be determined in the due process of Islamic law."

THE PRIME-TIME SMEARING
OF SAMI AL-ARIAN

ERIC BOEHLERT

JAN. 19, 2002—It may not provide him much comfort, but tenured University of South Florida professor Sami Al-Arian may be the first computer science professor ever mugged by four of the nation's most influential news organizations.

USF administrators fired the Kuwaiti-born professor after his appearance on a nationally televised conservative talk show revived discredited allegations of ties to anti-Israel terrorists. His crime? Not telling viewers that his views did not necessarily reflect those of the school. It was a tortured rationale that all but guaranteed future litigation.

As *Salon* recently reported, the Al-Arian episode raises disturbing questions about free speech, academic freedom, and the future of tenured status. But what's also important to understand is the crucial role the press played in the unfolding saga.

The University of South Florida is ultimately responsible for firing Al-Arian. But equally culpable are Fox News Channel, NBC, Media General (specifically its Tampa newspaper), and the giant radio conglomerate Clear Channel Communications.

In the wake of the September 11 terrorist attacks, all four media giants, eagerly tapping into the country's mood of vengeance and fear, latched onto the Al-Arian story, fudging the facts and ignoring the most rudimentary tenets of journalism in their haste to better tell a sinister story about lurking Middle Eastern dangers here at home.

The story went national when Al-Arian was invited on the Fox News Channel's *The O'Reilly Factor* show back on September 26. Host Bill O'Reilly revived inflammatory charges against Al-Arian dating back, in some cases, fifteen years. Those charges were that a now-defunct Islamic think tank that Al-Arian founded and ran in conjunction with USF operated as a sort of home away from home for radical Palestinians and terrorists. The charges had been thoroughly investigated and rejected by USF, and an immigration judge; the FBI has been looking for years and has never filed any charges.

Not even his harshest critics suggest Al-Arian has done anything in the last five years that could be even remotely construed as aiding terrorist organizations. The entire controversy sprang from the fact that viewers became enraged after old allegations were re-aired, albeit often in mangled form, by O'Reilly.

O'Reilly's accusatory and hectoring interrogation of Al-Arian, filled with false statements and McCarthy-like smears, climaxed in a chilling parting shot in which the host repeatedly told his stammering guest that if he were with the CIA, "I'd follow you wherever you went"— clearly implying that he believed Al-Arian was a terrorist. Not surprisingly in the fearful and hysterical climate after September 11, the show resulted in a torrent of angry calls, including death threats against Al-Arian, to USF.

Before firing him, USF placed Al-Arian on paid leave, saying his presence made the campus unsafe and pointing to an avalanche of hate mail and death threats.

But the Gulf Coast hysteria was entirely created by the media. Without the *Tampa Tribune*, which undertook a dubious seven-year crusade against Al-Arian, there would have been no story to begin with. Without *The O'Reilly Factor*—a showcase for noisy right-wing ranting whose producers apparently didn't even know that Al-Arian had been cleared of charges before they handed him over to their equally ignorant hanging-judge host—the controversy would never have been revived. Without incendiary, know-nothing Clear Channel radio jocks, led by a gentleman named Bubba the Love Sponge, there would almost certainly have been far fewer USF death threats. And without NBC's sloppy work on *Dateline* there would probably have been no firing.

The Al-Arian story reveals what happens when journalists, abandoning their role as unbiased observers, lead an ignorant, alarmist crusade against suspicious foreigners who in a time of war don't have the power of the press or public sympathy to fight back. It's called a pile-on, and this game first began in Tampa, seven years ago.

On April 21, 1995, *Tampa Tribune* reporter Michael Fechter wrote a news story about the bombing at the Oklahoma City Federal Building, which had been destroyed two days earlier by domestic right-wing terrorists. Law enforcement officials had yet to make an arrest, but Fechter had his own ideas. "More and more," he wrote, "terrorism experts in the United States and elsewhere say Wednesday's bombing in Oklahoma City bears the characteristics of other deadly attacks linked to Islamic militants."

Fechter seemed to be an odd choice to write the piece, since at the time the county news reporter had virtually no experience covering religion, politics, or terrorism for the *Tribune*. Instead, he wrote crime stories, covered local city council politics, and monitored neighborhood action groups.

But what readers didn't know was that Fechter had recently befriended controversial terrorism expert Steve Emerson—who has been accused of sloppy journalism and with having a pervasive anti-Arab bias—and behind the scenes was remaking himself into a self-styled authority on terrorism. The following month the *Tribune* would uncork Fechter's sprawling series about Al-Arian and the alleged ties between him, his USF think tank, and terrorists. The story would keep Fechter busy for the next six years, as he churned out nearly seventy stories on the topic.

But first, as a sort of dry run, Fechter wrote about the Oklahoma City bombing case. Taking the cue from his terrorist mentor Emerson, who made the same bogus claim on national television, Fechter pointed an accusatory finger at Muslims. Looking back, the glaring mistake should have raised a red flag among *Tribune* editors about their new in-house terrorist expert.

Thirty-seven days after the Oklahoma City miscue, Fechter's exposé landed on Page 1 of Sunday's May 28, 1995, paper. Picking up where Emerson had left off with his inflammatory 1994 documentary *Jihad in America*, which argued angry Muslims at home pose a larger danger to this country than Muslim terrorists abroad, Fechter breathlessly reported that Al-Arian had raised money for Islamic groups that had killed hundreds of people around the world. In addition, Fechter wrote that World Islamic Studies Enterprises, or WISE, the USF think tank Al-Arian helped create, had associated with, and even invited to the campus, known terrorists.

As would become Fechter's custom for years to come, the evidence presented was mostly circumstantial, with guilt by association being his weapon of choice.

That was the conclusion other area journalists came to over time, with the *St. Petersburg Times* and the *Miami*

Herald both agreeing that the *Tribune*'s charges against
Al-Arian were weak and revolved around questionable
journalism.

John Sugg, writing in the Tampa alternative newspaper the
Weekly Planet, was the most scathing, concluding, "The
Tribune has woven together unproven assertions, articles from
highly suspect publications, and out-of-context statements."

Those types of notices probably kept the story from
being picked up nationally at the time. Locally, however,
the *Tribune* series had an enormous impact, particularly on
Al-Arian's life. Spurred on by the paper's provocative
charges, local law enforcement agencies launched investigations, raided the WISE office as well as Al-Arian's home,
and arrested his brother-in-law for deportation.

How do we know government investigators were following the *Tribune*'s lead and not the other way around?
Weeks after the first of the paper's Al-Arian stories ran, the
professor's citizenship application was derailed by the
Immigration and Naturalization Service. (Al-Arian has
lived in America for a quarter of a century.) Al-Arian filed a
Freedom of Information request to see what secret evidence was being used to justify the delay. Two years later
the INS's evidence was revealed: *Tampa Tribune* newspaper
clippings.

Over the years the *Tribune* has supported Fechter, creating a separate Web page so readers could view his entire
series, and often cheerleading his work from the editorial
page.

And both the *Tribune* and Fechter enjoy staunch defenders in the community. "I felt the reporting of the
Tribune warranted a Pulitzer Prize for investigative reporting," says Norman Gross, leader of a Tampa area Jewish
media-watch group.

Gross says he recently met with *Tribune* editors on

December 19 and discussed the paper's coverage. The next day the paper ran an editorial entitled "USF Gets Rid of a Hatemonger," fervently supporting USF's decision to fire the professor. That was odd, since two months earlier a *Tribune* editorial, while denouncing Al-Arian's actions, suggested any talk of firing him was "ridiculous." After all, asked the *Tribune*, "Do we want a university where there is no free expression of ideas?" Apparently, after December 19, the paper's answer is yes. (Joe Guidry, who wrote the contradictory editorials, did not return calls seeking comment.)

The seeds of Al-Arian's firing were planted in Fechter's May 28, 1995, article. Some of the evidence Fechter cited in order to substantiate his claim that Al-Arian had ties to terrorists consisted of "rhetoric presented in the conferences" organized by the USF professor. Fechter also noted that Sudanese leader Hassan Turabi, whom he characterized as "the leader of a terrorist state," had visited the USF campus under Al-Arian's watch. Later, Fechter wrote ominously that Al-Arian had "lured" Turabi to USF.

Unfortunately for Fechter's alarmist thesis, on that same trip Turabi also met with Senator Nancy Kassebaum, R-Kan., Representative Lee Hamilton, D-Ind., and the editorial board of the *Washington Post*, and he spoke at both the Council on Foreign Relations and the Brookings Institution.

Al-Arian had also founded a Palestinian advocacy group called Islamic Committee for Palestine, or ICP. In his original May 28 article, Fechter, trying to tie Al-Arian to terrorism, quoted fiery articles from an ICP publication supporting the intifada and the 1993 World Trade Center bombing—though Fechter acknowledged that the magazine "included a disclaimer that views expressed were not necessarily the ICP's."

From Day 1, Al-Arian, while never shying away from his militant support for the Palestinian cause, has denied supporting terrorism or terrorist activities. "I have never raised a cent for Islamic Jihad," he said. He has acknowledged that ICP helped raise funds—$20,000 or $30,000 a year—for Palestinian charity organizations, and suggested in a letter to a friend that anyone looking to help Palestinians should send money to Hamas, the radical Islamic resistance group. Hamas, whose members have staged numerous terrorist attacks against Israel, has a political wing that distributes money to Palestinian widows and orphans of men killed in the conflict with Israel. It can certainly be argued that money raised for Hamas, regardless of its intentions, could end up supporting its terrorist activities. But it was only in 1996, after anti-terrorism legislation was passed, that it became a crime to send money to foreign groups classified by the State Department as terrorist organizations, such as Hamas.

In fact, what Fechter uncovered, and the rest of the media piled onto, was not a dangerous terrorist but a fairly mainstream—that is, pro-intifada—Palestinian, who in his hot-headed youth made regrettably inflammatory comments about Israel, but who has never been tied to any terrorist groups. What's noteworthy here is how eagerly the post-9/11 media conflated the Palestinian cause with bin Laden and al-Qaida, when in fact there is little actual connection, beyond a shared anger at Israel, between the two.

In a July 10, 1997, article, Fechter tried mightily to prove that a local Muslim travel agent was somehow involved in the 1993 World Trade Center bombing because one year before the blast he booked a flight for one of the suspects. Fechter wrote that the travel agent "advocated violence abroad against the enemies of Islam."

A correction in the next day's *Tribune* conceded that accusation was false.

In October of 1995 the Al-Arian story took on added urgency when Ramadan Abdullah Shallah, the former head of WISE who had returned to the Middle East months earlier, suddenly emerged as the head of Palestinian Islamic Jihad, a radical group that has engaged in many acts of terrorism against Israelis. The USF community expressed shock at the turn of events, and to this day there's been no proof that anyone in Tampa knew of Shallah's connections, if any, to the organization when he was at USF, or any proof that he was involved in terrorist activities at that time or subsequently.

That didn't deter Fechter, who on August 7, 1997, reported matter-of-factly that "Shallah now says he served as the terrorist group's second in command" while working in Tampa. The *Tribune* subsequently retracted that assertion.

At one point Fechter quoted an obscure Jordanian newspaper, *al Urdun*, that suggested that even if Shallah hadn't been tapped to run Islamic Jihad, another WISE researcher, Basheer Nafi, was next in line. Al Urdun later retracted the story, but Fechter continued to make the assertion in print.

Why? Fechter today insists, "If the article was untrustworthy, the retraction was, too."

While Fechter had no qualms about quoting from obscure Middle Eastern papers to support his charges, he was less willing to cite experts. Fechter has never quoted this November 1995 passage from Israeli journalist Ze'ev Schiff, generally acknowledged to be the nation's leading commentator on military affairs, who informed readers that Shallah "does not have a previous experience in terrorist actions. His background is predominantly political. . . . Nor is he considered a religious fundamentalist."

The saga took its second major turn when Al-Arian's WISE colleague and brother-in-law, Mazen Al-Najjar, was arrested for deportation. Although he had clearly over-stayed his student visa, Al-Najjar appealed. Rather than release him on bond, the government submitted secret evidence to the court, insisting that Al-Najjar had terrorist ties. A judge ordered Al-Najjar held without bond.

In a move that turned traditional journalism ethics on its head, Fechter, who had already been criticized by area Muslims for being biased in his reporting, was allowed to write a Sunday commentary for the *Tribune*, where he derided the "public sympathy campaign" being waged on Al-Najjar's behalf.

For more than three years Al-Najjar sat in jail without knowing what the evidence against him was. Finally, in 2000, a federal judge ruled that the use of secret evidence had violated Al-Najjar's constitutional rights and ordered a new bond hearing. After sifting through all the government evidence that, like the *Tribune* reporting, tried to tie WISE and its associates to terrorist activities, Judge R. Kevin McHugh, a former military judge, ordered Al-Najjar set free.

In his decision, McHugh set aside space to address the activity at USF: "Although there were allegations that ICP and WISE were 'fronts' for Palestinian political causes, there is no evidence before the Court that demonstrates that either organization was a front for the [Islamic Jihad]. To the contrary, there is evidence in the record to support the conclusion that WISE was a reputable and scholarly research center and the ICP was highly regarded."

To this day, the judge's passage, which knocked down the entire premise of Fechter's crusade, has never been quoted in full by any *Tampa Tribune* reporter. Readers only saw the whole quote when Al-Arian himself penned an Op-

Ed for the paper, one year after the ruling was issued.

That court decision, combined with an independent investigation launched by USF whose final 200-page report also found no proof of terrorist ties to WISE or USF, seemed to signal the logical conclusion of the Al-Arian saga. But the irrepressible Fechter returned last June with another in his series of "Tampa's a hotbed for Islamic radical" stories. "Tampa Links Cited in Bombing Trial" was the headline to the 1,800-word, Page 1 *Tribune* story.

Fechter reported that the name of Tariq Hamdi had come up during the trial of four men convicted of conspiring to destroy U.S. embassies in Kenya and Tanzania, where 224 people were killed in 1998. That's because Hamdi, now a journalist, had been hired as a consultant by ABC News to help secure an interview with Osama bin Laden in 1998. Prosecutors contended that Hamdi delivered to bin Laden's network a replacement battery for a satellite telephone. Hamdi was never charged with any wrongdoing.

What were the "Tampa links" that led the *Tribune* to play the story on Page 1? It turns out that Hamdi, a former grad student who left USF a decade ago, once served as ICP's office manager.

This past December, Fechter wrote another excited, Page 1 story about a document found in Al-Arian's home that detailed a "vast covert intelligence and training operation spread throughout the United States."

After reading all 1,400 words, readers learned the document was A) written twenty years ago by B) an unknown person C) seized by investigators in 1996 who D) confronted Al-Arian with it one year earlier and then took no action.

By then, the Al-Arian story, thanks to the post–September 11 interest in all things terror-related, as well as the professor's ill-fated appearance on *The O'Reilly Factor,* was big news again. But what the *Tribune* has never told its readers is the role Fechter played in helping O'Reilly's producers prepare for the show. He provided them with translations of a solicitation letter Al-Arian wrote seven years ago, as well as a composite videotape of meetings from the late 1980s and early 1990s.

Tribune editor-in-chief Gil Thelen defends the information sharing, calling it nothing more than a "professional courtesy," and denies that the paper needed to inform readers of Fechter's role as he covered the aftermath of Al-Arian's TV appearance, including the death threats, his paid leave, and then his firing.

But Dean Mills, dean of the School of Journalism at the University of Missouri, disagrees, saying, "If a reporter or newspaper played some role in another medium's program which became a news event, then they have an obligation to include that fact in their coverage."

When prepping O'Reilly's producers, Fechter never mentioned Judge McHugh's definitive ruling, which completely exonerated Al-Arian and WISE. "I felt confident that Dr. Al-Arian would be capable of pointing out the judge's writings on his own," wrote Fechter in an e-mail response to *Salon*. "My interest is in getting answers to questions [Al-Arian] does not want to face and that other reporters choose not to ask."

Incredibly—or maybe not so incredibly—O'Reilly's producers apparently never bothered to look into the legal disposition of Al-Arian's case. John Sugg, now senior editor of Atlanta's *Creative Loafing* newspaper, recently talked to Fox producers when they contacted him about appearing on the show for a follow-up segment about Al-Arian.

"They said they did not know there was exculpatory information or that a judge had examined this stuff," says Sugg. "They felt like O'Reilly got blindsided."

So much for the no-spin zone.

For weeks, O'Reilly played up the Al-Arian interview, returning to the topic fourteen different times. Despite assuring viewers that "we researched it pretty thoroughly," he routinely bungled the facts.

For instance, during his original interview O'Reilly insisted that former Tampa resident Tariq Hamdi was "on the [FBI] list of suspected terrorists," which is simply not true. On subsequent telecasts O'Reilly insisted that "to this day," Al-Arian "has contacts with Hamas and the Islamic Jihad" and remains "very tight" with the head of the Palestinian Islamic Jihad. Those are allegations not even Fechter or Emerson have dared to make.

Neither O'Reilly nor his producers returned calls for comment.

By the time USF fired Al-Arian, O'Reilly was trying to wash his hands of the situation: "I'm getting blamed for this guy losing his job. I don't want that blame on me," he told viewers.

O'Reilly's belated profession of blamelessness is ludicrous, but there's plenty of media blame to go around.

Tampa Tribune columnist Daniel Ruth helped by painting a picture of an unrepentant professor still spouting hate when he recently wrote that Al-Arian had made highly inflammatory, anti-Israel comments at a rally in 1998. Ruth was off by a decade: Al-Arian made the remarks, which he now says he regrets having made, as a thirty-year-old in 1988, the year the intifada began. The *Tribune* has yet to correct that error.

Certainly the veteran terrorism expert and NBC news consultant, Steve Emerson, would take credit, not blame, for Al-Arian's firing. Despite the fact no charges have ever been brought against the USF professor (on the contrary; he's met personally with both presidents Clinton and Bush in recent years), Emerson has been branding Al-Arian a terrorist for close to a decade. During a 1996 speaking engagement in St. Petersburg, Emerson, citing anonymous sources, assured the audience that Palestinian radicals at USF were involved in the 1993 World Trade Center bombing.

Testifying before Congress that same year, Emerson said that materials seized at Al-Arian's home constituted "one of the largest acquisitions of raw terrorist material ever found in the United States."

And during a 1997 speech Emerson laid it on thick, insisting, "From the safety of [his] Tampa office, Mr. Al-Arian operated a terrorist organization, raising funds, recruiting terrorists and bringing them into the country, devising terrorist strategies, and actually directing specific terrorist attacks." Again, Emerson's unspecified sources made it impossible to verify these sensational charges. Of course, if Emerson had real evidence to support them, Al-Arian wouldn't be sweating an appearance on *The O'Reilly Factor* today; he'd be doing hard time.

Despite that string of hollow indictments, producers at NBC's news magazine *Dateline* didn't hesitate to usher Emerson on the air last October for a segment to—what else?—accuse Al-Arian of aiding terrorists.

In her introduction, NBC's Jane Pauley recklessly stressed a connection between Al-Arian and September 11: "We're told that it's probable, if not certain, that there are still terrorists among us. Now investigators say there is evidence that an organization with ties to Middle East terrorists may have been operating in Florida for as long as a decade."

The "investigators" turned out to be . . . Steve Emerson. In fact, NBC never interviewed a single law enforcement official for its October 28 report. The *Dateline* piece consisted entirely of Emerson, who was given a prime-time platform to air his creative accusations. (Al-Arian refused to appear on the show.)

Emerson told *Dateline* reporter Bob McKeown that Islamic Jihad "had essentially relocated to the United States in the city of Tampa," where it was operating as "a shadow government" for the terrorist group.

Emphasis on shadow, since neither the FBI, the INS, the CIA, USF, nor the Tampa police were ever able to uncover it. Only Emerson.

Of course, Emerson never mentioned that Judge McHugh had looked at these allegations in 2000 and found no wrongdoing. It's not clear whether McKeown even knew about the judge's ruling.

Neither *Dateline* producers nor McKeown would comment about the segment. Hussein Ibish, communications director at the American Arab Anti-discrimination Committee, says he called McKeown twice after the piece aired, but never heard back. "If I'd been responsible for such a shoddy piece of journalism I wouldn't want to be held accountable," says Ibish. "It was indefensible."

Another key media player in this drama has been the *St. Petersburg Times*, the *Tribune*'s competitor across the Bay. Interestingly, the *Times*, which for years had offered a long-running counterbalance to the *Tribune*'s sinister take on Al-Arian, may have precipitated Al-Arian's firing when the paper seemed to turn on him after September 11.

"I've gotten the distinct impression that something has happened at the *St. Pete Times*. Their coverage [on Al-Arian] has just deteriorated," says Joe Mahon, a former Middle Eastern oil executive who has met with local editors in recent years on behalf of Muslims in the Tampa community.

That shift most likely stemmed from the fact that the

Times' Susan Aschoff, who worked the story for years, was taken off the beat on September 28, just as Al-Arian's appearance on *The O'Reilly Factor* was exploding into a big national story.

Aschoff wouldn't discuss the move. But according to Mahon, who spoke with the reporter last fall, she was told the move stemmed from her "incompetence." Yet ten months earlier Aschoff's editors had nominated her work for a Pulitzer Prize. (She's still with the paper, covering medical news.)

"She was clearly upset and did not know what was going on," says Mahon. "It puzzles me and I wonder if the paper was responding to pressure."

Norman Gross, who runs the local Jewish media-watch group, and who had complained about Aschoff's work in the past, was glad to see her go. "I just felt she'd become so taken with Al-Arian that she could no longer write a story without putting in a phrase or twist sympathetic to the cause."

Neither *Times* editor and president Paul Tash nor managing editor Neil Brown returned calls to discuss the newspaper's coverage.

The paper's November 1 editorial, "Behind Al-Arian's Facade," added to the perception that after September 11, *St. Petersburg Times* executives may have felt, at least from a P.R. standpoint, that they were on the wrong side of an emotionally charged issue involving Middle Eastern terrorism.

Taking its lead from NBC's *Dateline* broadcast, the paper lashed out at the USF professor for "playing his American hosts for fools for years," and "spewing the most hateful sort of venom in the company of fellow Islamic extremists." (The paper's editorial board still maintains that Al-Arian was unjustly fired.)

Robert Friedman, who wrote the unsigned editorial,

says it was based on new information aired by NBC. But Robin Blumner, a member of the paper's editorial board, insists that *Dateline* simply aired allegations already familiar to local readers. "It was all old news," says Blumner, who lobbied unsuccessfully to have the wording of the Al-Arian editorial toned down. (The fact is, one year earlier the *Tribune* had written about the information Emerson used for his *Dateline* segment.)

The final media players in the Al-Arian debacle were the local Tampa talk radio jocks, who vilified Al-Arian for months. "The Clear Channel stations, especially 970 AM [WFLA] led the charge against Al-Arian," reports Bob Lorei, news director at Tampa's WMNF. Clear Channel is the largest owner of radio stations in America, with approximately 1,200 outlets nationwide, and eight in Tampa.

WFLA host Tedd Webb highlighted his ignorance of the case when he stated publicly that ABC turned to "a professor from USF" to secure a bin Laden interview. (Webb was presumably referring to Hamdi, who is not "a professor from USF.") He has also echoed Emerson's claim that "the terrorist cell operating at the University of South Florida was the largest . . . in the world."

Then why no arrests? Webb had a conspiracy theory to explain that: "In an effort to bring peace in the Middle East between the Israelis and the Palestinians," the FBI never made a move on Al-Arian.

But Webb was the soul of journalistic probity compared to his R-rated Clear Channel colleague Todd Clem, better known as Bubba the Love Sponge. Even before Al-Arian appeared on *The O'Reilly Factor*, Bubba was falsely telling Tampa listeners that Muslim students at USF had been seen celebrating the September 11 attacks. University spokesman Michael Reich says the school called the station and spoke to representatives in the newsroom who conceded they knew the accusations were not true but that they had nothing to do with Bubba's program. The university's general counsel office then contacted Clear Channel's station manager, but to no avail. Bubba continued making the bogus claim, even insisting that he had a videotape to prove it. He never did produce a tape. WXTB program director Brad Hardin did not return calls seeking comment.

(Even as the horrific events of September 11 were unfolding, Bubba and his morning crew on WXTB managed to find moments of humor. Watching live TV shots of the World Trade Center engulfed in flames, Bubba suggested they crank call and tell workers there, "In case you guys don't know it, the building's on fire!" One sidekick joked, "You won't be able to go to Windows on the World for lunch today!")

One week after the terrorist attacks Bubba called a local doctor's office on the air and accused him of making anti-American comments. Three hundred angry Bubba listeners deluged the doctor with calls that morning, and his office was forced to close early. Unfortunately, the shock jock had the wrong man.

Then, after Bubba spent one October morning insulting Al-Arian on the air, the professor was hit with a wave of hate e-mails.

One would not think that Bubba the Love Sponge's role in fomenting a campaign of ignorant, hate-filled e-mails against a tenured professor would be something that University of South Florida administrators would highlight. But Jack Wheat, USF's special assistant to the president, recently answered an e-mail from a *Salon* reader who complained about the school's decision to fire Al-Arian with the following remarkable communication:

"Thank you for your message. Unfortunately, a good number of Americans do believe that he is speaking for the

University. We have received hundreds of communications indicating that from people whose mastery of syntax and argumentation suggest that they are quite intelligent. More troubling have been the barrage of computer viruses sent by people who are intelligent but warped. But most troubling have been the death threats, often stimulated by local media personalities such as Bubba the Love Sponge, that have breached the safety of the learning environment. Dr. Al-Arian has violated the professional obligations that are clearly delineated in the contract negotiated by the faculty union and the State University System of Florida."

Wheat could not be reached for comment.

Al-Arian's battle to get his job back at USF will likely end up in the courts. Perhaps while his attorneys examine the university's egregious behavior, they should train their attention on some of America's biggest media players as well.

STAND BESIDE HER

KING KAUFMAN

OCT. 22, 2001, ST. LOUIS—Neema (not her real name), an Egyptian woman, brought her second-grade daughter to register at an elementary school in the inner-ring suburb of Webster Groves last week. She says that as she pulled into the parking lot, where lots of parents were picking up their kids, two women blocked her with their cars, preventing her from parking. They also blocked her exit, she says, and she had to maneuver in reverse to get away. "And when we were leaving, some of the kids from that school were throwing plastic—well, thanks, my God, it was plastic bottles."

Though Neema dresses in Western clothes, she has always worn a *hijab*, the traditional head covering of Muslim women. "I have only put a very small veil on my head. We're required that by the Quran."

But Neema has stopped wearing her veil, and she doesn't drop her daughter off at school. She says she made these decisions partly so she doesn't make others feel uncomfortable—"just really to give peace and tranquillity for people"—but she's also scared.

"If I am in my country, and they are saying, 'Americans will bomb my country,' what am I going to do? I will try to do the best I can to avoid the bombing, right? So that's what I'm trying here," she says.

Recently, Neema has had some help in avoiding "the bombing," as she puts it. Local volunteers have come forward to act as escorts for those who have been threatened, or feel threatened, by knee-jerk reactions to their clothing or appearance. Similar ad hoc programs have sprung up, with varying degrees of formality, in several other American cities with large Arab-American and Muslim populations, providing company and a measure of protection in public for those afraid to leave their homes.

Violence and threats against Muslims and Arab-Americans, and those, such as Sikhs and Hindu Indians, who are often mistaken for them, have skyrocketed since the September 11 suicide attacks on the World Trade Center and the Pentagon. Within hours of the plane crashes, a mosque in Texas was riddled with bullets. Killings in California, Arizona, Texas, and Michigan have been attributed to the backlash. The FBI has opened more than 160 hate crime investigations since the incident. Various Muslim and Arab groups report that anywhere from 300 to 800 anti-Arab or anti-Muslim incidents have come to their attention since the attacks, ranging from verbal abuse to murder.

But, as President Bush noted last week, there's been another side to the situation. "I was struck by this, that in many cities when Christian and Jewish women learned that Muslim women, women of cover, were afraid of going out of their homes alone, that they went shopping with them, that they showed true friendship and support, an act that shows the world the true nature of America," Bush said in a nationally televised speech.

In St. Louis, longtime peace activist Bill Ramsey, who runs the Human Rights Action Service, a network of activists and a political letter-writing service, hastily rounded up nearly two hundred volunteers to accompany

Muslim and Middle Eastern people, most of them women, who were afraid to go out after the terrorist attacks. He had checked in with Arab-American colleagues and friends in the hours after the disaster to find that many were going to their children's schools to make sure the kids were not being harassed—and in some cases pulling them out of school—and making plans to hunker down at home.

Ramsey also learned from the local International Institute, an organization that helps immigrants and refugees settle in St. Louis, that the group just settled more than one hundred Afghans in the past six months, and also had a large community of Somalis and a large community of Iraqis that they were concerned about.

Angie O'Gorman, who directs the Immigration Law Project at Legal Services of Eastern Missouri, trained the volunteers in techniques of accompaniment developed for Central American refugees in the 1980s.

"It's basically good communication skills and learning how to use your body in ways that are not aggressive, even if you may be feeling angry," O'Gorman says. She says the idea is for the volunteer to place herself in a position to protect the person being threatened without becoming a threat herself.

Once trained, the volunteers were deployed at places like Soulard Market, a downtown farmers market favored by immigrants and refugees, among others, and at a recent international festival. They also made themselves available to accompany women to English lessons and on other daily errands. A day at the park was organized for families who had been too frightened to let their children out of the house.

Neema reports that she's had several offers of help from both Christian and Jewish organizations and individuals, and she's taken up one of them.

"I took only one Christian lady," she says. "She came last Friday and she was very nice." The woman brought her two children with her and the families went out together. "She even asked me can I wear my veil when I'm coming out with her, and I said it's better off I can leave it. That way we will not be bothered."

An immediate problem for the volunteers was that they needed to have a way to be recognizable to the people they're trying to help. Ramsey found the answer to that problem in a closet, where an old banner from a Central American campaign repeated a folk-art representation of a bird numerous times. The banner was chopped up, and each volunteer was given a piece of cloth with a bird on it to wear to Soulard. The bird symbol was also displayed at the International Institute, so it would be recognized, and eventually buttons were made for volunteers to wear. It's become the symbol of the accompaniment project.

At the market, the volunteers simply stroll around, giving people the traditional Muslim "*Salaam*" greeting, but otherwise leaving them alone unless the other person initiates a conversation. "It's sort of a delicate balance of watching out for people but not giving them the sense that *we're* stalking them," Ramsey says. "We're not doing this to get all involved and interrupt people's lives with our service. We're supposed to be there just making it easier for them to do what they're doing. We sort of keep our distance."

Immediately following the hijackings, Muslim and Arab customers stayed away from Soulard Market, say several vendors and volunteers. But many people—regardless of their faith or appearance—stayed at home in the wake of the trauma. And as "women of cover" have returned to the market, there has been nothing resembling an incident there.

Which is just fine with the volunteers. "Our job is to

intervene if something happens, but more immediately our job is just to create environments that people will trust so that they can go about their lives and routines," Ramsey says.

"I think the first day, everybody was scared so the words came out, but I think now everybody's figured out that people who are in America are mostly running away from that stuff," says Sam Rammaha, a Jordanian man interviewed at a crafts booth at the International Folksfest, a festival sponsored by the International Institute at which accompaniment volunteers were present. "I think we're cautious, that we expect [problems], but really it's not what people make it sound like. Most people who are prejudiced, they will just come out anyway, but in general everything is good. Thank God, as they say!"

Sahla Peterman, an Iranian college teacher shooting the breeze in a Persian food stall at the same festival, agrees. "I guess I've lived here long enough, I've been here twenty-six years," she says, "and you know, sometimes you get this feeling, like, you go to a store or something, that people stare at you, but for the most part people have been very supportive."

Ramsey believes, however, that some ugly incidents are going unreported. "I don't think we're getting the full story on how people are feeling and how much that kind of harassment is going on."

He says that about two weeks after the attacks on New York and Washington, he and others met with groups of refugees from Somalia, Iraq, and Afghanistan. "In one or two cases of those meetings, they would start to talk about things that were happening to them, and then they would say something to the effect, 'Well, this is just something we may have to swallow right now because we know this country is going through something it's never gone through before,'" Ramsey says. "So I'm certain that all acts of harassment are not being reported to the police, or even to the International Institute or to us accompanying them. I guess it's hard to get a statistical analysis of what's going on. We have a lot of anecdotal stuff."

It's worth noting that Iranians are not Arab, just as it's worthwhile to know that most Muslims aren't Arab, either. In fact, a huge number of Arab-Americans—maybe half or more—are Christians, not Muslims. But these distinctions are lost on most of the American public, especially those who would lump all of the above in with terrorists.

"A number of people are worried about [violence or threats], especially ladies, who are readily recognizable outside as a Muslim if they are covering their head with a scarf," says Muhamed Hasic, a Bosnian who is the imam at the Islamic Center, a mosque in St. Louis. "Also when they go to the store they receive completely different treatment. People look at them strange and all that."

Several women mentioned harassment at supermarkets in the weeks since the terrorist attacks. Neema says she's been followed around her local Schnucks by store employees.

"You find one guy or one woman behind you, watching what are you doing. Are you putting anything on the food? Do you have anything? Do you have any big bags, are you bringing things out of it? Or whatever. That's the main problem now, because of whatever they're saying, the biological weapon or whatever," she says.

Neema says the store employees don't actually ask those questions or say what they're doing, but that that's what she believes they're watching her for.

(Schnucks spokeswoman Lori Willis says she's "floored" by the charge. "This is the first such incident that's been brought to our attention. We'll certainly look into it." She

says that Schnucks not only trains its 16,000-plus employees not to discriminate, but also assures them that the company will stand behind them if they feel that customers are
mistreating them. "We've always made it very, very clear
that *no one* should be treated unfairly in our stores," she
says, "no associate, and no customer for certain. So this
would be completely going against all of the Schnucks policies and philosophies with which we do business.")

Another consequence of the current tension, Neema
says, is that she feels bound to hide her daughter's identity
as an Egyptian-American and a Muslim. She told the
school only that her daughter was born in Canada, she says,
and "I told her not to speak about religion, not to say anything, not to become identified as a Muslim or anything.
You have to be very careful. She was very confused, but I
did not know really how to approach her except to just
warn her. She kept saying, 'Why?' I told her that it's a bad
time now, and she might not make friends if she did. Kind
of sad."

Dianne Lee, a community college professor, says that
hearing about this sort of thing stirred her political fires and
caused her to get involved as an accompaniment volunteer.

"When I started seeing reports in the media about
Arab-Americans being singled out and how many
American citizens felt like the Arab-Americans, even if they
were citizens, should be forced to carry special I.D.," she
says, "I just really felt called to take a stand on this one, that
this is not OK. We need to stand with people and do everything we can to respect how horrendous what happened on
the eleventh was, but not allow ourselves to become perpetrators of evil because of it."

Kally Higgins, who works at an advertising agency, got
involved after seeing a flier in the Delmar Loop, a shopping area in nearby University City, close to Washington

University. She took an Afghan woman and her daughter grocery shopping and found the experience eye-opening.

"They were just wonderful," she says. "This little girl spoke English great. She was seven. So she was kind of the translator. It was really interesting. You know, I see on television how horrible it's been in Afghanistan for these women, and you feel that and try to imagine what it must have been like, and then suddenly I'm sitting there with two women, because she'd invited me into her home and there was another Afghan woman. To sit there and hear their stories of what it was like to be in Kabul and the Taliban taking over, it was pretty amazing."

With the accompaniment project entering its second month, Ramsey and O'Gorman, the volunteer trainer, both say they'd like to evaluate the program by meeting with both volunteers and members of the immigrant community and asking them how it's gone so far and what else can be done.

"I expect that that [the individual accompaniment] is going to increase," O'Gorman says. "As soon as people begin to trust that the folks that we have trained will actually be available and present to them, I think we're going to get a lot more requests from individuals to take kids to school, because a lot of these kids have been pulled out of school."

For the moment, there will be no more volunteer training, mostly because there are so many in place already that it has become hard to keep track of them. So far, they seem to be welcome in the Arab-American and Muslim community, where fear has decreased but not completely evaporated. For all of the good feeling that has been established since the tragedies of September 11, there is still a real danger of ignorance and fear creating dire situations for innocent people.

"I think a very, very high percentage of St. Louisans understand," says Hasic, the imam, referring to the fact that Muslims are not all terrorists, "but unfortunately, still, it doesn't matter how small a percentage: Those people who do not understand, maybe you just walk beside that one.

"One in a million, if you walk beside that one, it doesn't matter, you still could be really harmed."

BRINGING THE WAR HOME

DAMIEN CAVE

OCT. 19, 2001, BERKELEY, CALIF.—The Berkeley City
Council's call for a quick end to the bombing of Afghanistan
sparked a wave of outrage across the country this week. The
Berkeley resolution, which was passed on Tuesday, has
drawn the kind of obsessive coverage from Fox News that it
once lavished on Gary Condit's relationship with missing
intern Chandra Levy. The conservative *National Review*
denounced the ever-tolerant city for finding "something
new to tolerate: the murder of 6,000 Americans by fanatical
terrorists." Letters, phone calls and e-mails filled with fury
and disbelief poured into Berkeley's City Hall.

"In my eight years working here, I've never seen this
kind of outrage," says Susan Wengras, legislative aide to
Betty Olds, a City Council member who voted against the
resolution. "Parents in other cities are calling to say that
they've cut Cal off their children's list of potential colleges.
Others are talking about a boycott of Berkeley businesses,
and we've also gotten some letters from people saying, 'I
lost three friends. How dare you do this?'"

But while the media plays up the "only in Berkeley"
radicalism of the measure, many local observers say the real
surprise is how hotly debated it was and how relatively
moderate was its wording. The resolution barely squeaked
by, on a 5–4 vote, passing only after its language was soft-

ened; while the council's antiwar members favored an immediate cessation of the U.S. bombing campaign, the final resolution called on President Bush to stop the air raids "as soon as possible."

In fact, the Berkeley resolution doesn't show a city united in its antiwar opposition, but a city divided. "Deeply split," in the words of Mayor Shirley Dean, a moderate Democrat, who opposed the measure.

What's more, Berkeley is not alone. Other liberal college towns with a strong antiwar tradition—such as Madison, Wisconsin, Cambridge, Massachusetts, and Santa Cruz, California—are also experiencing a political identity crisis following the carnage of September 11. Aging activists whose antiwar convictions date back to the Vietnam War era still have influence in these communities, but their power to define public opinion and city policy has greatly diminished.

The change is partly demographic: The nineties boom brought more wealth and fewer radicals to these cities, attracting people who cared more about good schools than international politics. But even longtime residents say the September 11 attacks altered many people's convictions. Some liberals who marched against Vietnam believe that bombing Taliban and terrorist targets in Afghanistan is justified.

"This is not the sixties revisited," says Jane Bear, a Santa Cruz resident and former antiwar activist who attended a City Council meeting Wednesday that debated the current crisis. "We always said [during Vietnam] that if we were attacked on our own soil, and our own civilians were killed, that that would have changed everything. Now it's on our soil. Now the new generation has to do away with the rhetoric of the sixties and come up with a way to deal with what's going on."

Rethinking attitudes toward U.S. policy is no easy proposition in cities like Berkeley, where the municipal government has long condemned America's foreign affairs, from the Vietnam War to investment in South African apartheid. The Reagan administration's military involvement in Central America prompted the city to declare itself a sanctuary for refugees from El Salvador during the eighties, and more recently, the City Council passed a resolution that declared solidarity with the nation of Tibet. One day each year, the city flies the Tibetan flag over City Hall.

But the September 11 attacks have forced even the most liberal enclaves to reevaluate their political views. Berkeley's Wengras says that she marched against the Vietnam War and never expected to support Bush, whom she calls "a moron." "But this is a different time, a different war. We were attacked at home; we lost over five thousand innocent people. We can't let this go unanswered. How can you let people use human beings as missiles? When terrorists come and do this to us, we have to respond."

Berkeley City Council members who share Wengras's view tried to kill Tuesday's controversial resolution, but they settled for watering it down significantly. The original draft condemned U.S. foreign policy in Israel, Saudi Arabia, and Iraq, but opponents got that language removed. The final draft called for a halt to the bombing "as soon as possible," rather than immediately. And it contained a sentence offering condolences to families who lost loved ones in the attacks.

Because the press and public have come to expect radical measures from Berkeley, complains council member Linda Maio, they ignored the fact that she and her colleagues worked very hard on the language to make sure "it didn't look like we were trying to tie the government's hands," she says.

"We understand that you have to take out military installations, that you have to take out planes and weapons," Maio says. "It's not that the city opposed the start of the bombing but just that it should end quickly, 'as soon as possible.' When that is isn't up to us."

Nonetheless, the resolution has brought scorn and derision on the city; it has been widely denounced as naive, simpleminded, and even traitorous. Opponents have threatened to boycott the city, and that scares political leaders already coping with a local economic downturn. Mayor Dean says that a local lumber company lost a $60,000 contract, and that the Chamber of Commerce has received dozens of complaints. Some people have even asked the chamber to cancel their local restaurant reservations for them.

"I just went to KTVU [a local TV station] for [Fox News show] *The O'Reilly Factor*, and before I left, I checked my voice mail," Dean says. "Of the last twenty-six phone calls, twenty mentioned the boycott. I'm very worried about that."

Given the potential damage to the city, Maio says she has some regrets about even the watered-down resolution. "If I had known that it would have been mischaracterized as a condemnation of the bombing, I wouldn't have voted for it."

Madison, home of the University of Wisconsin, has also experienced a backlash against its deep-rooted antiwar convictions. After the Madison School Board attracted howls of protest for banning the Pledge of Allegiance from its schools on October 8, the board reversed its decision this week.

In Cambridge, Massachusetts, where pro-peace passions have traditionally grown as thick as the ivy in Harvard Yard, a patriotic mood prevails. Even though

Cambridge has had a so-called peace commissioner on the city payroll—charged since 1982 with promoting nonviolent problem-solving—the enormity of the September 11 attacks and the outrage about them have largely kept her quiet. The only war-related resolutions passed by the Cambridge City Council since September 11 put flags on city streets and guaranteed full pay to city employees called up to serve in the military.

The difference between the moods in Cambridge and Berkeley probably stem from the cities' relative proximity to the terror attacks' ground zero, says Terrence Smith, chief of staff for Cambridge Mayor Anthony D. Galluccio. "Two planes left from here; a lot of people from the Boston area died," says Smith. "It's harder to make those leaps to pacifism when you could run into someone on the street who lost a mother, a brother, or a father. The knee-jerk left-wing reaction is hard enough to support but it's even harder on the East Coast, in Boston, because of the proximity, because there are people walking our streets who lost people in the attacks."

Still, even in Berkeley and Madison, the municipal governments' antiwar moves didn't sit well with many residents. A week after Madison's school board banned the pledge, more than 1,200 packed a public hearing and after nine hours of debate, the board bowed to citizen pressure and voted to reverse its decision. "It was democracy at its best," says Bill Geist, a Madison resident who attended the meeting and called for the pledge to be returned to local schools. "There's a new breed of patriotism here. There are flags everywhere and for the first time, those who feel there's a peaceful alternative may believe that they'll be outnumbered."

Demographics—the city's shift from being a university town to one more focused on business—account for part of the shift, but not all. "The real energy came because of September 11," says Geist.

Dona Spring, the Berkeley council member who first sponsored the measure, didn't return calls for comment. But other veteran progressives in this antiwar capital aren't surprised by the angry local reaction. "Berkeley's been moving toward the center for some time," says Gus Newport, the city's radical mayor from 1979 to 1986, who was known for his peace trips abroad and his opposition to U.S. foreign policy. The reasons, Newport says, are obvious: College students aren't as radical as they used to be, and because of a state-mandated end to rent control and the nineties boom, property prices have spiked, bringing a more affluent and conservative class to what used to be known as "the People's Republic of Berkeley."

Still, liberal strongholds like Berkeley are not likely to become the Bush administration's most ardent supporters. Peace activists in these cities believe they will once again become centers of antiwar opposition if the conflict in Afghanistan drags on and grows bloodier. Right now, Santa Cruz "is about 50/50, 50 leaning toward supporting Bush," says council member Mike Rotkin, a longtime radical activist, speaking after the town hall meeting Wednesday. "But that's just because they don't have a real good understanding of what's going on. If you talk to them for fifteen minutes, you can usually open them up."

Mayor Dean of Berkeley agrees: "The support (for Bush) is tied to what's been going on; whether it will last depends on how the administration handles future events. If they go astray, you would see a strong antiwar movement appear in a flash."

But Dean expresses some dismay at her city's deeply ingrained antiwar attitudes. "Berkeley is still a liberal city, a lot more liberal than most cities," she says. "But what I see is a lot of folks from the sixties who are nostalgic and out of touch. They look back through rosy glasses and think of the unity of that era and they want to reach back for the good old days. They don't understand that this is not the Vietnam War. They don't understand or accept or don't believe that there is a difference. But there is a difference and it's pretty apparent. We got attacked on our soil and six thousand people were killed. The only crime they committed was that they went to work in the morning."

Additional reporting by Jakob Schiller.

A MEMO TO
AMERICAN MUSLIMS

M. A. MUQTEDAR KHAN

OCT. 18, 2001—In the name of Allah, the most Benevolent and the Most Merciful. May this memo find you in the shade of Islam enjoying the mercy, the protection, and the grace of Allah. I am writing this memo to you all with the explicit purpose of inviting you to lead the American Muslim community in soul-searching, reflection, and reassessment.

What happened on September 11 in New York and Washington will forever remain a horrible scar on the history of Islam and humanity. No matter how much we condemn it, and point to the Quran and the Sunnah to argue that Islam forbids the killing of innocent people, the fact remains that the perpetrators of this crime against humanity have indicated that their actions are sanctioned by Islamic values. The fact that even now several Muslim scholars and thousands of Muslims defend the accused is indicative that not all Muslims believe that the attacks are un-Islamic. This is truly sad.

Even if it were true that Israel and the U.S. are enemies of the Muslim world, a response that mercilessly murders thousands of innocent people, including hundreds of Muslims, is absolutely indefensible. If anywhere in your hearts there is any sympathy or understanding with those who committed this act, I invite you to ask yourself this question: Would Muhammad sanction such an act?

While encouraging Muslims to struggle against injustice (Al Quran 4:135), Allah also imposes strict rules of engagement. He says in unequivocal terms that to kill an innocent being is like killing entire humanity (Al Quran 5:32). He also encourages Muslims to forgive Jews and Christians if they have committed injustices against us (Al Quran 2:109, 3:159, 5:85).

Muslims, including American Muslims, have been practicing hypocrisy on a grand scale. They protest against the discriminatory practices of Israel but are silent against the discriminatory practices in Muslim states. In the Persian Gulf one can see how laws and even salaries are based on ethnic origin. This is racism, but we never hear of Muslims protesting against them at international forums.

The Israeli occupation of Palestine is perhaps central to Muslim grievance against the West. While acknowledging that, I must remind you that Israel treats its 1 million Arab citizens with greater respect and dignity than most Arab nations treat their citizens. Today Palestinian refugees can settle in the U.S. and become American citizens, but in spite of all the tall rhetoric of the Arab world and Quranic injunctions (24:22), no Muslim country except Jordan extends this support to them.

While we loudly and consistently condemn Israel for its ill-treatment of Palestinians, we are silent when Muslim regimes abuse the rights of Muslims and slaughter thousands of them. Remember Saddam Hussein and his use of chemical weapons against Muslims (Kurds)? Remember the Pakistani army's excesses against Muslims (Bengalis)?

Remember the mujahedin of Afghanistan and their mutual slaughter? Have we ever condemned them for their excesses? Have we demanded international intervention or retribution against them? Do you know how the Saudis treat their minority Shiites? Have we protested the violation of their rights? But we all are eager to condemn Israel; not because we care for the rights and lives of the Palestinians; we don't. We condemn Israel because we hate "them."

Muslims love to live in the U.S. but also love to hate it. Many openly claim that the U.S. is a terrorist state but they continue to live in it. Their decision to live here is testimony that they would rather live here than anywhere else. As an Indian Muslim, I know for sure that nowhere on earth, including India, will I get the same sense of dignity and respect that I have received in the U.S. No Muslim country will treat me as well as the U.S. has. If what happened on September 11 had happened in India, the world's biggest democracy, thousands of Muslims would have been slaughtered in riots on mere suspicion and there would be another slaughter after the culprits' identity was confirmed. But in the U.S., bigotry and xenophobia have been kept in check by the media and political leaders. In many places hundreds of Americans have gathered around Islamic centers in symbolic gestures of protection and embrace of American Muslims. In many cities Christian congregations have started wearing *hijab* to identify with fellow Muslim women. In patience and in tolerance ordinary Americans have demonstrated their extraordinary virtues.

It is time that we acknowledge that the freedoms we enjoy in the U.S. are more desirable to us than superficial solidarity with the Muslim world. If you disagree, then prove it by packing your bags and going to whichever Muslim country you identify with. If you do not leave and do not acknowledge that you would rather live here than anywhere else, know that you are being hypocritical.

It is time that we faced these hypocritical practices and

struggled to transcend them. It is time that American Muslim leaders fought to purify their own lot. For over a decade we have watched as Muslims in the name of Islam have committed violence against other Muslims and other peoples. We have always found a way to reconcile the vast distance between Islamic values and Muslim practices by pointing to the injustices committed upon Muslims by others. The point, however, is this—our belief in Islam and commitment to Islamic values is not contingent on the moral conduct of the U.S. or Israel. And as Muslims can we condone such inhuman and senseless waste of life in the name of Islam?

The biggest victims of hate-filled politics as embodied in the actions of several Muslim militias all over the world are Muslims themselves. Hate is the extreme form of intolerance and when individuals and groups succumb to it they can do nothing constructive. Militias like the Taliban have allowed their hate for the West to override their obligation to pursue the welfare of their people and as a result of their actions not only have thousands of innocent people died in America, but thousands of people will die in the Muslim world.

Already, half a million Afghans have had to leave their homes and their country. It will only get worse as the war escalates. Hamas and Islamic Jihad may kill a few Jews, women and children included, with their suicide bombs and temporarily satisfy their lust for Jewish blood, but thousands of Palestinians then pay the price for their actions.

The culture of hate and killing is tearing away at the moral fabric of the Muslim society. We are more focused on "the other" and have completely forgotten our duty to Allah. In pursuit of the inferior jihad we have sacrificed the superior jihad.

Islamic resurgence, the cherished ideals of which pursued the ultimate goal of a universally just and moral society, has been hijacked by hate and calls for murder and mayhem. If Osama bin Laden were an individual, then we would have no problem. But unfortunately bin Laden has become a phenomenon—a cancer eating away at the morality of our youth, and undermining the spiritual health of our future.

Today the century-old Islamic revival is in jeopardy because we have allowed insanity to prevail over our better judgment. Yes, the U.S. has played a hand in the creation of bin Laden and the Taliban, but it is we who have allowed them to grow and gain such a foothold. It is our duty to police our world. It is our responsibility to prevent people from abusing Islam. It is our job to ensure that Islam is not misrepresented. We should have made sure that what happened on Sept. 11 should never have happened.

It is time that the leaders of the American Muslim community woke up and realized that there is more to life than competing with the American Jewish lobby for power over U.S. foreign policy. Islam is not about defeating Jews or conquering Jerusalem. It is about mercy, about virtue, about sacrifice, and about duty. Above all it is the pursuit of moral perfection. Nothing can be further away from moral perfection than the wanton slaughter of thousands of unsuspecting innocent people.

I hope that we will now rededicate our lives and our institutions to the search for harmony, peace, and tolerance. Let us be prepared to suffer injustice rather than commit injustices. After all, it is we who carry the divine burden of Islam and not others. We have to be morally better, more forgiving, more sacrificing than others, if we wish to convince the world about the truth of our message. We cannot simply be equal to others in virtue, we must excel.

It is time for soul-searching. How can the message of Muhammad, who was sent as mercy to mankind, become a source of horror and fear? How can Islam inspire thousands of youth to dedicate their lives to killing others? We are supposed to invite people to Islam, not murder them.

The worst exhibition of Islam happened on our turf. We must take first responsibility to undo the evil it has manifest. This is our mandate, our burden, and also our opportunity.

DRAFTED INTO THE CULT OF WAR

CHRIS COLIN

OCT. 11, 2001—We were all driving back to Oakland, California, the morning after the wedding, through the suburbs and Silicon Valley, our suits and dresses on our laps. Then some crows flapped down from a tree and at that moment we heard that the bombing had begun. If there is a single instant when the hermit lets the fabric drape thick over his windows, when the quicksand gets its final grip around the explorer's chest, then it happened for me there in the back of the van, as the radio crackled and the birds preened grimly on the street.

NPR didn't know much yet: Bombs had hit Afghanistan from the sea and from land. It was dark there. Our planes dropped food. Osama bin Laden wasn't dead. In the absence of a thorough report, I looked out my window and felt myself join a dark, luckless cult I might not leave.

From an automotive standpoint, nothing actually separated the front seat from the back. But that morning something like lead fell down around my corner of the van. Others speculated, or tapped their feet, or recalled moments from the previous night's wedding. I said not much and listened to the radio.

We drove. A car of friends passed us on the left. Missiles from submarines were blasting out from waves and drying off en route to Afghan buildings. The car beside us made funny faces. "You guys look great," our driver yelled to them, and the echo in my head against the missiles was tinny at best. I did not think those guys, or any guys, looked great. I thought, instead, that the countdown had finally finished and we'd now been fired deep into space. More than that, we were the tragic kind of astronauts—the ones who ought not to burn dwindling oxygen saying foolish things.

If your personality has just a little room, I'm learning, this war will move in and spread out. It just visits at first, but soon it's on the lease, and eventually you can't recall life without it. Your personality isn't simply overwhelmed by the war; it *is* the war. Such transmogrification would make good science fiction if science fiction could somehow matter at a time like this.

"At a time like this" enjoys special prominence in the melodramatic vocabulary of newly transmuted war hosts. We get lumped in with the paranoid, the kooky, and the frightened sometimes—sometimes for good reason. Other times we're taken for the info addicts, uncomfortable with the amount of time lost switching from CNN to MSNBC. But these categories fail to discern our lack of nuance. We simply think about war all day. If two hours pass without a thought about it, the feeling is that of forgetting house keys, and we pat our pockets.

I belong to a cult whose ideology remains obscured. So far we believe in dread and cable news. We are, in part, the cult of updates, the cult of answers. We are not the cult of life as usual. We forget to check the transmission fluid. We're late with the bills because who can think of bills at a time like this? We don't do long-range planning because we can't picture the long range. If all the bleakness proves misguided, we say, terrific. In the meantime we catalog doom scenarios.

The architecture of doom is as secret as that of terrorism itself. One can identify specific fears—dead American
soldiers, dead Afghan civilians, smallpox at the shopping
mall—but the real dread comes from the unchartability of
it all. The dread can reconfigure every day, and could
stretch for decades. It could rest and then revive with the
single lurch of an airplane three years from now. The
appropriate analogy is that of the nightmare within the
nightmare.

I had made progress since September 11, had begun
taking the recycling out on Tuesdays again and remembering to talk about things besides terrorism. But the interlude
also allowed me to let my guard down, and once the draw-
bridge had been lowered, it became that much easier to
admit the mongrels.

We drove onward to Oakland—there is no other way to
mark the beginnings of war when you're on a freeway.
American flags hung from overpasses, and mysterious,
anonymous tractor trailers rumbled beneath them, hauling
either hamburger buns or anthrax spores. Above, a small
prop plane angled toward the city; it was a crop duster or it
was not.

Everything outside the immediate purview of the cult
either gets appropriated or overlooked: A sunset stub-
bornly incompatible with an anthrax plot becomes invisible. A gradual blinding began in the car, a narrowing of
vision that rendered the streetlights and background
mountains immaterial. Things that do not predict the outcome of the war lose their identifying characteristics. If it
can't speak to my agenda—the safety of loved ones, say—I
can only barely make it out. I am an extremist.

There are deeper implications for this entire arrangement. The situation is that of an existential wag-the-dog
scenario, in which a massive war (and the potential for

retaliation) distracts me from life itself, and all of life's thank-you letters, birthdays, and walks down by the field across from the fair. At an elementary level, this phenomenon has been detected by instruments of localized capitalism. Get back to your normal life, our mayors urge us, spend!

But we're not just neglecting to shop. We can't remember why those stores were built in the first place. Against a backdrop of approaching disaster, everyday scenery loses its familiarity and soon one is on the moon. As a boy in Washington at the end of the seventies, I saw an early version of this cult, those men and women sucked far into the world of Vietnam. These were the people who, for one reason or another, chose to spend their lives in tents in front of the White House. Some had political agendas, while others were just *being* Vietnam. Obviously many of them had actually fought in the war, but not all. They went crazy, people said, as compassionately as possible. But crazy didn't explain it.

One wonders, in 2001, whether one is headed for the tents. At a party recently, I met a nice woman and asked if we could talk about biological weapons. No, she said. So we stood there in the kitchen and looked at each other. I tried to think of something besides war. What do I like? I asked myself. What do I enjoy talking about? Presumably I have certain interests? I could recall no interests.

In the end, to fill the silence, I told her about the frantic black lab I'd seen at the beach last month, swimming farther and farther out to sea. My friends and I had joined the chorus of whistlers and yellers, waving crazily to lure the frightened dog back to shore. It was forty-five minutes before he finally found his way back, but when his tearful owner spread her arms for a big wet hug, the animal instead bolted down the beach as though mad from the sea.

The episode had been amazing to me before September 11, but I nearly fell asleep telling it now, and rushed through the good parts. We should have talked about biological weapons, I said finally. Yes, she said.

Back in the van, we finally reached Oakland and went home. We carried our suits and dresses inside, and drank tea in front of the television. Later other friends came over, and we walked in the neighborhood. We walked down Seventh, then up Wood, and then over on Willow. Let's go back, I said, and we did, and watched more television.

Collateral
Damage

THE KITSCHIFICATION OF SEPTEMBER 11

DANIEL HARRIS

JAN. 25, 2002—Within minutes after the collapse of the World Trade Center, inspirational songs, propagandistic images designed to feed the fires of patriotic fury, and poetry commemorating the victims began to proliferate on radio, television, and the Internet. The Dixie Chicks performed an a cappella rendition of "The Star Spangled Banner"; car-window decals appeared featuring a lugubrious poodle with a glistening tear as large as a gum drop rolling mournfully down its cheek; refrigerator magnets of Old Glory flooded the market ("buy two and get a third one FREE!"); and the unofficial laureates of the World Wide Web brought the Internet to a crawl by posting thousands of elegies with such lyrics as "May America's flag forever fly unfurled, / May Heaven be our perished souls' 'Windows on the World'!" Gigabytes of odes to the lost firemen and celebrations of American resolve turned the information superhighway into a parking lot:

My Daddy's Flag

Arriving home from work and a trip to the store,
My 5 year old daughter greeted me at the door.
"Hi daddy!" she smiled, "what's in the bag?"
"Well, daddy has brought home the American flag."

With a puzzled look she asked "What does it do?"
I answered, "it's our country's colors, red, white and blue.
This flag on our house will protect you my dear,
It has magical powers to keep away fear."

Does an event as catastrophic as this one require the rhetoric of kitsch to make it less horrendous? Do we need the
overkill of ribbons and commemorative quilts, haloed
seraphim perched on top of the burning towers and teddy
bears in firefighter helmets waving flags, in order to forget
the final minutes of bond traders, restaurant workers, and
secretaries screaming in elevators filling with smoke, standing in the frames of broken windows on the ninetieth floor
waiting for help, and staggering down the stairwells covered in third-degree burns? Perhaps saccharine images of
sobbing Statues of Liberty and posters that announce "We
will never forget when the Eagle cried" make the incident
more palatable, more "aesthetic" in a sense, decorated with
the mortician's reassuringly familiar stock in trade.
Through kitsch, we avert our eyes from tragedy, transforming the unspeakable ugliness of diseases, accidents,
and wars into something poetic and noble, into pat stories
whose happy endings offer enduring lessons in courage and
resilience.

And yet while kitsch may serve to anesthetize us to the
macabre spectacle of perfectly manicured severed hands
embedded in the mud and charred bodies dropping out of
windows, it may conceal another agenda. The strident sentimentality of kitsch makes the unsaid impermissible and
silences dissenting opinions, which cannot withstand the
emotional vehemence of its rhetoric. It not only beautifies
ghoulish images, it whitewashes the political context of the
attack which, when portrayed as a pure instance of gratu-
itous sadism, of inexplicable wickedness, appears to have

had no cause, no ultimate goal. Four months to Bush's "crusade," despite clear successes, we remain far from certain about what, in the long run, we hope to achieve.

Ignoring geopolitics, we sealed the incident off in an ideologically sterile vacuum, the perfect incubator for kitsch, which thrives on irrational simplifications of moral complexities. Rather than making sincere efforts to understand the historical origins of the event in a protracted international conflict, we erect a schematic narrative that pitted absolute evil against absolute good, our own unwavering rationality against the delirium of crazed fanatics. On the electronic bulletin boards on the Internet, the terrorists became cartoon villains whose "insane and beastly acts" were both unmotivated and unaccountable, the result of nothing more explicable than "malevolence," of the "dastardly cowardice" of "an inhuman . . . group that has no place in the universe." These "depraved minions of a hate-filled maniac" who subscribed to "the toxic theology [of] suicidal barbarism," "watched from a distance / And laughed in a hauty [sic] tone" at this "ungodly intrusional [sic] violation of human life," this "psychotic" prank ostensibly staged out of sheer spite.

If the perpetrators are monsters, the victims are not just innocent but angelic, diaphanous seraphs with harps who, after being crushed in the collapse, "rose again, / Through the smoke, and dust and pain. / To fly. To play above again / In the blue American sky. / The perfect, blue American sky." R&B vocalist Kristy Jackson has hit the charts with a commemorative single entitled "Little Did She Know" about a woman who, on the morning of September 11, sent her fireman husband off to work with a peck on his cheek, heedless of the fact that he would never return:

Little did she know she'd kissed a hero
Though he'd always been one in her eyes
But when faced with certain death
He'd said a prayer and took a breath
And led an army of true angels in the sky.

Little did she know she'd kissed a hero
Though he'd always been an angel in her eyes
Putting others first, it's true
That's what heroes always do
Now he doesn't need a pair of wings to fly.

The kitsch of extreme innocence also emerges in the selectivity of the roll call of the martyrs. We found the deaths of the emergency personnel far more riveting than the deaths of the office workers, even though the latter outnumbered the former by a ratio of approximately 12 to 1. It is difficult to make a martyr out of someone who is run down in the street by a bus, as the casualties in the two buildings essentially were, dying, not while manning gun turrets or lobbing grenades, but while filing expense reports and faxing spreadsheets. Such an unglamorous, clerical fate is not suited to instant martyrdom and hence our attention shifted away from secretaries and CEOs, who did nothing more intrepid than attempt to save their own lives, and gravitated toward a group that more adequately satisfies our folkloric requirements for heroism. The whole story was reshaped so that the narrative focus fell squarely on those whose bravery in the face of death allowed us to superimpose on the chaos and panic of that incomprehensible hour a reassuring bedtime story of valiant knights charging into the breach, laying down their lives for their countrymen as they fought against "the forces of darkness."

Much as the skies above New York were immediately "sterilized" to prevent further.attacks, so debate was sterilized to prevent further discussion of the disaster. Many patriotic stalwarts seemed to believe that dissent amounted to a disavowal of one's American citizenship, a McCarthyite accusation that created an atmosphere of fear and paranoia, a self-consciousness hardly conducive to the effective discussion of an emergency. Moreover, uncritical defenders of our foreign policy made liberal use of such words as "tasteless," "inappropriate," and "untimely" to describe the statements of anyone who questioned the wisdom of carpet-bombing Afghanistan, including the unfortunate host of the television program *Politically Incorrect*, who was forced to retract remarks deemed offensive to the Pentagon after his outraged sponsors, Sears and FedEx, summarily yanked their advertisements. Because other more despotic forms of repression have been outlawed in democracies, we now rely heavily on a lawful form of censorship, social pressure, a subtle method of coercion that legislates conformity by stigmatizing marginal opinions as the indiscretions of ill-mannered boobs who, while they may not literally break the law, trample on the more elusive statutes of "decency." It is ironic that, during a time in which we seem so preoccupied with the "tastefulness" of people's remarks, we exhibit an appalling insensitivity to the tastelessness of kitsch, which repeatedly and unapologetically rides roughshod over all aesthetic standards.

Instead of conducting open and uninhibited discussions, we state our opinions through symbols, through saber-rattling images of American eagles sitting on stools sharpening their claws; screen savers of rippling flags captioned "these colors don't run"; computer-manipulated photographs of the tear-streaked face of the Man of Sorrows superimposed on the Statue of Liberty; and votive candles that morph into the burning buildings themselves. It is appropriate that President Bush, a man known for the endlessly inventive infelicities of his speech, should communicate to the American public largely by means of symbols, by displaying the badges of dead policemen and staging photo-ops in which, bull horn in hand, he hugs firemen on piles of rubble and leads squirming first-graders in the Pledge of Allegiance after admiring a bulletin board of their drawings titled "The Day We Were Very Sad."

Symbols are the language spoken by those who are uncomfortable with words. Our leaders use them when they seek to stimulate, not thought, but adrenaline. They are the weapons of emotional obscurantism, paralyzing dialogue before we are plunged into war where doubts and hesitations have potentially disastrous consequences and where our actions must be swift, decisive, and unthinking. So much of the "discussion" of the World Trade Center is based on button-pushing, on a barrage of symbols designed to trigger reflexive, Pavlovian reactions, bringing us to our feet against our wills to salute the flag and burst as one into song, our intellectual independence shot down by salvos of patriotic kitsch.

In the course of the imagistic orgies that flared up after September 11, a brand-new American symbol was invented: the towers themselves. Poets and commentators anthropomorphized the skyscrapers as, on the one hand, "pillars of strength," which, like Atlas, seemed to support the weight of the entire United States; and, on the other, as wavering ghosts, which, like Hamlet's murdered father, seemed to call out for revenge, especially when they were superimposed on top of sympathy card images of disconsolate angels. The buildings quickly lost their material reality as architecture and became living beings, "two brothers" endowed with the capacity to move, to "reach," "stretch," and "stand tall." We even cast this prime piece of Manhattan real estate as Christ in a resurrection scene: No sooner do the buildings collapse than, like phoenixes, they rise again from their ashes, often in the form of the American eagle, soaring skyward out of the smoking rubble: "As the Eagle lay on the ground / In awe I witnessed a miracle, a rebirth! / The eagle rose triumphant."

The transformation of the Word Trade Center from a physical location into a turn of phrase, a "vibrant symbol of the bounty and pride of democracy," gave both terrorism and dissent a new dimension, that of heresy, of the desecration of holy idols, of buildings that quickly acquired the mystique of temples and, in many images, of New Age crystals, which, like gigantic prisms, emanated a throbbing aura of iridescent energy. As a result, those who advocated restraint became more than just opposing voices but iconoclasts and flag-burners, blasphemers who inflicted physical harm on objects that our high-flown rhetoric treated as sacred relics. We left the realm of reason, of bricks and mortar, and entered the realm of faith, of sacraments and graven images, of flags that have "magical powers to keep away fear." We scoff at the extremism of terrorists who are willing to die in the name of Allah, but we ignore the religious dimension of our own behavior that we justify not by carefully reasoned defenses but by animistic symbols as hallowed as the Koran or the Kaaba. Both the Islamic fundamentalist and the American patriot may share more than they care to admit.

Economic as well as political factors contributed to the proliferation of kitsch after September 11. Kitsch is frequently associated with fund-raising, especially fund-raising for diseases that afflict children, whether it be the doe-eyed poster children of the first muscular dystrophy campaign, or Ryan White, the heroic young AIDS victim who, after being

railroaded out of his bigoted hometown, was canonized as
the patron saint of AIDS charities, largely by means of the
attention lavished on him by *People* magazine. And yet,
appearances notwithstanding, AIDS affects far fewer children than it does adults. Similarly, on September 11, only
three victims were below the age of thirteen (all passengers
on the hijacked planes). That's a surprising statistic, given
the disproportionate number of relief agencies that, after the
attacks, were launched specifically to help children, the cash
cows of the tragedy's nonprofits, which have primed the
pumps of American generosity with ad campaigns featuring
images of bereft toddlers superimposed on apocalyptic photographs of the ruins. Even during an event in which children are only indirect casualties, they are the ones brought
in to shake the tin cans. They, and not adults, are easiest on
the eyes, the most photogenic of panhandlers, issuing
importunate entreaties with a mere kiss on the cheek or
squeeze of the hand. Children are the unpaid workmen of
kitsch, its drudges and slave laborers. Many did, of course,
lose a parent, but many parents lost something equally
important: their lives. Once again, the primary victims of the
tragedy were shuffled off to the sidelines to make room for a
cast of more narratively appealing objects of compassion,
much as the rescue workers were elevated into the starring
roles of this *Towering Inferno*, since their deaths were more
dramatic than the banal denouements of file clerks collapsing at the watercooler and stockbrokers suffocating in bathroom stalls.

What distinguishes the professional fund-raiser from
any other sort of commercial advertiser is that he has
nothing to sell other than his complimentary toasters and
his tote bags, his "Never Forget" T-shirts and his
American flag car window clings. Because the altruist
receives nothing commensurate with the money he gives,

nonprofit organizations must ensure that they provide an adequate emotional boon to their benefactors, an intangible feeling of pride, a "warm glow," the sole "product" that the fundraiser really "sells." Charities must induce the consumer to do something that goes against his capitalistic instincts, to give something for nothing, a dilemma that leads them to employ the full rhetorical arsenal of kitsch, providing a particularly rich and satisfying spiritual reward in the complete absence of a material one. Charities are so kitschy precisely because they are an industry that packages the warm glow, the well-earned satisfaction we experience after limping to the finish line of the AIDS walkathon sponsored by AmFAR or adopting a wide-eyed Central American waif through the Save-the-Children Fund.

But in the midst of epidemics and natural disasters, many Fortune 500 companies try to pass themselves off as charities, to slip into wallets already lubricated by the grease of legitimate, fundraising kitsch, such as Burger King, which is helping to "rebuild the American way of life" by selling $1 flag decals with their shakes and fries. After September 11, the airwaves were flooded with corporate condolences from firms that should perhaps have donated to the FDNY's Widows and Orphans Fund the millions they squandered on prime-time television spots advertising their good Samaritanship, expressing their "horror," and dispensing their "thoughts and heartfelt prayers." Charity impersonators infiltrated the ranks of the Red Cross and the Twin Towers Fund, camouflaging their commercials as public service announcements, while hordes of unscrupulous entrepreneurs set up shop by promising to donate to the orphans of dead firemen 20 percent, a full one-fifth, of the proceeds they collected from the sale of their WTC coffee mugs and their "United

We Stand" posters of the towers wrapped like an enormous Christo work in 110-story flags ("Please support our country, every purchase helps. God Bless America"). Even a pornographic Web site that offers paying clients images of big-busted Asian women promised to donate 10 percent of its proceeds to relief agencies.

If there was something duplicitous about Wendy's asserting its intentions of selling hamburgers to make "our beloved nation stronger than ever," Coca-Cola blowing its own horn about the fruit juices it supplied the rescue workers, and Chase Manhattan Bank hanging a four-story American flag on the facade of its Midtown offices, there was something equally duplicitous about the consumers who responded to these blandishments and shopped up a storm under the thin pretense that, given a company's outpouring of concern, they were "giving" rather than "buying," donating their hard-earned dollars to a caring, compassionate organization that offered something a little more enticing than a thank-you note, a toaster, and a tax break. We discovered that we could have our cake and eat it too, enjoy that laptop or that surround-sound stereo system and simultaneously bask in the warm glow. If corporations engaged in charity impersonation, consumers engaged in a similar fraud: benefactor impersonation, with both parties participating in a mutually beneficial game of self-flattery.

The marketing of self-congratulation finds a particularly susceptible consumer niche in a culture permeated with pop psychology, with its ever-more clamorous calls for emotional candor and its dire warnings about the dangers of bottling up potentially explosive feelings of anger, pain, and grief. Soon after the attack, Oprah's Oxygen Media posted on its Web site a video of Cheryl

Richardson, a self-styled "life coach," who advised viewers to "get your feelings up and out of your body in order to assist in the healing process," as if our emotions were toxic substances or medieval "humours," which exert damaging pressure on our internal organs, poisoning our systems if they are not purged or drawn out by professional blood-letters. Throughout the crisis, the constant refrain of politicians, celebrities, and even housewives was the necessity of beginning the process of "healing," which, in the current context, has nothing to do with recuperation, but precisely the opposite: with wallowing, indulging in the unnecessary prolongation of our misery, in the drama of living in a state of high alert.

What's more, the word "healing" promiscuously extends the status of victim to the general public and hence the privilege of being coddled, consoled, and pitied, as if we were all casualties and had all narrowly escaped being crushed in the collapsing towers, rather than merely sat safely in our living rooms glued to our television sets.

The mandate to "allow yourself to cry the wounded animal sounds and write in your grief journal," to quote one of several mourning "rituals" Oprah offered her audience after September 11, shows how the contemporary notion of mental health has weakened the inhibitions that once held our sentimentality in check, our sense of shame about self-disclosure, about losing control in public. We have reached unprecedented levels of mawkishness, levels that exceed even those attained by such lachrymose Victorians as Dickens and his devoted readers who wept copiously over the untimely death of Little Nell, a tragedy that would appear to bear some resemblance to the September 11 attack, which, according to one commentator, was so moving that it "burst the clogged, stereotypical male tear duct wide open."

We believe in the putative healthiness of creating external embodiments of internal states through "art" and "play" therapies, activities that lead to a proliferation of folk ceremonies and homemade tchotchkes: commemorative quilts, the largest hug ever staged in human history (thousands linked arms in a field after the tragedy), and the work of the so-called "Crayola Coalition," a group of schoolchildren nationwide who commit their hopes and fears to paper and send them to the rescue workers (often with the help of McDonald's, which includes original artwork—surely an indication of how highly such drawings are prized—in each bag of Big Macs and French fries it distributes at ground zero).

We are now taught that it is detrimental to our peace of mind, indeed, to our sanity, to experience emotion apart from its communication, its "release," and must therefore never remain alone with our feelings but seek out an audience to receive our discharges, our cathartic unburdenings, the messy, unhygienic ruptures of our blockages. What we are witnessing in the kitschification of the World Trade Center is how the pressure to externalize, to emote, "to get your feelings up and out of your body" results in emotional exhibitionism, emotional pornography, a need to play to the galleries and ham up our shock and horror as histrionic spectacles that we relish in and of themselves. Internal states retain their authenticity only if they retain some of the solitude in which they are originally experienced, only if there is no audience that needs to be entertained by the trembling of our chins, only if our real responses remain inaccessible to others in the privacy of our consciousness.

The Internet bulletin boards provide one of the most unrestrained examples of the emotional exhibitionism that pop psychology sanctions. The anonymity of the Web eliminated any need for a censoring mechanism to contain the exuberance of our grief and the result was a crying contest to see who could utter the loudest lamentations, the most piercing keens:

"I felt . . . disbelief, horror, sadness, and the relentless shedding of tears . . . Would I ever be able to enjoy a sunrise again? . . . Would food ever taste good to me again?"

"I flipped the tv to the news early Tuesday while putting a workout video in the vcr . . . needless to say, I never did work out that day . . . Every time I hear or see the news, I cry . . . the flags flying all over my city make me cry . . . hearing our national anthem through various media makes me cry . . . hearing people going around trying to find their loved ones makes me cry . . . knowing how many lives were directly affected . . . makes me cry . . . I've been crying since Tuesday."

When the crying subsided, bulletin board contributors offered each other a profusion of papal blessings ("may God bless each & every one of you," "may the Lord cause His Countenance to shine upon you") and engaged in one of the most complex and disingenuous acts of mourning seen in the aftermath of the World Trade Center tragedy: They posted condolences to the victims' families, electronic sympathy cards in which they told the orphaned children of firemen that "I just wanted you all to know I cared" and wrote poetry to the bereaved husbands and wives and despairing mothers and fathers:

> "We care that you are lonely and blue,
> So we are sending this hug especially for you."

One unnerving thing is missing from this soothing murmur of comforting words: the people being comforted. It is doubtful that the survivors of the tragedy spent the hours after September 11 poring over the thousands if not millions of notes that appeared on the Web and one must therefore conclude that we posted them for our own benefit, that we were both the senders and receivers of these love letters, and that we took turns playing for each other an audience of devastated widows and orphans. We were acting as aesthetes of grief, competing to see who could utter the windiest sighs, who could beat their breasts and gnash their teeth most piteously. Kitsch was created as the ante was steadily upped and the emotional pornography of an exhibitionistic culture reached its climax, its money shot. Just as Puritans once vied with each other in demonstrations of their piety, so we competed to prove who could *feel* the most, who could "express" the most intensely, showing off a new type of secular piety as unctuous as the zealotry of seventeenth-century religious purists.

The Internet samizdat offered not only a talent contest for the self-appointed pallbearers of the tragedy but an art gallery in which grass-roots designers displayed their click-and-drag doodles and daubs. The images in this electronic museum are based on what might be called the aesthetic of jumble, the haphazard look that results when preexisting images available in such computer programs as Clip Art are carelessly juxtaposed or even rendered transparent and placed on top of each other, forming an arty if often illegible mess. With a click of the mouse, files can be copied and pasted so that the same American eagle can be endlessly recycled and combined in countless permutations with the same angel, the same candle, the same red-white-and-blue ribbon, and the same dove carrying the same olive branch. The deadening unoriginality of Internet kitsch is largely the result of the computer's capacity to clone pictures and photographs, thereby minimizing the user's need to invent his own graphics and reducing his role to that of a collector, the rag picker of the World Wide Web who scavenges through various databases in order to assemble a collage of ready-made imagery.

The aesthetic of jumble and the prefab look that it creates become a metaphor of the intellectual vacuity of the Internet samizdat where opinions are replicated and then pasted in like Clip Art, the same denunciations of the terrorists' "evil" appearing cheek-by-jowl with the same panegyrics of the firemen's selfless heroism, the same expression of American indomitability with the same torrential spate of tears. As an experiment in democracy, the Internet has failed, for while it is true that the voiceless may have found their voices in a forum in which it is always open-mike and people are free to say virtually anything they'd like, in fact they do little more than repeat the clichés of their leaders, mouthing slogans that are the literary equivalent of the graphics created in the wake of the attacks. The photo-ops of President Bush and the inflammatory symbol-mongering that has dominated the discussion of the attack become the editorial Clip Art of the bulletin boards, the source of the generic patriotism and jingoistic hawkishness that the contributors right-click and copy, presenting them to the public as revelations. Much is made of the radical potential of the Web, which has restored to common people the means of being heard above the deafening corporate voices of the media, but when we really listen to these quieter, uncensored voices, what we hear is smiley faces and little red cabooses, Santa Clauses and carved pumpkins. The Internet is the grave of free speech, a monument to our lack of thought and autonomy. Freedom to speak amounts to freedom to repeat, to select a picto-

graph from an archive of icons, here a whimper of stereo-
typed anguish, there a defiant cry of militaristic fury.

The same voice echoes from server to shining server.
The response to the World Trade Center attack was a
celebration of consensus, of the exhilarating unanimity of
what one bulletin-board contributor aptly characterized as
"Americans banning [*sic*] together, soaring [*sic*] flags, showing pride." People from every corner of the globe weighed
in with their expression of sorrow and solidarity, from the
residents of "the little inupiaq Eskimo village on the shores
of the Bering Sea in Deering, Alaska" to the Australian
chapter of the Jackie Chan Fan Club: "on behalf of the
member of the Australian Jackie Chan Fan Club, our
thoughts, prayers, and hearts are with all of our brothers
and sisters in the United States."

Within a matter of days, memories of the tragedy
seemed to fade as horror gave way to the unadulterated
joy of togetherness, which lent the bulletin boards an air
of morbid conviviality, the stately funeral procession
quickly lapsing into a riotous Irish wake. "How I wish
I could embrace you all!" one contributor bursts forth,
while another shouts "we love you all!!!" and still another
recommends hugging as a palliative to grief, for "a hug
heals more pain than the eye alone can see." One contributor was so overwhelmed by the spirit of good will
created by the tragedy that she wrote a poem in which
she imagined the victims of the attack "choosing" to die
in the World Trade Center well before their birth, vol-
unteering in heaven for a divine mission, that of rallying
all nations together in a common cause against evil:

> In the halls of Heaven an offer
> was made to thousands
> of angels one day:

"You can go to the earth and help unite the world
But you won't be able to stay."
The angels stepped forward.

Behind the kitsch of our grief is a horrible, seemingly inhuman fact: We are not as dejected as we profess but in fact excited, a repulsive notion that we hide from ourselves, burying our euphoria deeper and deeper in sentimentality, becoming all the more long-faced the more gleeful we are at having come together as one.

Why do we experience pleasure during such crises? Surely not because we are sadists at heart, prurient, unfeeling ghouls who gloat over the sufferings of others. Instead, such an inappropriate reaction is the natural outcome of the fact that we no longer consciously experience on a daily basis a very acute sense of belonging to any community, even though the infrastructure of a highly complex society lies behind our most insignificant actions, from opening a tap and raising the thermostat, to flushing a toilet and flipping on a light. And yet, the communities we live in have become invisible, despite their omnipresence; the thousands who work in our water departments are never seen, we have no contact with those who keep our furnaces running, and the electric company appears only when the meter reader rings our bell. What's more, our government operates so efficiently that it has all but disappeared from our lives, leaving us with an eerie sense of being free agents acting alone in an unpopulated wilderness full of automated amenities. A society that seems to run by itself, that does not require us to perform any civic duties, is plagued by feelings of isolation and is particularly prone to bouts of pathological collectivity in which we hold old-fashioned neighborhood socials around a centerpiece of mangled corpses, a hideous incongruity that we hide behind a tearful mask of kitsch. In an atomized society, any crisis becomes a catalyst for instant togetherness in which the pleasure of companionship far exceeds the depths of sorrow and our fierce tribal instincts reemerge with a vengeance, having been thwarted by the curse of autonomy that afflicts advanced Western cultures.

DAN RATHER'S TEARS

STEPHANIE ZACHAREK

SEPT. 18, 2001—The hardest thing to watch about Dan Rather's guest appearance on the David Letterman show Monday night—the first Letterman show since last Tuesday's attack—wasn't that Rather broke into tears twice. It was the way he *apologized* for crying.

"I'm a professional. I get paid not to do that," Rather said briskly to Letterman and the audience, directly following the commercial break that Letterman quickly called after Rather first lost his composure. Rather had been talking about the time he'd spent with rescue workers at the World Trade Center site, when, it seemed, he simply lost touch with whatever internal mechanism it is that keeps *any* of us on an even keel in times of distress. It could happen to anyone—it just happened to strike a man whose livelihood depends on a measure of detachment from the events around him, and he scrambled to regain his footing like a cat who's fallen off a windowsill.

Rather knows what his role is, and his determination to fit into that role, rigidly and stalwartly, is what made his apology—an apology he repeated during the course of the appearance—so wrenching. He knows that America, and the world, expects detachment from its newspersons.

But that was in the old days, before last week. The newsroom is not, and never will be, an appropriate place

221

for outpourings of emotion, a fact Rather is more conscious of than anyone. But at a time when people around the world are trying in vain to process the meaning of an inexplicable event, the tried-and-true newscaster's facade, maintained at all costs, seems disingenuous at best. Rather's moments of reckoning on Letterman were something else again, a different and intensely personal kind of reporting: He has never seen anything like what he saw last week, and his refusal to pretend otherwise may have manifested itself in tears, but it was really a shout—a voice calling out to us in the middle of what has come to seem like a vast, dark hole.

The American news media, after showing remarkable professionalism, urgency, and levelheadedness on the day of the attack and immediately following, have returned to their usual pattern of turning every story—even this one—into a melodramatic arc, an ongoing, never-ending miniseries complete with marketing-slogan titles ("America Rising"; "America's New War"), special logos, and even syrupy theme music.

Local newscasters here in New York try valiantly to lend gravitas to their reports—it's impossible to be a New Yorker and *not* be perpetually cognizant of the smoldering mass grave downtown—but they're really just going about their jobs in the only way they know how. Their methods include trying to maintain calm, measured, but not sleep-inducing tones (keep those viewers alert and awake! As if any of us have actually been sleeping these days) and furrowing a brow or otherwise affecting concern whenever appropriate. Before last week, many of us were annoyed but grudgingly tolerant of the puppet show that so much TV news has become. This week, the puppet show is its own unbearable travesty—it's not that the TV news media doesn't grasp the scope of the tragedy and the events it's likely to set in motion. It's just that they know no other way to *be*.

Rather's two moments of spontaneous, bone-rattling despair on Letterman weren't signs of weakness, cracks in judgment, or evidence of an inability to be impartial. They were a newsman's personal and immediate reckoning with how to *be*—a nonverbal acknowledgment that no one, not even those who have been trained to keep their composure at all costs, is immune to the emotional fallout of events like last week's. That should be a comfort, and not an embarrassment, to the rest of us.

Rather's appearance on Letterman was as a news personality, not a news anchor; he was wearing a different hat. His views of last week's attack didn't make for particularly incisive news analysis: He spoke of the inevitability of American retaliation, a statement that probably seemed jingoistic to some viewers but wasn't particularly strident considering most Americans' simmering (and ongoing) anger and confusion. He made it clear that the enemy was not Islam itself but a relatively small contingent of religious extremists. He spoke of those extremists' "jealousy" of America and Americans, for its riches and apparent unassailability. And he made no bones about the attack as a manifestation of pure "evil"—a word that in the past week has proved to be resolutely practical in attempting to explain the inexplicable.

Rather maintained his evenness until he told Letterman that a song Americans have sung since they were school kids, "America the Beautiful," will never sound quite the same to him: "Oh beautiful for patriot's dream / That echoes through the years / Thine alabaster cities gleam / Undimmed by human tears." His voice broke as he got to that last line.

The United States is peopled by all kinds of patriots:

Repressive ones, even-handed ones, annoying ones, lazy ones. The most sensible patriots, and the ones that are most needed now, are the ones who have come to terms with the difference between the real America—the messy one, the one that often makes mistakes, the one that has plenty of enemies—and the dream America that we sang about as school kids. Nonetheless, there's a place where those two Americas intersect. In the space of that verse Rather saw that America, that inextinguishably bright oval in the Venn diagram, and the sight of it was too much for him, in that moment, to bear.

He pulled himself together and apologized again. "Yeah, you're a professional, but good Christ, you're a human being," Letterman told him without missing a beat, clutching for his hand. Rather, a consummate professional whether you like him or not, might never cry on-camera again. But in the midst of a world gone wrong, a world where so little feels good or right or natural, it's no small relief to see a human being and not a puppet in the news-caster's seat.

CONFESSIONS OF
A 9/11 WIDOW

A.R. TORRES

JAN. 25, 2002, NEW YORK—"Every baby is born with bread under his arm." Eddie reminded me of this Spanish saying whenever we talked about our shaky financial future. I was due to have our first baby in the fall, and we were concerned because I'd be unable to work at that point.

As it turned out, the saying proved true: When our son was born in October, I no longer worked. But there was enough money to take care of all of our expenses, and the promise of more money to come. Eddie, who died on September 11, became the bread under our son's arm.

It is a bizarre time in my life: My beloved husband goes to work and dies when a plane hits his building. Then, as I attempt to deal with the loss, and learn the art of single motherhood, checks arrive in the mail, in various amounts, on a regular basis. One day I may receive $1,500 from the Cantor Fitzgerald Relief Fund and $1,000 for supplemental needs from the Red Cross. Another day I may receive more—from the United Way September 11th Fund, the New York Crime Victims Board and Social Security. And while the money comes in—from government agencies, charities, and special funds set up in the aftermath of the tragedy—there is an additional chunk of change to be had from the Federal Compensation Fund, provided I accept it rather than choose to sue.

The arrival of each check reminds me of the debate about why 9/11 families are so significant, specifically as compared with families touched by the Oklahoma City bombing, and all other tragedies, past and future. Who deserves how much? I don't know. But it is certain that I am fortunate, along with the rest of the unfortunate affected by September 11, to be associated with this particular tragedy instead of one that is somehow less important in the public imagination.

The checks also make me think about the way Eddie died, compared with all the possible ways he could have died but didn't. I think about the near misses of the year: What if Eddie hadn't gotten up after falling face first when he went skiing last winter? What if he had fought the crazy, threatening guy at the pizza place last spring? What if he had hit the embankment on the parkway, with me in the car beside him, last summer?

A death of happenstance rather than of terrorism would have yielded significantly different results. Certainly there would not be all these checks in the mail. Instead it would have been quiet and calm. I would not have found myself so high in the hierarchy of the nation's sadness and sympathy, a grieving widow with a post-9/11 baby, a newly minted American icon. This is the last thing I could ever imagine being; the last thing I could ever possibly want.

The only thing familiar to me these days is walking my ten-year-old dog, if, that is, I don't bump into the neighbors who either offer consolation for the death, or congratulations for the birth, or, very awkwardly, both. When I make a foray through Manhattan, I feel assaulted by the post-9/11 flags and all the rest of the godblessamericana.

It's a marketing motif for store-window displays, some of them doubly dizzying dioramas of flag fashion in front of flag backgrounds. Frayed flags hang off antennae; there are little pins, patches, lots of jewelry.

The flags and WTC-ware keep me stuck in a place I don't want to be. They stifle me so that my wounds cannot even begin to heal. Each item takes me back to how this all began, the phone call from my brother asking, "Didn't Eddie just start working there?" My tragedy is personal, but I am forced to discover its terrible dimensions on the nightly news, in the daily papers, and in every publication on the newsstand.

It may even be that I was forced to witness my husband's final moments on the printed page. About a week after the tragedy, with no news about Eddie, I looked at a friend's *Time* magazine. I had shielded myself from the images, listening to the radio instead for all the new developments. But this time, for some reason, I looked.

In the magazine, there was a photo with little people in the air, like fairies, on their way down from the tower. One person seemed to be hanging off the building, just about to jump. It was hard to see the details, but he had on a shirt the color of the shirt my husband wore that day— that jewel-colored electric blue that was so popular among the corporate casual. The man in the photo also had the same hair and skin tone as my Eddie. And there he was, grim-expressioned, ready to sky-dive with no parachute.

A few days later, detectives called me to say Eddie's body had been recovered. His death certificate read: "Immediate cause: Multiple blunt trauma to head, torso, and extremities." He had jumped.

I still think about that image in *Time*. I'm sure that if I really want to verify it, *Time* would help me and perhaps would even be able to provide me with a whole series of photos, the entire sequence of the fall, fully documenting his actual death. I am sure the images would help me—force me—to accept Eddie's death, still so un-real. But at the moment, I want nothing to do with them.

Now I am waiting for the WTC movie to come out, hoping it won't be about me. I feel so exposed. I cynically imagine a request from *Playboy* to pose on red, white, and blue satin, patriotically baring myself to suckle my post-9/11 son. And then I seriously wonder who will be the first among the families to do it.

Along with flag-waving, donating to victims' families is now part of America's patriotic duties. America wants us to be OK, economically sound, happy, and sane. If we're OK, somehow, by extension, all Americans will be OK too. It's America's way of healing.

I'd like to think that for every flag, there is at least $1 that may come my way. For every word in print, $5; for every sound bite, $500; and for every image, $1 million. In this way, I see the money I receive as royalties from feeding America the sort of media that it desperately needs to consume, day after day. It is the bread under my son's arm, a blighted blessing that feeds us, day after day.

If Eddie had lived, we probably would have financial problems now, unless, of course, we won the lottery. They used to say, especially when the lotteries reached crazy amounts, that you have a better chance of being killed in a terrorist attack than winning the jackpot. If so, does that mean that my odds have now improved?

As I accept the money that admittedly helps—a lot—and stomach the sympathy that goes with it, I wait for the time when our stories will grow stale and I am left alone to normalize my life. After all, despite the emotional stirrings aroused by September 11, America is still the home of the quick fix. Then again, as this new world birthed by the tragedy matures, I'm not so sure that I will be allowed to withdraw into anonymity. September 11 may instead expose me forever, and leave my loss like ground zero, wide open to the public.

MISSING WOMEN

LAUREN SANDLER

DEC. 6, 2001, NEW YORK—"You want to know the routine?"

Charles Christophe takes a deep breath, stifles his tears, and recites the details of his new life. "We wake up. I bring her to day care. Then I go into the city to look for office space in midtown. By six I'm back. I buy the groceries. I pick up Gretchen from day care. I feed her. I give her a bath. I put her in bed. We read books until she falls asleep. I do the laundry. I go to sleep. The weekends are the same; we are together.

"I tried with a baby sitter, but she doesn't feel comfortable," he says, words away from a resumption of sobbing. "She cried, 'Mommy, Mommy, Mommy.' She's barely learned to say 'Mommy.' "

Gretchen's first birthday was September 13, two days after her mother was killed in the attacks on the World Trade Center. That night Christophe bathed his young daughter for the very first time, straining to listen for the phone as Gretchen splashed and screamed for her mother. He was certain it would ring at any moment, that Kirsten couldn't get to a phone, that perhaps she was stuck on the train home.

"She always calls. She's always good in a disaster. She always knows what to do," says Christophe, who still refers to his wife in the present tense.

He went down to the basement to get some of Kirsten's breast milk out of the freezer—she had saved a two-month supply, pumped at the nursing station on the 104th floor of Tower Two. She had called from her office that morning to say that the first tower had been hit by a plane, that she was OK. An hour earlier Christophe had kissed her good-bye in the lobby and rushed off to his office a block away on Broadway. He had been late for a court date.

Three weeks later, Kirsten Christophe's body was identified with the help of DNA derived from a sample of Gretchen's baby-fine hair. And Charles was forced to accept that suddenly, officially, unimaginably, he was a single father.

"This is my life now," he stutters. "It breaks my heart."

Many of us have navigated beyond our immediate and emotional reactions to the events of September 11. We have crammed the horrifying images and attendant incomprehension into a mental closet that won't quite lock behind us. The door still flies open from time to time, jimmied by the force of an unexpected visceral reminder.

But Charles Christophe lives behind that door, stranded there with hundreds and hundreds of other men. For them, the closet is sealed shut against their former lives. They used to be husbands and fathers, balancing the roles with the help of their wives, their children's mothers. Now they are widowers and single fathers, their lives composed of constant and inconceivable challenges, both logistical and emotional.

Americans have endured the loss of male veterans of war in staggering numbers. But we have never experienced the loss of hundreds of women, many of them mothers, in a single day in what is now described as an act of war.

It is impossible at this stage to know how many wives died that September morning—even the total number of those killed is disputed by the hundreds every day. Originally it was estimated that more than a thousand women died in the attacks. That number has slipped into the unknown hundreds, still a figure of historical significance. Out of the 36,568 Americans killed in the Korean War, only 2 were women. In Vietnam, just 8 of the 58,204 who died were female. And in the Gulf War, when 383 Americans were killed, a total of 15 women were lost.

"When soldiers die, there's usually a woman taking care of the family. It's a different ballgame," says Rabbi Earl Grollman, who has written more than twenty books on grief and mourning.

Many of the women who died on September 11 worked at home as tirelessly as they did in their WTC offices. They did the laundry, cooked the meals, shopped for groceries, cleaned the house. They curated their families' social lives and orchestrated their daily routines. Their families don't experience their loss just through the disappearance of a familiar laugh, a tender touch, or a quirky sense of humor. The emptiness created by their deaths stretches to fill each corner of the daily lives of the people they left behind.

For the women's husbands, this means that, in addition to the overwhelming task of grieving, they confront daily demands and myriad tasks, many of which are completely unfamiliar. At the same time, they are in many cases the sole caretakers of young children struggling with inner suffering, as well as a need to return to their old routines.

"Everyone's sense of safety has been shaken, and children more than ever need routine to have a sense that the adults will be there and be in charge," says Ronnye Halpern, a widow who coordinates bereavement services at Cabrini Hospital in Manhattan. "Children haven't formed inside themselves an internal kind of structure, and routines do that for them on the outside, which can be very reassuring. Baths, meals, whatever can be established—it's going to be different than it was before, but you do find a new way of living. That's the task for everybody."

And it is an incredibly painful task for widowers, who are aware of the necessity of routines but are struggling mightily to establish some. "Dinner is the most difficult time of every day," says Harold Weiss, who lost his wife, Margo, in the attacks. She had been in her office for only ten minutes before the first plane hit her building. She was on the phone with a friend at the time, discussing two-year-old Jason's first day of school. "We still haven't resolved how we have to do meals in the long term," says Weiss. "At least in Manhattan there's a lot of takeout available."

But dinner is easy compared to some tasks that seem almost insurmountable. "We're at the stage where my nine-year-old daughter is thinking of her body changing," says Weiss through tears. "What do I do then? What will the rest of her life be like? Everything from brushing her hair in the morning," he says, pausing to get his breath. "My God, I had never even brushed her hair."

"In all of this, the grief is devastating, of course, but maybe it is the raising of daughters which is the most terrifying," says Clark University professor Cynthia Enloe, who studies the experience of widows and war. "I never hear women who are suddenly widowed with young children talk about this kind of fear. They may be completely overwhelmed financially, but they don't ever seem to be scared about how to be a parent," she says. "It's usually very different than this. They draw on the help of those around them. They're not so alone."

Christophe hasn't consciously rejected help, but circumstances have made his new life unbearably solitary. He quit his job after the attacks to search for his wife and care for his daughter. He mentions a few friends who live near him in Maplewood, New Jersey, one of whom escaped Tower One and accompanied Christophe on his hunt for his missing wife in those frenzied first few weeks.

"He's the one who has understood it the best, but there's not so much time to see him now," says Christophe. "I have to find an office, to get back to work and start paying the bills now, not just take care of Gretchen." In addition, Christophe's family is far away. His father, also a widower, lives in Europe. His wife's family lives in the Midwest. Kirsten's sister came for a couple of weeks after the attacks, then her mother took over, but she needed to return home soon after to care for her own husband, who was diagnosed with cancer this summer. She'll return for the Christmas holiday, but will have to leave her son-in-law alone with Gretchen soon after. Thanksgiving was a couple of hours at a friend's house, then home to bathe Gretchen and put her to sleep.

"When I was notified about the body I was by myself," says Christophe. "You have to go to the cemetery, find a place for the grave. How do you know what to do alone?" His thoughts, as always, return to his wife. "We were so close, so happy. We talked all the time. Even on business trips, we'd be on the phone for hours. My cell phone bills! And now there's no one."

Christophe sought out a therapist in the first days, but since then has done his grieving alone, lost in the demanding schedule of his new role as a single parent. "I needed to talk to someone just a few times, because I was going to explode. So there was a kind of release of what was inside of me, but then I had to get on," he says.

This is typical of how men tend to mourn, say those who counsel them, especially in the first six months or year of mourning. Women, in contrast, tend to be quicker to reach out for support, both among their friends and in more structured bereavement groups. "Women will talk and cry with other women, but men in general go back to work. Men will change the subject when asked about how they're doing," says Grollman. "In any support group, if men make up ten percent of the people there, you're lucky."

"They're still in shock, just trying to get through what they have to do each day," says Halpern. Few people, women or men, she says, are seeking treatment. "Last year I had a wait list for my groups. Now, it's like pulling teeth." Bereavement groups set up around the city have reported a complete absence of new widowers—evidence of the gender divide in mourning.

"They won't ask for directions—you think they're asking for help?" asks Halpern. "Men are taught to act strong, to focus on moving beyond it. Defenses have always been given a bad rap, but they're what help us survive."

In fact, says Halpern, it's hard to imagine how men like Christophe would manage the daily pressures of sudden single fatherhood without the aid of emotional shock to push them into their new tasks. "I guess you could call it a sort of blessing," Halpern concedes. "Women need the process; men need to have their plan."

Rabbi Grollman worries about how long these men will bottle up their shock and deal with it alone. "Grief is grief, and if men want to grieve in a different way than women do, they should be allowed to," he says. But the longer they keep it to themselves, the harder it can be to manage. "It becomes a kind of emotional constipation," he says.

Some people believe that the very public nature of the calamity and the first days of mourning that followed it may have made the process of recovery even more difficult. "Men tend to have a very difficult time with group shows of grief," says Scott Campbell, co-author of the 1996 book

Widower: When Men Are Left Alone. "In this situation, I think it was very helpful at first to have the whole country, the whole world even, mourning with them. But a few weeks later people moved back to their lives, and they were left to deal with it all alone, in perhaps a more intense way, coming down from that initial feeling of support."

For men who do enlist help, it tends to be an intensely private enterprise. Weiss has sought therapy for himself and for his daughter, but their counselor comes to their Manhattan apartment and speaks with each of them separately. He is fortunate to have resources to assist with the logistics—his mother moved into his Upper West Side apartment building to help out, and he has two baby sitters whom his children love. This extraordinary support has allowed him to spend more time engaging in his grief rather than in the multitude of daily parental pressures that burden fathers who are newly single and grieving.

"I think that my experience in this process is learning that men are a lot more emotional than you'd think, but it's very private, and very raw," he says.

Weiss, like Christophe, speaks of a devastating loneliness that has intensified with the holidays, even as he is surrounded by loved ones. "Having gone through a holiday weekend with loving family all around, I still felt so lonely, so strangely lonely that day," Weiss says of a difficult Thanksgiving—a day his wife used to relish. "Because of the nature of what I was missing, of course. She's just not replaceable."

This painful fact is evident not just in Weiss's heart, but everywhere in his life now. He has had to hire a wake-up call service, since Margo never forgot to set the alarm clock, but he always did. "Margo was the center of our family," he says. "She took care of all of us, took care of everything. What's so cruel is that she probably felt better about herself and was looking forward to the future more just before she died than at any other time in her adult life. And she was beautiful. God, she was just so beautiful."

After Thanksgiving, Weiss decided to begin the heart-breaking process of going through Margo's closet with his daughter, Parker. He felt it was time to try to move on, but it was a process he quickly aborted. "I barely began," he says. "Everything brings back a memory, memories of when she wore a particular dress, how stunning she looked. I was so lucky. And then there are other things I know she never wore. That's really hard, too. I can't really do it yet.

"To see it all, you'd think she's still living here. I'm still expecting her to walk down the street," continues Weiss, his voice trembling. "But obviously, I know intellectually that that's not going to happen." It will be up to nine-year-old Parker to select which of her mother's outfits she would like to save. She has already chosen her mother's wedding dress and shoes.

"I am really focused on my children and what is best for them. Everything else is secondary," says Weiss. And it's clear that while he is responsible for making major household decisions and delegating all he can, he wants Parker to decide how she'll respond to her mother's loss. Her first choice was to write a eulogy for her mother's memorial service in September, which she courageously delivered herself.

"She was very poised and brave," says Weiss. "It wasn't morbid, just her words and thoughts about her mom, and how she's extraordinarily impacted by this." Parker also opted to change her Halloween costume. She was planning to go as a vampire in Victorian dress, but felt that day that her creepy garb hit gruesomely close to home. She went trick-or-treating instead dressed as a forties movie star. Her heroic date for the evening, appropriately, was a fire-fighter—two-year-old Jason's costume of choice.

Parker doesn't want to talk about her mother's death yet—and Weiss doesn't push to her to do so, outside of her private therapy. She has thrown herself into a routine of gymnastics, piano lessons, and chorus, feeling more comfortable outside the sad confines of the family's apartment.

Weiss feels the same misery, which he fears will only intensify if the family stays home for the holidays. Weiss, although Jewish, has assembled a beautiful collection of ornaments over the years. Each winter he, Parker, and Margo would decorate their tree together. This year, the box of ornaments will be left behind in New York when the family travels to California to spend two weeks with Margo's family.

And in the new year, the Weiss family will make an even more difficult trip. They'll go to Hawaii, where Margo was raised, so Jason and Parker can see for the first time where their mother spent a childhood very different from their newly tragic ones. "We planned this trip long before all this. And now we feel like we just have to go. You never really have a chance to say good-bye," says Weiss.

In the three months he has been a single father, Weiss has learned what to pack to take care of toddler Jason and knows not to forget Parker's hair-detangling spray. "I think she's figured out by now that I'm never going to be very good with her hair," he says. "I can never be her mother for her. And the only thing I can ask for from her, from myself, from everybody, is just an enormous amount of patience—just time and patience."

THE ISLAND OF MOURNING

TERRY GOLWAY

NOV. 20, 2001, STATEN ISLAND, N.Y.—When politicians and celebrities visit ground zero to pay tribute to the spirit of New York, they're probably not thinking of the tree-lined streets of northern Staten Island, or the tracts of new row houses that have sprouted up around the infamous Fresh Kills landfill in the island's southwest corner, where World Trade Center debris is being trucked. The city's least-populated and most suburban borough is home to neither the glamour nor the power that the world associates with Manhattan. But it, along with the Rockaways, is the city's ground zero of grief. Nearly 200 Staten Island residents, in a borough of about 400,000, lost their lives September 11. Of that number, 81 were firefighters. Two months after the terrorist attack, small shrines of flowers and the artwork of schoolchildren decorate the borough's firehouses, and firefighters still are gathering in their dress blue uniforms outside the borough's churches, still saluting widows holding their husbands' helmets, still eulogizing fallen brothers. To add to the horror, the remnants of Staten Island's Rescue Company 5, decimated on September 11, were sent to the Rockaways on November 12 when American Airlines Flight 587 crashed, killing at least 260 people.

If, in the aftermath of the World Trade Center attacks, there is a new cultural moment known as blue-collar chic,

Staten Island is its epicenter. It is the city's whitest borough and its most Republican. It is heavily Catholic, predominantly Italian, filled with cops, firefighters, and other uniformed workers. It is almost aggressively middle-class in its values and cultural interests. It is a place easily dismissed, at least before September 11, as the home of big hair, clunky minivans, and brawny do-it-yourselfers.

But there's an infinitely more complex and more human narrative at work in the borough's tidy backyards, thriving public schools, and flourishing civic life. The stories of some of the borough's lost firefighters fascinate not only because of the courage they displayed, but the stereotypes they shattered. Lieutenant Charles Margiotta, forty-four, one of a locally famous athletic family, was on his way home after working the 6 P.M. to 9 A.M. overnight shift when he heard about the terrorist attack September 11. A graduate of Brown University, Margiotta double-majored in English and sociology and played for the school's Ivy League championship football team in 1976. He worked for General Motors for a few years after college, but it offered him little satisfaction, so he joined the Fire Department in 1981. The morning of September 11, driving home, he heard about the attacks and drove to the nearest firehouse, the headquarters of Rescue 5, and jumped aboard a rig headed for downtown Manhattan. He died there, leaving a wife and two children.

Sean Hanley, thirty-five, had grown up hearing stories about his maternal grandfather, who died fighting a fire in Brooklyn in 1939. Undeterred, he followed in his grandfather's footsteps five years ago, and on September 11, he, like Margiotta, had finished up a night tour and was headed home when the planes struck. He drove himself to the World Trade Center, and died.

Even the Fire Department of New York can't teach such

selflessness. It springs from family, parish, and community, from values that honor courage more than money, sacrifice more than ambition, family more than status. Those same values are helping the borough heal from the September 11 tragedy, but even here, it will be slow going.

If we really want to understand the lives of the Charles Margiottas and Sean Hanleys of our world, we will have to put aside our media-encouraged clichés about narrow working-class life. Staten Island may send Republicans to Congress and the City Council, but the borough's firefighters are old-fashioned union men (even those with college degrees) who haven't forgiven their onetime union leader, Thomas von Essen, for crossing over into management to become Mayor Rudy Giuliani's fire commissioner. The two- and three-car garages may indicate suburban individualism run riot, but many of the borough's two-dozen-plus towns cling fiercely to their collective identities. Tottenville, in the borough's southern tip, prides itself on its little shopping district and small-town values; St. George, just across the harbor from downtown Manhattan, is grittier, more urban, and almost—almost—chic.

Staten Island can be a parochial place, like so many ethnic or blue-collar enclaves, but the flip side of parochialism is a sense of community that no city of transient careerists can match, or perhaps even comprehend. The obituaries in the local newspaper, the *Staten Island Advance*, chronicle not just the lives of individuals but the life and heartbreak of a vibrant community. This firefighter coached youth soccer teams; that one ran charity golf outings. One arranged his work schedule around his children; another organized an annual family reunion. Staten Island, it becomes clear, is a place where nobody bowls alone, to use sociologist Robert Putnam's shorthand for modern anomie. It is a place where the firehouse ethic of brotherhood and fraternity rules. Before Sept. 11, that ethos was condemned as ridiculously out of date: patriarchal, clannish, and parochial. Now, however, those supposed weaknesses help explain the strength of a community and a profession.

On a sunny weekend in late October, nearly thirty firefighters descended on a century-old house in the island's West Brighton section, where the aging parents of firefighter John Santore have lived for more than forty years. The house needs a new roof, and Santore, who lived nearby with his wife and kids, had been planning to replace it this fall. Of course, he wasn't going to do it himself—he was counting on help from his brothers in Engine 24 and Ladder 5 in Manhattan. But on September 11, weeks before he could put the roofing party into action, John Santore and seven co-workers from Ladder 5 scrambled up to the thirty-seventh floor of the World Trade Center's north tower. They were evacuating office workers when the tower fell. His body was found in the rubble four days later.

Dennis Taaffe and John Santore both started as firefighters on July 11, 1981, and they worked together in the lower Manhattan fire station that houses Engine 24 and Ladder 5. "We planned to retire together," Taaffe said. With just over two decades on the job, they were closing in on that magical date: Most firefighters retire after twenty-five years, when they're eligible for a half-pay pension.

Taaffe and another colleague of Santore, Cosmo DiOrio, understood that their friend's parents had lost not only a son, but a protector, a repair man, a nurse, a grocery shopper, a mechanic—and the man who would repair their roof before winter arrived. So they posted a sign on the firehouse bulletin board asking for volunteers to do the work John Santore left behind. They bought shingles and plywood, loaded ladders onto pickup trucks, and got the job done.

DiOrio called this coming together "the firehouse way." More than any other civil service job, and more than most white-collar jobs, firefighters depend on each other, not to meet a deadline, not to maximize a profit, but for simple survival. They work, eat, and live together in small units of five or six, much like combat squads. Not surprisingly, then, firehouse friendships don't end at the firehouse doors. DiOrio, for example, owns a small ski house in upstate New York with several firefighter friends.

"We do everything together," said DiOrio's wife, Gerri DiOrio. "Our kids all know each other. We go on vacation together. It's a way of life. My friends are firefighters' wives. We're always there for each other." She turned forty on September thirteenth, but her husband couldn't join her for a planned celebration. "He was at the World Trade Center site, searching for people," she said, adding, "I didn't expect him to be anyplace else."

"It's not an ordinary co-worker relationship," said Taaffe. "This isn't a nine to five job where everybody goes his separate way at the end of a shift. At the firehouse, it's more personal. We call each other 'brother,' and that's not an accident."

In the cultural moment since September 11, it's not even politically incorrect. The Fire Department of New York has few women—no more than 50—in its 11,000-member force. It also remains a bastion of white ethnic Catholics, particularly the Irish. In the world that no longer exists, it seemed to matter that the survivors of most dead firefighters had names like Liam and Paddy and Bridget and Margaret Mary. Now, with nearly 350 firefighters to bury or memorialize, what matters most is their courage.

The firehouse culture of shared bonds, of astonishing bravery and of extraordinary selflessness, no longer seems an anachronism. In fact, it now seems worthy of imitation. "This is one of the last jobs on earth where men rely on each other to stay alive," said novelist Peter Quinn, whose father was a Democratic congressman and judge in the Bronx. "And it reflects something in the Catholic working-class ethic, that life is not all about fame and financial success, that doing something noble and providing for your family was more important. It's a parochial-school world-view that in the past led people to become priests. In fact, joining the Fire Department is about as close as you can get to being in a religious order but still having a wife and kids."

On Staten Island, a borough of old town centers and tacky strip malls, the city of unquenchable ambition and seven-figure bonuses seems much farther than the five miles that separate its northern tip from downtown Manhattan. "Staten Island," DiOrio said, "is one of the last small-town communities. It's a place where people know each other and help each other." They know each other from church—usually, a Roman Catholic parish—from a fraternal organization or a Rotary Club or a PTA or a beer-league softball team.

"The nature of the community means that you have a lot more support for these firefighters and their families than you might have for some poor kid who was a junior broker at some stock trading firm," said journalist Chris Franz, political editor of the borough's weekly newspaper, the *Staten Island Register*. Ultimately, then, the firehouse way is, in fact, the Staten Island way. Which came first is an issue left for others to ponder.

About a dozen miles away from the Santore house, St. Clare's Roman Catholic Church in the island's Great Kills section is preparing for one last memorial mass for a parish firefighter. St. Clare's lost 11 firefighters and 19 civilians on

September 11, a total of 30 parishioners leaving behind parents, children, spouses, and grieving friends and families. The church is about a quarter-mile from the local firehouse, an aging brick building draped in mournful purple bunting and seemingly sagging from the weight of grief and loss. Monsignor Joseph Murphy has presided over the funerals and memorial masses. These have been, he said, the most sorrowful weeks of his life. "I've been a priest for forty-eight years, and I've never experienced so much personal grief," he said. "It has been the most painful period of my life."

The Fire Department masses and funerals have an added poignancy. Most of the firefighters were young, with young families, and many were active parishioners, rather than occasional churchgoers. As he presided over these terrible rituals, Monsignor Murphy says he has borne witness to the unwavering courage of the Fire Department of New York and its extended family. "It is a privilege to see how much these men wish to honor their brothers," he said. "Sometimes tears come to my eyes to see the sorrow."

To help his grief-stricken flock, Monsignor Murphy asked parishioners to help their friends and neighbors cope with their sorrow. The response, he said, was extraordinary. "Hundreds of people volunteered to provide financial assistance or other kinds of help," he said. "We set up six support groups for different categories of people affected by September 11. The response has just been remarkable."

No doubt the opinion-makers and taste-enforcers in faraway Manhattan will soon grow weary of firefighter chic, of the travails of St. Clare's Parish. But long after the magazine writers and camera crews have left, this borough of small towns will remember the wounds inflicted on neighbors—wounds that will never fully heal. Only those reared on irony and detachment can speak of closure. The firefighting families of Staten Island, who vacation together and pray together and grieve together, know that the pain of losing a child, a spouse, a parent never goes away. There will be no closure for the hundred-plus children Staten Island's firefighters left behind.

But just as nobody mourned by themselves on Staten Island, nobody will be left to heal by themselves. Firefighter Taaffe, after helping to replace the roof on the house of his dead friend's parents, said he'd be back in springtime to help with other chores. "They won't ask for help," he said of John Santore's parents, "but we'll hear about it, and we'll be there for them."

NOT EXACTLY FATHERLESS

KEVIN J. SWEENEY

NOV. 21, 2001—The events leading to my father's death
were not shown on live television. Aside from the phone
calls to family and friends, and the generous obituary written for the hometown weekly, there was no way for the
larger community to know that something profoundly sad
had happened. My dad died alone, of congestive heart failure, at six o'clock on a Thursday morning, at Stanford
University Hospital. It was 1962, and I was three years old,
the fifth of his six children.

There is little in the way of detail to connect my father
to those who died on September 11. While there was a
frantic last phone call—from a doctor telling my mother to
come quickly—it came minutes too late. His occupation
did not match the lofty pursuits of so many who worked in
the twin towers: He was a former diaper deliveryman, and
his last job was as a city maintenance worker—a street
sweeper.

But like many of the men who died on September 11,
my father was young (thirty-eight), and in the prime of his
life, and he left a young wife and young children—abruptly.
These are details that bring tremendous sadness; at times I
am nearly swept away by it as I read the endless stream of
obituaries in the *New York Times*. But I recall, as I mourn
these losses, that even though my childhood was marked

indelibly by a sad event, it was not a sad childhood. I was a
pretty happy kid. And, so far, I've been a pretty happy
grown man.

It might be because I have not been fatherless, not
exactly, even though my mother never remarried.

Several years after my father died, I began to worry
about what I might lack as someone who grew up without a
dad. I remember, at the age of seven, worrying about
whether I could ever be a good father if I didn't have a
father. In the hazy minutes between bedtime and sleep, I
would linger over the fact that I would not have the classic
point of reference—my old man—in crucial moments of
maleness or parenthood. I really don't know why I saw this
particular need. It may have come from the image of television fathers, the ones who sat on the edge of the bed and
had the perfect words to close the week's episode. It may
have come from Catholicism, a grand influence in our
household, and its emphasis on male leaders. It may have
been that I missed my dad terribly, and replaced my sadness
with a worry.

Whatever my motivation, I figured out a plan. It was
mysterious, in that I am not entirely sure how I came up
with it, and it was secret, in that I told no one else.

I picked out three men from our working-class community and decided that they would teach me how to be a
father. None of them would know about their surrogacy,
but I would watch them closely. And sometimes my surveil-
lance would extend to contact: They were all friends of my
family and I would be in a position, from time to time, to
ask them for advice or hang out with them.

I watched Jim Gaffney, Sherm Heaney, and Chick
Kelly for many years. When our families got together, I
would loiter in the living room with the grown-ups,
watching the fathers go about their business. I watched the

dads in the park with their own kids, and in the stands, when I played ball. I watched the fathers watching their sons. I watched them shake hands, hug, and kiss. I watched them be husbands, watched how they treated their wives. I saw how kind they were to my mother. Their words would break through the cacophony of a christening party or a wedding and I would listen carefully: These were the words of a good father, I would think, a father that I myself had chosen.

Sometimes I would seek them out, ask their advice, tell them my jokes, talk. I would never reveal the specialness of our relationships—I couldn't bear to tell them how great the stakes were. But I was always around.

Jim Gaffney was a graceful dad—DiMaggio with kids running around. He picked up checks with a kind of cool—and financial reserve—that one didn't see very often in San Bruno, California. He wore knit slacks and neat cardigan sweaters—he cared, without pretense, about how he looked.

Sherm Heaney taught me the first rule of the dad: Show up. He was always there for his kids. Always. He never shouted from the stands, but he always had a lot to say after the games. He was interested, he had specific questions that proved he was watching.

Chick Kelly looked like the lineman he was back when they played football in tiny leather helmets. The warm sting of his handshake tingled for whole minutes. He was a butcher and would show up at our house every so often with a ton of meat. He introduced me to steak. He was strong, but he had a soothing voice. I never heard him raise it. Even when he had something difficult to say. This I know from experience.

I had two very wild years in high school. I don't know how much my mother knew about what I was up to—

though I knew she was troubled—but Mr. Kelly knew at least as much as she did; perhaps one of his sons had given him the details. One evening, he pulled me aside and said, without raising his voice, that my actions were hurting my mother and that he would not tolerate them.

"You're not becoming the man you want to be," he said. "You're not on the way to becoming the man I know you can be." He said that he knew there was something in me, that I had shown him I had the potential to be a good man. I wasn't on the right path, he said, but he had faith that I soon would be. He told me that he knew that I could make better choices.

I was astonished and grateful. For him—and my mom—I started making better choices.

That conversation with Mr. Kelly, in which I said very little, was the only time I had anything like a father-son chat with any of the men I chose. But there were plenty of other times with them that made me feel less fatherless. Mr. Heaney always had questions not just for his own son, but for me—specific questions about things I was interested in or the stuff I was doing with my life. Mr. Gaffney, when dropping off his wife at our house to visit with her girlfriends, would pull me out to go see a movie. (*Tora! Tora! Tora!* wasn't on my mom's list of must-see cinema.)

There were risks, I suppose, in choosing three dads on my own. But the three men I chose served me well. On my good days as a dad, I can see their influence. On my bad days, I recall that they had some bad days too. And they aren't finished with me. Chick Kelly showed me how to die—his death was long, painful, and, amazingly, beautiful. Sherm Heaney, the lone survivor, now gets to show me how to be an old fart.

I realize that I have nothing to offer the mothers who find themselves suddenly alone, except maybe to say that your kids aren't just resilient, they are likely to be creative in their grief. But I do have advice for the men in the Bronx and Queens and Staten Island and all around New York and Arlington who might find themselves haunted by kids who keep hanging around, or look like they might want to: Laugh at the bad jokes and tell some that you remember from fourth grade; ask about their batting stance and whether it changes with two strikes; go to a movie—even the new Martin Lawrence movie—then go again. Look them in the eye when you ask how they're doing.

And remember: You don't need to be perfect. You just need to show up.

Start
Making
Sense

AMERICA THE SCAPEGOAT

MEERA ATKINSON

NOV. 30, 2001—It was five days after the attacks. My husband and I had fled Manhattan for his brother's place upstate to escape the acrid air and collect our shattered nerves. I was still having trouble eating and sleeping, and I'd brought my passport along, just in case World War III broke out overnight and I decided to slip across the border into Canada and fly home to Australia.

I was not one of the stoic New Yorkers. In fact, I was not even a New Yorker. But when I got an e-mail forwarded to me by a friend in London, I was upset on behalf of all 8 million of them.

The e-mail, written by a Chinese man, was an angry tirade against America and on behalf of Afghanistan and world peace, written in incongruently inflammatory language. The words "I don't give a shit," referring to the terrorist attacks and the suffering of Americans, stand out in my mind. The writer said that America had brought the attacks upon itself with its foreign policy, that Americans were soft and spoiled, that it was high time they got a taste of their own medicine.

I responded by telling my friend I'd found the piece nasty and offensive, and requested that she not send any more of the same ilk. I received a haughty reply stating that she and her friends were merely engaged in a rigorous international discussion, the implication being that there was something wrong with me, that I lacked the intellectual mettle to participate. I didn't know it then, but it was the first of many skirmishes to come. While flags sold by the millions and Americans spoke of their newfound sense of unity, I found myself at first divided and torn between cultures—and then, increasingly, alienated from my own.

When I was twenty and living in Sydney, my ardent lifelong love affair with American culture—partly born out of my youthful desire to escape what felt at the time like a suffocating, isolated island—crystallized into an intense obsession with New York City. A few years later Australia grew on me, and my fantasies of living in New York faded into a nostalgic whimsy. But when I met and fell in love with a New Yorker, I found myself dreaming of New York again. While I waited for my visa to come through I watched *Sex and the City* and tried to picture myself in its scenes.

Moving to New York also meant moving to America. I remember watching the news the day the U.S.S. *Cole* was bombed, the feeling of dread it raised in me, the sense of foreboding. I remember commenting to my father that Americans didn't realize how hated they were, and that one day it would all blow up. I remember phoning my then long-distance fiancé and expressing my fears of life in New York, of violent crime, and of living in a hemisphere beset by war. I remember the self-possessed calm in his reassurance that no one would be foolish enough to attack America itself, and the thin relief with which I tried to believe him.

Looking back now, I realize that our differing views of this potential arose partly out of geography. Australia and New Zealand are the most isolated "Western" countries on the planet. It is a distance that affords a uniquely clear outlook. At the same time this isolation casts a shadow of parochialism. The combination can result in a tendency to judge other nations and world events harshly and simply. It is this tendency with which I have been wrangling these past weeks.

I arrived in New York in December last year, and we married soon afterward. I was just feeling that I had finally arrived, and the beginnings of a bond with the city, when the planes flew into the towers, the Pentagon, and a sunny Pennsylvania field. The entire world was in shock, reeling with grief, gripped by fear, and overwhelmed by the psychic shift heralded by the "new reality." In the days following the attack I seemed to be in tune with my Australian friends back home, except that I was traumatized, having gone through it firsthand, or at least from the madness of the Empire State Building midtown. I shared my friends' concern that America might lash out in a bloodlust of retaliation. I recoiled from the American desire for revenge confirmed in polls. I agreed that the attacks were a wakeup call that demanded America reexamine its role in the Middle East, that it was an opportunity for America to own up to some of its more undeniable mistakes and wrongdoings and make amends.

But as the weeks passed and we all began to process the ordeal, review our history, and come to terms with the post-attack world and the war on terrorism, I became aware of an unsettling division—between those who find America a convenient scapegoat and those who do not.

Polls will tell you that the majority of people in Australia and other Western, allied nations support America's war on terrorism. Many of those heartily support the commitment of their own troops. But what the polls don't tell you is that there is a sizable and extremely vocal minority who don't, and that beyond even this there is and has been, for as far back as I can remember, a palpable anger and hostility toward the U.S. in general. This minority is not confined to university campuses but stretches across a broad spectrum of society. Of course there is the "foreign policy is not a popularity contest" standard by which to measure this opposition, but if September 11 and the "new reality" have taught us anything, it is that the hatred much of the world feels toward the U.S. can no longer be ignored.

That largely impoverished, uneducated, and oppressed nations hate America is more or less understandable. Some of these nations are ruled by American-backed undemocratic and highly corrupt governments, and most of them have lived for generations with the riches of the modern world in view but out of reach, informed only by a government-controlled media. Anti-American sentiment in the Middle East is easy to fathom. But why does this hatred manifest itself in countries like Australia, Britain, and France—affluent nations that have much more in common with America than with Middle Eastern and Third World nations?

In my recent dialogue with Australian family and friends, some predictable reasons have been given. One aunt declared that Australians' critical view of Americans dates back to World War II, when American troops were seen as "oversexed, overpaid, and over there." An Australian expat posting on the Web site Australians Abroad agreed. "My grandparents hated the Yanks and would tell stories of the Yanks coming into Brisbane on R&R and yelling out to the Diggers who were leaving on another train that they'd 'take care of their women for them,' " he said, before going on to confirm that some of those American soldiers did indeed "take care" of the Diggers' women and that a few were shot for their troubles. No doubt experiences such as these must have helped form some national opinion, but there are just as many stories of camaraderie between Australian and

American soldiers, and just as many Australians who feel a genuine sense of alliance with America. A cousin was quick to defend Australia's relationship with the U.S. "We know America would come to our aid if needed," she said. "It did when the Japanese invaded and Churchill said, 'Let them take it, we can get it back later.' " Run-ins during World War II or any other time don't account for the pervasive and vicious anti-American sentiment that has peaked in the wake of September 11.

The ANZUS Treaty, marking the Australia–United States alliance, was signed in 1951. The Australian prime minister, John Howard, was reportedly the first world leader to offer military support in the war on terrorism. Australian troops followed America into Korea, Vietnam, and the Gulf War. Australia has participated in U.S. intelligence gathering consistently since World War II. There is therefore a sense that Australia, a relatively peaceful nation, has been dragged into America's troubles repeatedly. Many Australians feel a pronounced anger toward the bind our military dependence on America presents. But why are some Australians so unwilling to acknowledge the rewards of this arrangement? Why are they so insistent on casting themselves as the hapless weak brother of the big buff bully? It is a clear case of risk and reward, and though the risks are real, and the dependence frustrating and unempowering, the rewards are great.

The refusal of the anti-American movement in Australia to address them is symptomatic of a largely complacent society. Australia is a wealthy country with a small population that couldn't possibly defend its coastline if it came under serious attack. It is a country that pays high taxes but which also enjoys good services. It has one of the most comprehensive health and welfare programs in the world. Its citizens live with the certainty that if they require medical care and cannot afford it, they will be given it, that if they reach retirement age without sufficient means of support they can draw a comparatively generous pension, that if they lose their job they can claim unemployment benefits until they find another.

All this is possible because it doesn't have to spend massive amounts of money on national defense. Many who were born and raised in post–World War II Australia, as I was, have little or no appreciation of the need for self-defense. In general Australians feel themselves so far removed, so relatively safe in their isolation, that they tend to view America as paranoid and hysterical when it comes to military defense. In my youth I, too, held this view; I indulged in the idealist, utopian fantasy of a world with no need for defense, imagining that Australia in particular need not concern itself with such unsavory preoccupations. My grandparents knew otherwise. I still hope for a future free of nuclear threat, for the realized potential of real world peace. But if and when it comes, it will come about as a result of a powerful organic human revolution. I am fairly sure it will not come about by pure fantasy, denial, and anti-government jingoism. One thing is certain: We are not there yet, and it's not only the U.S. that lags behind in this evolution.

The current antiwar, anti-American sentiment in the West is not confined to Australia, however. Its voice can be heard right across Europe. The London friend who had sent the "I don't give a shit" e-mail went on to explain in further exchanges that the view of America she shared with many Brits was based on a kaleidoscope of grievances. "America's intervention in world affairs is often corrupt, abusive, and hypocritical. U.S. foreign policy is highly destructive and sanctimonious," she declared, citing an article published in the *Guardian* in late September by Arundhati Roy as supporting evidence.

This friend, born and raised in a country settled as an English penal colony that grew into its own identity by resisting the class-based, culturally egotistical tendencies of the motherland, patiently explained why British culture was superior to American culture, with no visible sense of irony. She actually went so far as to make the claim that "We [Brits] are not as hysterical or ignorant as the U.S." It's probably accurate to say that the British, due to their proximity to Europe and the broader view of their media (at least their elite media) are more informed about the rest of the world than Americans, but this hardly precludes "ignorance" in general. And to claim that the British are less hysterical than Americans when the memory of the British reaction to Princess Diana's death is still fresh to us all is bold indeed. The enormous crowds and mass wailing in London in 1997 was far more extreme than New Yorkers' reaction to September 11, and it was not three but roughly four thousand people killed, not by accident, but by mass murder.

My London friend opened her litany of complaints with the perception of a U.S. public deluded by a pure-hype propaganda-machine media, and went on to cite America's military presence in Saudi Arabia, its conduct of the Gulf War, its responsibility for the starvation deaths of 100,000 Iraqi children as a result of economic sanctions (I've always wondered why this popular statistic only cites children, as if adults don't starve, or matter), and all the other well-known sins of America committed in the name of oil security. She climaxed with the widespread complaint against U.S. support of Israel, wound down with accusations of free-trade blackmail and two-faced global emissions policies, and finished with a description of the U.S.-led war on terrorism as a typical American aggression bound to add fuel to the fire.

In other discussions, a Canadian friend living in Australia wrote with absolute conviction that America's military action in Afghanistan was motivated solely by a desire for revenge and punishment, that self-defense "has nothing whatsoever to do with it." Someone else told me I sounded "like an American" simply because I questioned the caustic tone of the many recent anti-American letters to two major Australian newspapers. This same person attached to their message an article that posed the theory that America's war in Afghanistan is all about oil in the Caspian Sea, along with the heavy-handed Arundhati Roy piece, presumably to enlighten me. One letter in the *Sydney Morning Herald*'s online edition stood out from the others. It was written by a Jewish woman who had gone to a peace march in Sydney's Hyde Park staged by the usually cuddly Friends of the Earth. She was horrified, she said, to find herself surrounded by a furious crowd chanting poisonous slogans against the U.S. and Israel. People calling for peace with voices of hate is perhaps the ultimate bleak irony of the current antiwar, anti-American movement.

There have been other long-distance frictions too numerous to mention. Of course some of these criticisms are valid and earned, but many are misguided and vulnerable to challenge. Few who cast these aspersions seem willing to acknowledge that even the most educated and informed among us rarely get the full political picture—and many of those who are the loudest in their denunciations have far less than that. Yet even when they lack deep knowledge and information, many anti-Americanists are all too willing to assume the very worst of America in any given conflict, often downright whitewashing the other party.

It's not my aim to embark on an in-depth analysis of these charges or the degree to which they stick or don't stick; suffice to say that we all know the U.S. is not now, nor has it ever been, perfect. This is hard to accept; we don't want our superstars, or our superpowers, to be flawed, human, like the rest of us. What bothers me most about the anti-American sentiment I've encountered is not the criticisms themselves, simplistic as they frequently are, but the dogged superciliousness and smugness with which they are frequently expressed. There is a lack of real recognition of America, for better and for worse, inherent in this attitude. And there is an unsettling ease with which the United States of America is made the scapegoat for the flawed policies of the First World, the failings of some nations of the Third World, a library's worth of historical complexities, and the guilt of the privileged First World individual.

It is the fashion, it seems, to hold the U.S. responsible for the hardships and struggles of the entire planet, some of which were germinating or already had a long history before America's existence. For example, many of the problems of the Middle East and Third World can be more rightly laid at imperial Britain's doorstep. Granted, America has stepped in where Britain stepped out, but that doesn't justify holding a New World country solely responsible for problems born of the Old World.

Anti-Americanism's broadest complaint is also its most powerful argument—that the U.S. is too wealthy, too materialistic, too concerned with its own economic health to the detriment of the world's poor. The most powerful nation on the planet runs a laissez-faire economic system that dominates global economics. In Australia, where capitalism has long been tinged with socialism (though this hybrid is much diminished now), America's version of capitalism is viewed as ruthless. But if the problem is U.S.-led globalization and corporatization, there needs to be some acknowledgment of the way the rest of the world is participating. Furious finger-pointing at America ignores the option and responsibility of nations, communities, and individuals to resist and protest what they find objectionable. The money in a citizen's hand does more voting than we ever get to do in a polling booth. Our consumer dollar is, now more than ever, a powerful political tool.

Too much anti-Americanism rests on bad faith. A psychological sleight of hand makes it possible for the anti-American movement across the West to enjoy privileges while avoiding a sense of responsibility for them. America has blood on its hands: The rest of the world, apparently, does not.

For some years now I have refused to eat at McDonald's and Burger King because I object to what I view as the unethical corporate practices of U.S. fast-food chains. Neither do I buy products tested on animals, in protest of the global animal experimentation industry. I know many others who act similarly on their principles. But I have never heard of a person who refuses to use oil-dependent modes of transportation in adherence to their stance against America's oil-driven policies in the Middle East. I've met the odd rare individual who refuses to own a car because of their concern for the environment, but never anyone who boycotts oil across the board—or even who devotes significant time to trying to change oil-friendly governmental policies. Why? Because it's a luxury people simply refuse to give up. Foregoing a lousy cheeseburger and shopping cruelty-free doesn't require a great sacrifice—to live without using oil in the world as it is today would. That people don't wish to make this sacrifice is understandable, but that they demonize the U.S. despite their dependency on oil that may have been procured in association with U.S. policies is somewhat dishonest and hypocritical. Righteousness, it turns out, is the drug that soothes the fears and frustrations of exiled terrorist gurus and Sydney peaceniks alike.

I am more inclined to respect the voice of anti-Americanism when it produces more than simplistic critiques and—at its worst—hate speech. In other words, I am more inclined to respect it when it manifests an active rather than a reactive element. Unlike classic imperialism achieved by military-led expansion and domination, cultural and economic imperialism requires willing colonists. It is possible to resist so-called U.S. imperialism, as the small community of the Blue Mountains, northwest of Sydney, did several years ago when it successfully fought a bitter battle against the opening of a McDonald's in its quaint historic town. It is possible; it's just that most people would rather not bother. Victimhood is more appealing than self-responsibility, and when the villain is a big bumbling superpower it's an easy play.

Of course, being part of the problem doesn't oblige a person to silence. People have a right to be angry with the U.S. and its policies when they feel they're immoral, but they also have a responsibility to own up to their implicit participation. It's a democratic right to voice protest, but it's a matter of personal integrity to do so not from the moral comfort of a high horse, but while standing on one's own two feet.

Some anti-Americanists already do this, of course. Some, like socialists and anarcho-syndicalists, go further and campaign for radically different political and economic systems. But looking around at the anti-Americanists in my midst I see no home garage print-runs of the *Die-Hard Communists Weekly* or grassroots kitchen campaign meetings. I see people plucking the fruits, and treading the established paths, of capitalism.

And what of the confusions and contradictions of the

left wing in the first world? In the two or three years preceding the attacks of September 11, I received a string of e-mail petitions from alarmed feminists and leftists protesting the atrocities committed by the Taliban and calling for its brutal regime to be brought down. I signed and passed on every one without ever believing the petitions would literally achieve that end. It seems that others, though adult and educated, did believe in the power of these petitions to cause the Taliban to review in full the practices of its government. This is the only sense I can make of the turnaround of many of these same people, who are now on the front lines of the current antiwar movement. Some who were aware of conditions in Afghanistan under the Taliban's rule and who rallied against the world's complacency became, once America set out to topple the Taliban, its most ardent defenders, calling for peace at any cost, and casting America as the brute.

I understand that these people are not really defending the Taliban; rather they are expressing concern for the innocent, already long-suffering Afghan people, and rightly so. But why the political backpedaling? Why oppose the forcible removal of the Taliban when they are clearly far too determined and well established to be removed by other means? This confusion, born of a demand that the sufferings of others be rectified coupled with a refusal to tolerate the realities of what is required to achieve that change, results in an impossible demand that the U.S. is accused of failing to meet again and again.

I came across an explicit example of this when reading an article in which a prominent member of a women's rights organization publicly retracted a previous statement to the effect that she wished someone would forcibly take the Taliban out. Sounding somewhat like a small and frightened child, she explained that she "didn't really mean it," that it had merely been an expression of frustration and not of a real and concrete desire for military intervention. That the U.S. military action in Afghanistan and its result-ing refugee crisis and civilian causalities are painful, even tragic, goes without saying. But to believe in a world where dangerous people and tyrannical governments miracu-lously disappear seems infantile.

When I asked my French neighbor about the anti-American sentiment in France, she said there is a profound sense of "they had it coming" among the French left. When I asked her what the roots of French anti-American sentiment were she said simply, "Envy, jealousy. We think of Americans as arrogant, vain, self-centered. It is what France was two centuries ago: the center of the world." While I doubt this is all that fuels the anti-American senti-ment there and across the West, there is likely some plain old jealousy in the mix. It's not an envy as tortured and confused at that of the Middle East, because we in the West are neither as uniformly religious or as economically deprived as the peoples of those nations. But it is tempting, it seems, to resent those more powerful and dominant, and to rally a reactive cause in response.

Some of this resentment boils down to that most basic of human emotions—hurt feelings. Beyond the "Tall Poppy Syndrome"—the famous Australian pastime of cutting gloating achievement, blatant success, and perceived arro-gance down to size—Australians often feeling overlooked by America and Americans. I remember feeling disap-pointed that I didn't see Australia, a country with a fascinat-ing history and political life, covered at all in the American media for months following my arrival. Even now I'm lucky to catch a passing reference or a feature in a travel section. And I've felt personally slighted more than once socially, when someone's eyes glazed over upon hearing the word

Australia. Typically they'd vaguely mention Paul Hogan or
kangaroos before losing interest completely. This hurt is, I
think, a factor in the anti-American feelings of many peoples, especially Australians who get little attention on the
world stage. It's a legitimate complaint, but it scarcely justifies the virulent condemnations that have emerged after
September 11.

Another comment my French neighbor made, recount-
ing how a friend of hers in France had exclaimed bitterly
on the phone, "They have six cases of anthrax and it's the
end of the world. What about Rwanda?" illustrates another
confusion of the left in relation to the U.S.—the damned if
you do, damned if you don't principle. America is criticized
for not being a benevolent superpower when it doesn't
intervene, and criticized for being the world police when it
does. It is cast as an abusive cop when it steps into conflicts
such as Kosovo, or accused of criminal negligence when it
fails to act, as it did with the genocide in Rwanda. The U.S.
itself suffers a certain amount of confusion in its foreign
policy that gives rise to mixed messages, but whichever way
it goes on any distant conflict the left seems insistent on
meeting the U.S. with skepticism or conspiracy theories of
ulterior motives.

Certain factions of the American left are no less virulent. A country, particularly a powerful one, needs a mind-
ful and vocal conscience, and when it's doing its job, as it
did during the Vietnam War, it's a vital watchdog. But
September 11 seems to have reduced even some Americans
to sloppy accusations and irrational outbursts.

A prime example of this "America is the devil" silliness
appeared in the November 20 *Village Voice*. James Ridgeway's
"Mondo Washington" columns titled "The Ugly American:
Bully Spends Billions Blasting Nation of Refugees," "The
Lost Colony: Afghanistan's Huddled Masses," and "Brown

Out: U.S. Drops Bigger Bombs on Darker People" were the most stunning displays of frenzied knee-jerking in the name of journalism I've witnessed in a long time. In one short page he managed to hold the U.S. government responsible for the deaths of 7 million Afghan refugees (most of whom are not even dead), to refer to Afghanistan as an American "colony," and to suggest that the use of the dreadful "daisy cutter" in the bombing campaign was inspired by a racist impulse to "get rid of these nasty tan bugs."

As Christopher Hitchens pointed out in the December *Atlantic Monthly*, some in the American left and other "progressives" "have grossly failed to live up to their responsibility to think; rather, they are merely reacting, substituting tired slogans for thought." Or in Ridgeway's case, hysteria for thought. There's a certain laziness involved. It's not necessary to challenge oneself and grapple with impossible problems, it's not necessary to read extensively across a wide range of views (not only those that confirm one's most comfortable and staid thinking and beliefs), or to educate oneself on the intricacies of history and geopolitics in order to be certain which governments should be held accountable for what sufferings, when one can, without going to all this trouble, satisfy one's need to assign blame and take the high moral ground by making the U.S. accountable for everything, even deaths that haven't happened.

After many trans-Pacific and Atlantic conversations I've come to see the escalating anti-Americanism as the product of, to varying degrees, a tendency toward black-and-white thinking, a heartfelt concern for the suffering of disadvantaged peoples, and the denial of our own most rapacious capitalist selves—as projected upon and epitomized by the U.S. The stridency of this habit of thought is laced with wishful thinking and is driven by a lack of equanimity fostered by the new reach of global terrorism. People are afraid. They want to believe that if only America had not responded militarily, if only it had seen the error of its ways and had met the terrorist demands by pulling out of the Middle East, everything would be all right. They would not have had to send their troops, they would not have to fear future attacks on their own soil, they could go to sleep in the knowledge that World War III is an imaginary nightmare rather than a present-day potential.

It's an understandable conclusion, one I also entertained in the awful days following the attacks. The problem with it is that it underestimates both America and the terrorists who have declared war on it, if in totally different ways. I've been struck by the apparent sense of confidence some anti-American Westerners have in the terrorists. I've even stumbled across a few apologists. They seem to hold the view that the terrorists are somehow reasonable in their endeavor, that they would surely end the terror if they got their way. One Australian, again posting on the Australians Abroad Web site, stated, "Remember even the fanatics of 9 Sept [sic] didn't do this to maximize kill ratio . . . hitting a sports stadium with gas would have taken out thousands more." Apart from the fact that "hitting a sports stadium with gas" is not as easily achieved as this poster imagines, it's a preposterous notion that the perpetrators of this attack were in any way concerned with minimizing civilian casualties. The poster went on to argue his point by claiming that the terrorists had chosen "light flight loadings" guided by the same noble impulses. Apparently the idea that they'd chosen lightly booked flights because it meant less chance of passenger resistance and therefore a greater chance of success was not familiar to this well-meaning young man. But this fantasy of "almost" freedom fighters with an "almost" just cause is as prevalent as it is problematic.

What we know about bin Laden and al-Qaida suggests a very different potential. The theory that bin Laden's true focus lies in leading a fundamentalist Islamic insurgency right across the Muslim world seems to have some weight. If that is his mission statement, America's abstention from military action and wholesale backing out of the Middle East might well have had two immediate consequences: an oil crisis and a series of successful insurgencies. The world economy would have become unstable, and a significant portion of the world would soon be under the rule of fiercely repressive Taliban-style governments—but this time with nuclear capabilities. Who knows if they'd stop there? Islam has a proud history of expansionism. I suspect that then the anti-Americanists—Australians, English, Europeans, feminists, and peaceniks alike—would have a sudden change of heart.

I realize this is a dark and somewhat alarmist scenario. We have no way of knowing if it could have happened because America did, predictably, attack. And, of course, as the antiwar movement would be quick to point out, the U.S.-led action in Afghanistan carries its own risk of inciting insurgencies. However, they could not proceed as quickly and as smoothly as they might have had the U.S. simply withdrawn from the whole region at bin Laden's demand. I'm not suggesting that a U.S. withdrawal from Saudi Arabia is impossible or undesirable, only that there are problems with the assumption that America's "understanding" and tolerance of the terrorist cause as stated could or would have spared further conflict and escalation.

While many of my friends overseas promote stereotypes of America and find affirmation from each other in doing so—Americans are blinded by their own inflated self-image, they fall prey to their government propaganda mindlessly with no self-examination, they revel in their ignorance of other parts of the world, etc.—I see a different America. I see a grieving, vulnerable America shocked out of its self-absorption, an America that is indeed questioning, debating, and attempting to understand the root causes of its predicament, seeking to educate itself about Islam and Muslim cultures, seeking to defend itself against further attacks. I see an America that has welcomed more people from more countries around the globe than any other country in the history of mankind. I see an America whose embrace of democracy and vision of freedom, however less than perfectly realized, beats in every American heart. I see an America that deserves compassion in response to its misfortunes, and acknowledgment of its virtues and better strivings, however often they may fail or produce unforeseen consequences. And I see a world that would be less without it.

THE BLOODY JORDAN RIVER NOW FLOWS THROUGH AMERICA

GARY KAMIYA

SEPT. 17, 2001—Americans are preparing for the long, arduous, and necessary task of bringing the perpetrators of Tuesday's unspeakable horror to justice. But as we do so, we must also ask ourselves why this happened—and why it might happen again. Striking back at those who have viciously attacked us is a first step. But if we don't address the underlying reasons why we were attacked, we will invite more hatred, and in the end more attacks. We can turn our country into Fortress America, but no fortress can defend against zealots willing to die. In the end our best, our only real defense will be winning the hearts and minds of those who hate us.

Of course, some of those minds neither can nor should be won. Some people from less fortunate nations hate America because it is the world's only military and economic superpower. Others detest us because of our all-conquering culture. Others see us as godless infidels simply because we don't subscribe to their psychotic version of Islam. There is nothing we can or should do about any of these things.

Those who carried out Tuesday's attacks were clearly driven, in large part, by religious fanaticism. The perpetrators were Arab terrorists, linked to the Saudi dissident Osama bin Laden. Bin Laden and his followers are zealous Muslims who regard America as the enemy of Islam, and therefore an entity of essentially metaphysical evil. There is nothing we can or should do to lessen the medieval fury of such monomania. Bin Laden's zealots' hatred for America is an article of faith: Nothing will change it.

But as we look down the long, dangerous road that lies ahead, we must remember that there is one specific grievance that rankles in the breasts of millions of Arab and Islamic people in the world. And until that grievance is resolved, there is a greater possibility that one of those people will decide to strike a terrible blow at the United States.

The critical issue is the Israeli-Palestinian conflict—a conflict in which the United States plays a reluctant central role. Until a just resolution of that conflict is realized—one that provides a homeland for the Palestinian people and security for Israel—it will be far more difficult for America to put together a truly committed coalition to fight terrorism, one that is not simply held together by coercion. And there is a far greater chance that military action against Islamic states will backfire, inflaming a significant portion of the world's population against us and breeding thousands of terrorists where there once were dozens.

This is bin Laden's master strategy. We cannot allow it to succeed.

To ensure that it does not, America must boldly take the lead in the Middle East. We must pressure Israel to take the concrete steps necessary to provide justice for the Palestinian people.

The Israeli government is incapable of taking such steps. The latest evidence came Friday, when, incredibly, Prime Minister Ariel Sharon canceled scheduled peace talks with Palestinian Authority president Yassir Arafat at the same time that he was launching Israel's most aggressive military action in the last year against Palestinians. These are the actions of a man more interested in scoring political points by letting his adversary twist in the wind than in searching for peace. The Bush administration, which in the aftermath of the attacks had asked Sharon to get the peace talks moving again, was left in the usual American posture—wringing its hands impotently.

It's time for this to change.

It is legitimate to ask whether shifting America's Mideast policy, in the aftermath of a horrific terrorist attack, would not signal to terrorists that they had won. The answer is no. This is not appeasement, nor a surrender to our enemies. Moving toward a just resolution of the Middle East crisis, one that preserves Israel's security while providing a nation for the Palestinians, is simply the right thing to do—as it was before Black Tuesday, and as it will be after we hunt down and bring to justice the evil men who made a cold-blooded decision to kill thousands of innocent people. The difference is that after Tuesday, doing the right thing has acquired a different urgency.

For far too long, the United States has pretended to stand on the sidelines of a conflict in which we are not neutral, passively endorsing a situation in which bottled-up Palestinian rage has grown and grown until it has exploded in a terrible paroxysm of violence, bringing horror to Israelis and Palestinians alike. And every day that the situation remains unresolved plants the seeds of more Arab and Islamic hatred—of Israel, and of Israel's best friend, the United States. Tuesday's horrific attack might have taken place even if Israel and the Palestinians were at peace. Nor would Mideast peace assure us that no more terrorist attacks would take place. But this we know: As long as mil-

lions of Islamic and Arab people hate America because of
its Mideast policies, we will be in danger.

The plight of the Palestinians is the single most important issue to most Arabs. Professor Shibley Telhami of the
University of Maryland conducted a poll in which citizens
of five nations—Egypt, Saudi Arabia, Kuwait, Lebanon,
and the United Arab Emirates—were asked how important
the Palestinian issue was to them personally. In four
nations, 60 percent said it was the most important. In
Egypt, reviled throughout the Arab world as the state that
made peace with Israel, 79 percent said it was.

Nor are such sentiments confined to the Middle East.
In small anti-U.S. demonstrations Sunday in Rawalpindi,
Pakistan—the Muslim nation that is the key to our diplo-
matic and military efforts to apprehend bin Laden—
demonstrators chanted slogans attacking the U.S. over the
Palestinian issue.

What does this have to do with America? Everything.
It is difficult for Americans, thousands of miles away from
a conflict for which they feel no responsibility, to realize
how people in the Middle East—indeed, in much of the
Third World—view us. For many, perhaps most Arabs—
including those in the moderate states, as well as that vast
majority of the Arab world that is well disposed to the
American people—America is virtually indistinguishable
from Israel. The bitter joke in the region is that Israel isn't
a client state of the United States—the United States is a
client state of Israel. The refugees in the squalid camps in
Gaza may not know that Israel is the primary recipient of
our foreign aid, receiving $2 billion annually in military
aid, but they know Israel could not do what it's doing without us. The jets that fire missiles into Palestinian buildings, the tanks and helicopter gunships that enforce Israeli
control of the occupied territories in the West Bank and

Gaza, might as well have big pictures of Uncle Sam painted on the side.

And people ask, "Why do they hate us?"

If this were a case of good vs. evil, the righteous Israelis fighting for their survival against the evil Arabs, it would be a cause worth America enduring the hatred of millions of people. But it is not. No one in the world, aside from some segment of the Israeli public and, apparently, the U.S. government, believes this. The Third World doesn't believe it. The United Nations doesn't believe it. Our European allies don't believe it. And most Americans don't believe it—although in the horrifying spasm of mindless anti-Arab sentiment that is gripping the country now, who knows if that will continue to be true.

Let us be absolutely clear: If Israel is not a moral exemplar, neither are the Palestinians or the Arab states. There are no heroes and villains here. Nothing can condone the Palestinian terror attacks against Israel, any more than anything can condone the intransigence on both sides that has led to them. The day has long passed when anyone could seriously look at the Israeli-Palestinian conflict as anything but a train wreck, a horrifying collision in which every noble impulse and belief immediately runs into its opposite.

A people persecuted for thousands of years, subject to the most horrifying act of genocide visited upon any group in human history, finally finds a homeland where they can be free—only to discover that another group of people, with equal claim to the land, was already there.

Another impoverished and oppressed group of people, driven from their ancestral homes by an occupying force into wretched refugee camps, or left on the margins of the society created by that occupying force, turn in their desperation to religious fanaticism and suicidal violence.

On both sides, leaders without the courage to make peace. Decent men and women on both sides driven to hopelessness and hatred. And endless blood.

That is the situation. But it may still be possible to find a way out of this tragic deadlock—if America has the courage to step in. Only the United States has the power to broker a deal that will provide lasting peace between Israel and Palestine. Hitherto, we have lacked the will to do so. Perhaps Tuesday's horrific events will provide the impetus to find that will.

Exactly what the final form of a peace settlement between Israel and the Palestinians should or will take is impossible to say. Nor is ultimate success assured. The hatred and mistrust is deeper than ever; perhaps a point of no return has been reached. But the effort must be made. And the crucial initial step is obvious, as it has been for many years: Israel must immediately stop building new settlements in the occupied territories.

Freezing construction of new settlements is the critical step called for in this spring's Mitchell Report on Mideast violence—a reasonable, evenhanded document that assigned blame to both Israel and the Palestinians and was completely ignored by all parties, most glaringly the only one that had the power to make it happen, the United States.

Israel's construction of settlements in the occupied territories taken in the 1967 war violates international law, including the Fourth Geneva Convention, which, in the language of the Mitchell Report, "prohibits Israel (as an occupying power) from establishing settlements in occupied territory pending an end to the conflict." U.S. administrations from Reagan to the present have opposed the settlements. Their existence is the first point brought up by Palestinians in conversations about Israel.

It is true, as the Mitchell Report acknowledges, that

the Palestinians bear their share of the blame for contin-
uing to launch attacks against Israel. But playing the
blame game at this point is a sterile exercise, and the
stakes are Israeli and Palestinian lives. To break the cycle
of violence a bold step must be taken. A freeze—or, better still, a freeze combined with a dismantling of existing
settlements—would be the single most positive step
Israel could take toward restoring trust between itself
and the Palestinians. As an editorial in the Israeli newspaper *Haaretz* said, "A government which seeks to argue
that its goal is to reach a solution to the conflict with the
Palestinians through peaceful means, and is trying at
this stage to bring an end to the violence and terrorism,
must announce an end to construction in the settlements."

There should be no illusions that this by itself would
bring peace. Although most Israelis agree that no new settlements should be built, months of bloody terror have
eroded their trust in the Palestinians. And they are led by
Ariel Sharon, a hard-liner who knows no response to terror
but counterterror. Sharon has refused to stop building the
settlements, saying he does not want to reward Palestinian
violence and citing security concerns. But until the
Palestinians are given genuine hope, there will be no security for Israel.

Faced with this stalemate, the Bush administration has
done nothing—not only on the settlement issue, but on
anything relating to the Middle East. Fearing it will humil-
iatingly fail as the Clinton administration failed before it, it
skulks haplessly on the sidelines. The mightiest country in
the world is reduced to mumbling earnestly, "The cycle of
violence must stop," as bombs keep exploding and people
keep dying.

It's time for America to start throwing its weight

around—not just with the Islamic states like Pakistan that offer secondhand harbor to terrorists, but with Israel. There should be no great difficulty in getting the Israelis to do what we want: Just tell them that if they don't, we won't give them any more money. It's remarkable how persuasive $3 billion a year can be, the total amount of military and civilian aid we lavish on our Mideast partner.

At the same time as we lean on the Israelis, we also must squeeze Arafat. The Palestinian leader and those who follow him must be told that further outbreaks of violence will abrogate the whole deal. And he must also be told that at the end of the day (and it's going to be a very short day) the Palestinian people are not going to get significantly more than what they almost got at Camp David—that tragic missed opportunity for whose failure, as incisive articles in the *New York Times* and the August 9 *New York Review of Books* have demonstrated, Arafat, Barak, and Clinton must all shoulder the blame.

The U.S. must give the Palestinians muscular assurance that their basic needs as a sovereign state will be met. Those needs are summed up by Rob Malley and Hussein Agha in the *New York Review of Books:* "a viable, contiguous Palestinian state on the West Bank and Gaza with Arab East Jerusalem as its capital and sovereignty over its Muslim and Christian holy sites; meaningful sovereignty; and a just settlement of the refugee issue."

But just as the Israelis must give something up, so too must the Palestinians. There is no other realistic path to peace. They will not get everything they want. They must be told that they will not get universal right of return for all those Palestinians who were displaced by the creation of the state of Israel, or control of all of the West Bank or Jerusalem.

Arafat is a gravely flawed leader, torn between realism

and maximalist mythology. After he failed to embrace the imperfect but viable solution offered by Barak and Clinton at Camp David, even many liberal Israelis concluded that he was not seriously interested in making peace. But he is a better partner than anyone else on the horizon. And a bold American move at this crucial moment—with Arab leaders realizing that after Tuesday, the rules of the game have changed forever—could shake Arafat, and the moderate frontline Arab states, out of their anti-American posturing and into constructive action. Neither the PLO nor any Arab state wants a future in which a deadlocked Israeli-Palestinian conflict breeds endless terrorism, which in turn unleashes the full might of American military force against the Arab world.

As for the Israelis, the deal would also guarantee that America would stand behind their core demands. Those are, again in Malley and Agha's words, "its continued existence as a Jewish state; genuine security; Jewish Jerusalem as its recognized capital; respect and acknowledgment of its connection to holy Jewish sites."

Would America be putting Israel at risk by, in effect, forcing it to blink first? Not if America stood behind its words. If the Palestinian Authority in the interim period toward full statehood proved unable or unwilling to control radical rejectionists, America would stand behind Israel in its retaking of the occupied territory previously ceded to the Palestinians. In effect, everything would return to the previous, bloody status quo.

And if there is some risk in the deal—so what? The situation now is intolerable.

There is, of course, no guarantee that this plan would succeed. But it would be a way of breaking the bloody deadlock in the region. It would offer hope. And, crucially, it would take place in the context of a broader diplomatic initiative to the Islamic world, a mission in which we will need every card we can play. It would make a clear and emphatic statement to the Islamic states—at precisely the moment when we might be taking military action against Islamic regimes that harbor terrorists, a move that could inspire a new generation of terrorists with an implacable hatred of America—that it is a new day, that Israel is not the tail that wags the American dog.

No one can say that stepping into the Middle East quagmire will stop future terror attacks against the United States. The world is full of angry zealots with a laundry list of grievances. Bin Laden and his maniacal ilk might continue to plot mayhem against us no matter what we do. But it could help, and it is the right thing to do.

It is also the wise thing to do. Enraged politicians, pundits, and citizens are calling for America to lash out indiscriminately, to bomb states that harbor terrorists even if innocent people are killed—rabid reactions epitomized by columnist Ann Coulter, who wrote, "We should invade their countries, kill their leaders and convert them to Christianity."

That way madness lies. As we move into uncharted territory of extraordinary difficulty, hunting down the elusive and bloodthirsty foes responsible for history's worst act of terrorism, we must ensure that our efforts do not ignite a conflagration of anti-American hatred throughout the Arab world. To do this we must convince that world that we are genuinely interested in brokering a fair and comprehensive peace between Israel and the Palestinians.

There will be those who point to the televised images of Palestinians celebrating the attacks as proof that these people hate us too much to ever be partners in peace. Such a reaction is understandable, but it is wrong. No one can condone celebrating the murder of innocent people. But hopeless, desperate people are driven to do ugly things. In their hearts, the Palestinians, like the Israelis, like Americans, like all the people of the world, want the same things. Peace. A country. A decent life. The little girls in Nablus lighting candles in memory of those who died in New York City are the real face of the Palestinian people. Our goal must be to act in such a way that some day, if an earthquake rocks Tel Aviv, those little girls will light candles for its victims, too.

On Tuesday, America turned into Israel. The sudden, obscene horror. The nightmarish images. The anguish of families torn apart, of cherished lives suddenly snuffed out.

On Tuesday, America also turned into Palestine. The same horror. The same images. The same anguish.

Today, the Jordan River runs through the center of every city in America. Palestinians and Israelis have waded through that river of blood and tears for decades: On Tuesday, we received our terrible baptism. Like the human beings who live in Jerusalem and Ramallah, we know we are not safe, not any more. We must finally accept that what happens in Ramallah and Jerusalem on Monday will happen in New York and Washington, or San Francisco and Chicago, on Tuesday.

If America succeeds in unifying the world against terrorism, while helping bring peace to the world's most dangerous and intractable conflict and draining the venom from old hatreds, the unthinkable tragedy that has befallen us might yield a lasting good.

AMERICA IS THE BIGGEST TERRORIST STATE: A CONVERSATION WITH NOAM CHOMSKY

SUZY HANSEN

JAN. 16, 2002—Noam Chomsky and Susan Sontag will always be remembered as the two leading American intellectuals who said the wrong thing after September 11.

For Sontag, it was her now infamous *New Yorker* magazine slap at the idea that the terrorists were cowards. For Chomsky, it was statements like this one: "The terrorist attacks were major atrocities. In scale they may not reach the level of many others, for example, the bombing of the Sudan with no credible pretext, destroying half its pharmaceutical supplies and killing unknown numbers of people (no one knows, because the U.S. blocked an inquiry at the U.N. and no one cares to pursue it)." To many, it seemed Chomsky was shrugging off the September 11 attacks on the United States because our country commits atrocities just as terrible and often worse.

To those abroad who consider American power grossly abusive, Chomsky is a voice of reason—an American activist who reads their newspapers, keeps track of their suffering, and never lets his countrymen forget about it. In his 2000 book, *A New Generation Draws the Line*, he railed against our policies in East Timor and Israel, and most importantly, our intervention in Kosovo. What brought the U.S. to the battered region of Yugoslavia, Chomsky wrote, was not a humanitarian drive to stop Slobodan Milosevic from ethnically cleansing yet another Muslim population, but in fact the interests of our foreign policy elite. His critics argue that this is typical; the Chomsky position reflexively brands American foreign intervention as self-interested or imperialistic, regardless of what else might be at stake. But Chomsky's remarks after September 11 struck many as beyond the pale, even those accustomed to his relentless style of dissent.

Chomsky's latest book, *9-11*, is a collection of interviews about the "war on terrorism"—a characterization of the current conflict he rejects. The legendary seventy-three-year-old linguist and political essayist spoke to *Salon* last week from his office at the Massachusetts Institute of Technology, where he has taught since 1955.

In your public comments after September 11, you drew comparisons to our bombing of the Sudan following bin Laden's attacks on overseas American targets. Were you implying that we brought this on ourselves?

Of course not. That's idiotic.

That wasn't your intention?

Nobody could possibly interpret it that way. [I said] look, this is a horrendous atrocity but unfortunately the toll is not unusual. And that's just a plain fact. I mentioned the toll from one bombing, a minor footnote to U.S. actions—what was known to be a pharmaceutical plant in Sudan, providing half the supplies of the country. That one bombing, according to the estimates made by the German Embassy in Sudan and Human Rights Watch, probably led to tens of thousands of deaths.

I said, look, this is a horrible atrocity but outside of Europe and North America, people understand very well that it's just like a lot of history.

I'm kind of simpleminded. I believe in elementary moral truisms—namely, if something is a crime when it's committed against us, it's a crime when we commit it against others. If there is a simpler moral truism than that, I'd like to hear it. I think it makes sense to remind people of it.

Were you surprised by how people commonly interpreted your statement?

No, not at all. I expect the intellectual classes to behave exactly like that. That's their historical role—to support state violence and defame people who try to bring up moral truisms.

You don't think that your statements downplayed what happened on September 11?

By saying that this was a horrendous atrocity committed with wickedness and awesome cruelty, but we should understand that the toll is regrettably not unusual? What's unusual is the direction in which the guns were pointing. I think we should be honest enough to understand that.

You've said repeatedly that the United States is a leading terrorist state. What is your definition of terrorism?

My definition of terrorism is taken from the U.S. Code, which seems to me quite adequate. It comes down to the statement that terrorism is the calculated threat or use of violence with the aim of intimidating and provoking fear and damage in order to achieve political, religious, ideological and other goals, typically directed against civilian populations.

Do you distinguish between different kinds of terrorism, and if so, how?

There are different kinds. The U.S., of course, did declare a war on terrorism twenty years ago. The Reagan administration came into office announcing that the war on terrorism would be the core of U.S. foreign policy. To quote Reagan and George Schultz, terrorism was condemned as a war carried out by depraved opponents of civilization itself, a return to barbarism in our time, an evil scourge. They were concerned primarily with what they called state-sponsored international terrorism. So the Oklahoma City bombing was terrorism but not state-supported international terrorism.

I take terrorism to be just how they define it. By that standard, it's uncontroversial that the United States is a leading terrorist state. In fact, it's the only state that was condemned for international terrorism by the highest bodies: the International Court of Justice in 1986 [for backing Contra forces against Nicaragua] and the supporting resolution of the Security Council which followed shortly after that. The United States vetoed it.

How do you distinguish between what you consider U.S. terrorism and al-Qaida's terrorism on September 11?

One is state terrorism and the other is private terrorism.

How do you think both cases should be addressed?

Nicaragua dealt with the problem of terrorism in exactly the right way. It followed international law and treaty obligations. It collected evidence, brought the evidence to the highest existing tribunal, the International Court of Justice, and received a verdict—which of course the U.S. dismissed with contempt. The court called upon the United States to terminate the crime and pay substantial reparations. The U.S. responded by immediately escalating the war; new funding was provided. In fact, the U.S. official orders shifted to more extreme terrorism. The Contra forces were encouraged to attack "soft targets," as they were called, or undefended civilian targets, and avoid combat with the Nicaraguan army.

It continued until 1990. Nicaragua followed all the right procedures, but of course, couldn't get anywhere because the U.S. simply did not adhere to it. In that case, there was no need to carry out a police investigation. The facts were clear.

And al-Qaida?

In the case of something like al-Qaida terrorism—I presume like everyone else that al-Qaida was responsible for September 11, or some network very much like it— the right approach has been laid out by others. For example, in the current issue of *Foreign Affairs*, there's an article by the preeminent Anglo-American military historian, Michael Howard, a very conservative figure, who's very supportive of U.S. policy and British policy.

I don't agree with a lot of what Howard says about history, but his recommendation seems to make sense. He says that the right way to deal with criminal atrocities like the al-Qaida bombings is careful police work; a criminal investigation carried out by international authorities; the use of internationally sanctioned means, which could include force, to apprehend the criminals; bring the criminals to justice; ensure that they have fair trials and international tribunals. That sounds to me like sound judgment. It's also been proposed by the Vatican and innumerable others. So it's not only my opinion.

Do you think that American force is justified in the case of self-defense?

Sure, anybody is entitled to self-defense. That's Article 51 of the U.N. charter. However, it's very hard to find such cases. Nicaragua, for example, was entitled to the use of violence in self-defense. They didn't follow that but they would have been entitled to because they were certainly under attack.

Nicaragua's not the only case. All through Latin America, there's sharp condemnation of the criminal atrocities of September 11. But it's qualified by the observation that although these are horrible atrocities, they are not unfamiliar. The Jesuit University in Managua's research journal, *Envio*, says that yes, [September 11] could be called Armageddon but we're familiar with our own Armageddon. They describe the assault on Nicaragua, which was no small thing. Tens of thousands of people were killed and the country was practically destroyed during the Contra war.

So you don't think our war in Afghanistan is an example of self-defense?

Is the United States under an armed attack?

I would think so.

Article 51 [of the U.N. charter] is very explicit and I believe it's correct. It says force can be used in self-defense against armed attack. Armed attack has a definition in international law. It means sudden, overwhelming, instantaneous ongoing attack. Nobody believes the U.S. is under armed attack.

[Note: After the attacks, NATO allies invoked Article 5 of the North Atlantic Treaty, which states, "An armed attack against one or more of them in Europe or North America shall be considered an attack against them all."]

If the United States wanted to appeal to Article 51, it could. The United States could easily have obtained Security Council authorization for its use of force in Afghanistan but purposely chose not to. It would have gained authorization [and] Britain would go along reflexively, France would raise no objections, Russia would be enthusiastically in favor of it because Russia is eager to gain U.S. support for its own massive atrocities in Chechnya. China would have gone along for similar reasons—support for its own atrocities in Western China. So there would have been no veto. But the U.S. preferred not to have authorization, just as the U.S. preferred not to ask for extradition.

What would motivate the U.S. to do this?

My speculation is that the U.S. does not want to establish the principle that it has to defer to some higher authority before carrying out the use of violence.

It's a very natural position on the part of a powerful state; in fact, I think it's probably close to universal. If a state is powerful enough, it wants to establish the principle that it can act without authorization. In fact, that's official U.S. policy, announced very clearly by Clinton and Madeleine Albright: The U.S. will act multilaterally when possible, unilaterally when deemed necessary.

I don't suggest that the United States is different from any other country in this respect. Andorra would do it too, if they could get away with it. But unless you're a powerful state, you can't get away with it.

Why do you think that the attack on September 11 was not an armed attack on our country?

First of all, the United States itself does not claim it was an armed attack. It claims it was an act of terrorism, which is not an armed attack. An armed attack is an act of war. So nobody claims that it was an armed attack. But post–September 11 there is no armed attack. The only thing coming close was the anthrax scare but that's apparently domestic.

You have to currently be under attack and you don't think we are?

Yes, armed attack is ongoing, overwhelming attack. But my opinion doesn't really matter. If the U.S. believed it was under armed attack, it could go to the Security Council under that principle. The U.S. doesn't want to. The fact of the matter is it's not under armed attack and nobody claims it is.

Is there anything about the Islamic threat—we've heard so much about their hatred of the West—that requires our intervention and use of force?

I tend to agree with radical rags like the *Wall Street Journal* on this. Right after the September 11 bombing, to its credit, the *Journal* was the first and almost the only newspaper—the *Christian Science Monitor* did it too—to have a look at what opinion was really like in the Islamic world. The *Journal* turned to the people it's concerned with: wealthy Muslims. They had an article—I think it was called "Moneyed Muslims"—that evaluated the attitudes of very pro-Western, pro-American elements in the Islamic world: bankers, international lawyers, people who worked for multinational corporations. [The article] asked them what they thought of the United States.

They expressed their attitude...they're very strongly in favor of major U.S. policies—in fact they're part of them. But they were opposed to the United States because of its systematic opposition to democracy in the Islamic world, its undermining of democratic elements, its support for oppressive, corrupt, and brutal regimes. They're strongly opposed to its policy of severely harming the civilian population of Iraq while strengthening Saddam Hussein. And they remember, even if we choose not to, that the United States supported him through the worst atrocities. Of course, they oppose the decisive U.S. support for what has been a harsh and brutal military occupation for thirty-five years in the Palestinian territories. They oppose all those policies and that's very widespread, not only in the Islamic world but in much of the Third World.

Take Latin America. There were international Gallup polls taken after September 11. The question was: Should military force be used when everyone understands that that military force is going to severely harm civilians? Support was not very high, even in Europe. But in Latin America it was particularly low. The latest figures I've seen come from *Envio*, the research journal of the Jesuit University in Managua. According to them, figures ranged from a high of 11 percent in Venezuela and Colombia to a low of 2 percent in Mexico. Well, Latin America has experience with U.S. power.

But you don't think that the threat from the extremists in the Islamic world justifies our use of force?

The threat is terrible. In fact, the people who the *Wall Street Journal* was interviewing hate these guys. They're their main enemies. People like Osama bin Laden are aiming at them.

I want to be clear: Are you saying that because we're guilty of abuses against the Islamic world and elsewhere, the use of U.S. force to disable these violent extremists is not justified?

I thought Michael Howard's proposal was quite reasonable and that could very well have involved the use of force. If you have criminal atrocities, it is legitimate to use force to apprehend those who are guilty and give them a fair trial. Incidentally, notice that nobody, including you and me, believes that that principle should apply to us. So we're all hopelessly immoral, including me. None of us believes that that principle should have been applied to the people who were condemned by the world court.

You endorse a criminal pursuit of bin Laden and his cohorts—but why don't you believe that the war in Afghanistan is justified in the wake of September 11?

The war in Afghanistan targets Afghan civilians, and openly. The British defense minister put it very clearly in a front-page article in the *New York Times*. He said we are going to attack the Afghans until they finally realize that they better overthrow their government. That's a virtual definition of international terrorism.

Can you give an example of a situation where military force is justified?

Force was justified when Japan bombed Pearl Harbor and Germany declared war against us. If you try to think of the last fifty years, have there been military interventions which really did bring massive atrocities to an end? There are actually two cases, both in the 1970s. In 1971, India invaded what was then East Pakistan and put an end to horrendous atrocities. In 1979, Vietnam invaded Cambodia in self-defense and drove out the Khmer Rouge and terminated their atrocities. Why aren't those called humanitarian interventions? Why isn't the 1970s called the decade of humanitarian intervention when there really were two cases that ended massive atrocities?

There's a simple reason for that: The interventions were carried out by the wrong parties—not the United States. And secondly, the U.S. strenuously opposed both of the interventions and punished those who carried them out. If we're honest, we would say yes, there were two humanitarian interventions in the last fifty years.

So you do think that violence can bring peace?

Yes, the Second World War brought peace. I was a child, but I did support the war at the time, and in retrospect, still do.

Do you not think that we're under the same sort of threat now?

We, under a threat? No, nothing remotely like it. We're under the threat of a criminal conspiracy which ought to be dealt with like a criminal conspiracy, pretty much the way Michael Howard said. We're probably under a bio-terror threat. Whatever the anthrax story was, I don't take it lightly and I think that's a serious threat.

What can or should be done about someone like Saddam Hussein, someone who has access to weapons of mass destruction?

Not only weapons of mass destruction but here it's exactly the way Clinton, Bush, Blair, and everyone else says. He not only is a monster but his is the only existing country that used weapons of mass destruction, namely chemical warfare, against its own population. All that's missing in that description is three words: with our support.

Does that mean we should not go after him now?

Wait a minute. That's not a small point. He carried out a huge massacre of his own population with our support. The U.S. continued, as did Britain, to support him right through the worst atrocities, turning against him when he disobeyed orders. That doesn't make him less of a monster. But we should tell the truth. We should not conceal those three words which everyone else in the world knows.

What should we say?

We should say, "Yeah, we supported him in his worst atrocities; now we don't like him anymore and what should we do about him?" And, yeah, that's a problem.

My own feeling, to tell you the truth, is that there was a great opportunity to get rid of Saddam Hussein in March 1991. There was a massive Shiite uprising in the south led by rebelling Iraqi generals. The U.S. had total command of the region at the time. [The Iraqi generals] didn't ask for U.S. support but they asked for access to captured Iraqi equipment and they asked the United States to prevent Saddam from using his air force to attack the rebels. The U.S. refused. It allowed Saddam Hussein to use military helicopters and other forces to crush the rebellion.

You can read it in the *New York Times*. It was more important to maintain stability—that was the word that was used—or as the diplomatic correspondent of the *New York Times* put it, the best of all worlds for the United States would have been for an iron-fisted military junta to seize power and rule in Iraq the way Saddam Hussein did. But since we couldn't get that, we'd have to accept him. That was the main opportunity of getting rid of him. Since then it hasn't been so simple. The forces of resistance were crushed with our help, after the war.

Since then, there's a question of whether the Iraqi Democratic opposition forces could mount some means of overthrowing this monster. That's a tricky business. The worst way of doing it is to undermine opposition to him. That's exactly what the sanctions do. Everyone who observed the sanctions has concluded—including the humanitarian administrators, Dennis Halliday and Hans von Sponeck, who know more about it than anyone else— that the sanctions have severely harmed the civilian population and strengthened Saddam Hussein. People under severe sanctions and trying to survive are not going to carry out any action against an armed military force.

So how would you feel about it if we were to continue the war on terrorism there?

There's no war on terrorism. That's a term of propaganda. There cannot be a war on terrorism led by the one state in the world that has been condemned for international terrorism and supported by major terrorist states like Russia and China. We can call it something but we can't call it a war on terrorism.

But do you think that we should move against Iraq now?

No, I agree with virtually the whole world, including our closest allies, that a military attack on Iraq would be a terrible mistake.

Why?

Same reason that everyone in the world, including England, is telling the U.S. government not to do it. They apparently have no evidence whatsoever that would tie Iraq to these atrocities, so an attack on Iraq would be for some other reason that existed before. If those reasons were there before, why didn't the U.S. do it then? For one thing, they're not going to do it because they don't want to get rid of Saddam Hussein; given the likely alternatives, they don't want to break the country up.

What real difference do you think it would make if we were more honest about some of the things that we've done? It seems like one of your main complaints is against American rhetoric and propaganda.

If we were honest, then we could at least evaluate what we do sanely. If we're dishonest, we know that whatever we do, only by the merest accident will it be justified. The first elementary step is honesty. After that you can go on and consider complicated issues on their merits.

Do you think that U.S. foreign policy always narrowly serves our national self-interest?

No, I don't think it's national self-interest. That's a term of propaganda. It implies that it's in the interest of the nation. No state acts in the interest of the nation. They usually act in the interest of powerful internal groups that dominate policy. Again, that's a historical truism. I don't think Nazi Germany was acting in the interest of the German people. In the case of the United States, we know who the planners are and where they come from, and yes, I think they usually act in their own interest. It's not very surprising.

Do you think foreign interventions might ever be driven by a mixed bag of motivations?

Sure, every atrocity in history, including Hitler's invasions and the Japanese conquests, was a mixed bag. Take

Italy's invasion of Ethiopia, look at the rhetoric. They were going to Christianize and uplift the natives and end slavery and bring liberty and freedom to the benighted Africans. Certainly the U.S. State Department believed it; they approved of it. It's always a mixed bag.

Is it your position that we're driven by imperial designs?
No more than any other country. It happens that the U.S. is overwhelmingly the most powerful country in the world and has been for fifty years, so of course its reach is far greater. Luxembourg might be driven by the same goals but can't do much about it.

What would our imperial interest have been in Kosovo, then?
I take the official reasons very seriously. I tend to be rather literal; I assume people are telling the truth. The official reasons were three that were repeated over and over again by Defense Secretary [William] Cohen in his congressional testimony a year after the war. The first was to prevent ethnic cleansing. The second was to ensure the stability of the region. And the third was to establish credibility. The first we can dismiss because it's agreed on all sides that ethnic cleansing took place after the bombing began.

But Milosevic had already carried out ethnic cleansing in other regions of Yugoslavia before Kosovo and he was pressuring the Albanian population in Kosovo, so the threat—and intention— was clearly there.
Well, yes, but there's a very detailed record of this. The State Department has presented extensive documentation, as has NATO, the Kosovo observers, and so on. There were plenty of atrocities going on. In fact, the British government, which was the most hawkish ele-

ment of the coalition as late as January 1999, attributed most of the atrocities to the Kosovo Liberation Army. Look, it was a very ugly place—there may have been two thousand people killed on all sides in the preceding years and a lot of people displaced. But that was not the ethnic cleansing anyone's talking about. The United Nations High Commissioner for Refugees had no registered refugees at the time the bombing was started.

The massive ethnic cleansing and atrocities began a little bit after the withdrawal of the monitors on March 22. But it really began after the bombing on March 24. That's just not contested. We can contest whether it was a consequence of the bombing. General Wesley K. Clark, the commander, announced that a predictable consequence of the bombing would be ethnic cleansing. Maybe he's right, maybe he's not. So we know that the bombing was not undertaken to prevent the ethnic cleansing that followed it. Clark himself, three weeks after the war, was asked over British television whether the reason for the bombing was ethnic cleansing. He said of course not. Ethnic cleansing was never a factor.

So we're left with the next two reasons: ensuring stability and maintaining credibility. I think those are probably the reasons. Maintaining stability has a very special meaning. It doesn't mean that the area is quiet. Stability means under Western control. What does maintaining credibility mean? It means making sure that people are afraid of you and what you're going to do.

What would the alternative have been? If the West had not intervened, Milosevic could have carried on with his atrocities unmolested.

In Kosovo, right before the bombing, there were two positions on the table. One was the NATO position, the other was the Serbian government position. They both called for an international presence in Kosovo but they differed on what that should be. The NATO position was that it had to be a NATO-led international presence with a free run of all of Serbia. The Serbian position was vague. If you take a look at the peace treaty, it's a compromise between the two positions. Suppose they had pursued the possibility of the compromised solution which, in fact, was reached on paper at least. Could that have worked? Well, we don't know because it was refused.

I'm not a pacifist. I think use of force is sometimes legitimate. However, if someone is calling for the use of force, they have a heavy burden of proof to meet. The burden of proof is always on those who call for the use of violence, in particular extreme violence. That's a moral truism. The question is, was that burden met? Try to find some argument which meets that burden of proof. Don't take my word for it, check the facts. You'll find that the literature on this almost entirely overlooks the crucial evidence which is the extensive, detailed evidence from Western sources on what was happening up to the bombing. The only book I know that covers this is my own.

Second, take a look at the arguments that are given to justify the bombing. Either they claim that ethnic cleansing and atrocities were going on before the bombing—which we know is false—or they claim the bombing was carried out because ethnic cleansing was going to take place. Well, by that argument you could justify anything.

Couldn't NATO have been basing its actions on what we'd all seen Milosevic was capable of in Bosnia and Croatia?

They could have. But by that argument, if you really believe that, then they should have been bombing

Jakarta, Washington, and London. Which of course nobody believes.

At that very same time, Indonesia was carrying out much worse atrocities in East Timor. Furthermore, the Indonesian generals were announcing very loudly and clearly that unless the planned referendum went their way, they would just wipe the place out. Britain and the United States were still supporting the Indonesians, who had wiped out a third of the population. So according to the argument you're proposing, you're saying that the United States should have bombed themselves and Indonesia. We don't believe that.

Let me repeat a moral truism. If there is a principle that we apply to others, we must insist that the principle apply to us. If there is a principle that justified the bombing in Serbia, formulate the principle and ask— does it apply to us?

But as the world's largest superpower, we are called on, sometimes by countries that have criticized us, to intervene in conflicts. What role is the world's superpower supposed to play?

The first, simplest role it should play is to stop participating in atrocities. In 1999, for example, one role the U.S. could have played is to stop participating in the atrocities in East Timor. Britain could have played the same role. That would have made a big difference. In fact, when the U.S. finally did inform Indonesia that the game was over on September 11, after the worst had happened, they instantly withdrew. The power was always there.

Take another case. There was much talk about how NATO couldn't tolerate atrocities like those in Kosovo right near its borders. A small fact was overlooked: NATO was not only tolerating but in fact supporting

much worse atrocities right within its borders—
namely, Turkish atrocities against the Kurds inside
Turkey. Eighty percent of the arms were coming from
the United States. They peaked in the late 1990s and
led to tens of thousands of people killed and 3,500
towns and villages destroyed. There were 2 to 3 million refugees. One way the greatest superpower could
act is by terminating its massive and critical support
for these atrocities.

*Some of your positions, on Kosovo for example, have led people
even on the left to suggest that you think no matter what the
U.S. does it's unacceptable simply because the U.S. is doing it.*
If people believe that, that's because they insist on pure
propaganda and refuse to look at the facts. You can easily see whether in fact I said that. I didn't. And I don't
believe it. I can't help what intellectuals decide to
believe. If they want to fabricate propaganda images
and believe what they say or they hear in gossip, that's
their metier.

*As you know, people like you and Susan Sontag have gotten a lot
of outraged reactions to some of the things you've said after
September 11—again, even from some on the left. What do you
think about the future of the American left?*
It's certainly much better than it's been in the past. The
outraged reactions are coming mostly from intellectuals, liberal intellectuals. But that's standard. It was
much worse in the sixties. In fact, liberal intellectuals
typically tend to support the use of state violence. Who
initiated the Vietnam War? Liberal intellectuals, that
was Kennedy's war. Back in those days, in the early
sixties, I remember very well attempts to raise even
the most mild criticism of the war at that time. You

couldn't get four people in an auditorium to listen to you. In Boston, which is a pretty liberal city, we couldn't have a public demonstration against the war until about 1966 without it being physically attacked by people and protected by police. It's incomparably better.

THE MAKING OF A HAWK

DAVID TALBOT

JAN. 3, 2002—From the Gulf War on, the hawks have been on the right side in all the major debates about U.S. intervention in the world's troubles. The application of American military power—to drive back Saddam Hussein's invasion of Kuwait, stop Slobodan Milosevic's genocidal campaigns in the Balkans, and destroy the terrorist occupation of Afghanistan—has not just protected U.S. interests, it has demonstrably made the world safer and more civilized. Because of the U.S.-led allied victory in the Persian Gulf, Saddam—the most bloodstained and dangerous dictator in power today—was blocked from completing a nuclear bomb, taking control of 60 percent of the world's oil resources, and using his fearsome arsenal (including biological and chemical weapons) to consolidate Iraq's position as the Middle East's reigning force. Because of the U.S.-led air war against Milosevic, the most ruthless "ethnic cleansing" program in Europe since the Holocaust was finally thwarted—first in Bosnia and then in Kosovo—and the repulsive tyrant is now behind bars in the Hague. And in Afghanistan, the apocalyptic master plan of the al-Qaida terror network was shattered by America's devastatingly accurate bombing campaign, along with the medieval theocracy that had thrown a cloak of darkness over the country.

304

These demonstrations of America's awesome firepower were clearly on the right side of history. In fact, the country's greatest foreign policy disasters during this period occurred because the U.S. government failed to assert its power: when President George H. W. Bush aborted Operation Desert Storm before it could reach Baghdad and finish off Saddam (whose army had only two weeks of bullets left) and when he failed to draw a line against Milosevic's bloody plans for a greater Serbia; and when President Bill Clinton looked the other way while a genocidal rampage took the lives of nearly a million people in Rwanda and when he failed to fully mobilize the country against terrorism after the 1993 World Trade Center bombing and the later attacks on American targets abroad—a failure that extended through the first eight months of Bush II.

Despite their eventual success, each U.S. military response in the past decade—even to the brazen sky terrorism that leveled the World Trade Center and devastated the Pentagon—has sparked passionate opposition in political, media, and cultural circles. Conservative commentators like Andrew Sullivan, Charles Krauthammer, and the *Wall Street Journal* editorial board have blamed current antiwar resistance on the left and its tradition of pacifism and criticism of American hegemony. And it's true, any liberal who came of age during the Vietnam War, as I did, feels some kinship with these implacable critics of American policy, even a lingering sense of alienation from our own country's world-straddling power. But most of us, at some point during the last two decades, made a fundamental break from this pacifistic legacy. For me, it came during the savage bombing of Sarajevo, whose blissfully multiethnic cosmopolitanism was, like New York would later become, an insult to the forces of zealous purity. Most liberals of my generation, however, feel deeply uneasy about labeling themselves hawks—to do so conjures images for them of General Curtis "Bombs Away" LeMay, it suggests a break from civilization itself, a heavy-footed step backwards, toward the bogs of our ancestors. What I have come to believe, however, is that America's unmatched power to reduce tyranny and terror to dust is actually what often makes civilization in today's world possible. I want to retrace my journey here, for those who might be wrestling with similar thoughts these days.

In truth, the opposition to assertive American foreign policy over the past decade has come from liberals and conservatives alike (as has support for interventionism), and while the Susan Sontags and Noam Chomskys have become convenient targets for pro-war pundits in recent months, the most effective critiques of American power since Vietnam have come not from Upper East Side salons and Berkeley's ivory towers but from within the government itself, including even the Pentagon.

Ever since the Vietnam War, the foreign policy establishment has been suffering from what the astute analyst Robert Kagan calls a "loss of nerve." This failure of will within the foreign policy elite—and Washington's struggle to escape the shadow of Vietnam—is the theme of David Halberstam's recent best-seller, *War in a Time of Peace: Bush, Clinton, and the Generals*. As in his Vietnam classic, *The Best and the Brightest*, Halberstam builds his new book around portraits of key policymakers. But unlike his Vietnam book—which laid the blame for the debacle on arrogant interventionists like Robert MacNamara and the Bundy brothers—Halberstam's new book is clearly sympathetic toward foreign policy boldness. The irony here has not escaped observers like Kagan, who in a withering essay in last month's *New Republic* pinned much of the establishment's loss of confidence on popular critics like Halberstam himself. According to Kagan, prominent writers like Halberstam "fixed it in the popular mind, and in the elite mind, that 'the best and the brightest' were dangerous. To be among the best and the brightest was to stand accused of criminal incompetence. And what did that mean about America? If our best and brightest could not be trusted not to destroy us, then we were doomed. Could American power be wielded with a measure of confidence? No, it was impossible to wield power at all. Was national greatness a possibility if the best among us were fools?"

Though he doesn't concede that his thinking has undergone any revision, Halberstam's views have clearly changed with time. The heroes in *War in a Time of Peace* are the hawks in the Clinton administration—Secretary of State Madeleine Albright, Balkans negotiator and later U.N. Ambassador Richard Holbrooke, and Kosovo air war commander General Wes Clark. Both Holbrooke, who served as a young diplomat in Saigon, and Clark, who commanded an army company and was wounded four times in one battle, were shaped by Vietnam. But unlike other future political and military leaders who came of age in the crucible of that jungle war, neither of these men was incapacitated by it. Despite America's failure in Vietnam, both men recognized how important it was for the country to play a strong global role—and their hawkish views of the Milosevic killing machine in the Balkans finally helped convince Clinton to strike back at the dictator, who despite all the dire predictions from GOP doves like Trent Lott and Newt Gingrich (and perennial Vietnam-era peace crusaders like Tom Hayden) promptly wilted.

But, as Halberstam makes clear, the hawks were an embattled minority during the Clinton years—as they were during most of the senior Bush's administration. Whether it was the cynical James Baker, who famously concluded that America did not "have a dog in that fight" and thereby allowed the Balkans war to take its savage course, or the ineffectual Warren Christopher ("Dean Rusk without the charisma," as Democratic Party insiders mordantly summed up Clinton's choice for secretary of state), America's foreign policy was led during these years by men who believed it must operate within very narrow constraints.

The man who gave this limited foreign policy a name was Colin Powell, whose high-level service has stretched from the first Bush administration to Clinton's to that of the junior Bush. With its demand that no military action commence unless it faced certain and swift victory, the Powell Doctrine placed the bar so high it nearly assured U.S. paralysis. As one of George H. W. Bush's presiding commanders, Powell had emerged from the Gulf War a national hero. But in fact, as Halberstam observes, it was Bush himself who had to push Powell and his other reluctant advisers into the war with Saddam. Powell had advised the president to forfeit Kuwait and draw a line of defense around Saudi Arabia. And after Saddam's army was defeated, Powell urged Bush to conclude the war with Saddam's regime still intact. As Clinton's top military commander, Powell continued to play the "reluctant warrior" (a term Halberstam says was used against him by one critic but which he happily embraced), using his stature to intimidate the young, inexperienced president. He scared the Clinton team away from intervening against Milosevic—as he had the Bush administration—with his chilling predictions of a Balkans quagmire. "Under Bush, and again under Clinton, when the top civilians asked what it might cost to intervene militarily, Powell would show his lack of enthusiasm by giving them a high estimate, and they would quickly back off," writes Halberstam. "The figure never went under two hundred thousand troops." Powell was similarly dismissive of what airpower could do against the Serb dictator—despite its decisive role during the Gulf War. "When I hear someone tell me what airpower can do, I head for a bunker," he snorted after a meeting with civilian Bush officials. Years later, as the decade came to a close, Milosevic's military machine would finally be broken by U.S. airpower after just ten weeks of bombing. By then, some 200,000 people had been killed in the region and 3 million made homeless.

Powell's skepticism about armed action was widely shared within the military's high command, which was more scarred by Vietnam than perhaps any other arm of government. Indeed, if hawkish commentators are looking for the headquarters of American pacifism, they need look no farther than the Pentagon. "There the memory of Vietnam was a little longer, because almost all of the top army people, unlike those at State, had served directly in that war and the experience had been a bitter one in almost all instances," writes Halberstam. "The Pentagon had an all too personal understanding of what happens, first, when the architects of an interventionist policy underestimate the other side, and second, when so many of those in the political process who were its architects soon orphan their own handiwork and go on to other jobs, leaving the military to deal with a war that no one could get right."

The most telling showdown between the hawk and dove factions of the U.S. government came during the Clinton administration debate on Balkans intervention, when then-U.N. Ambassador Albright—who as a child of Europe's tragic history was painfully aware of the threat posed by Milosevic—confronted the cautious Powell. "What's the point of having this superb military that you're always talking about if we can't use it?" she burst out. "I thought I would have an aneurysm," Powell later recalled in his autobiography. "American G.I.s were not toy soldiers to be moved around on some sort of global game board." (This confrontation illustrates the political tension over military policy that has characterized the past decade. In the shrewd assessment of conservative commentator Bruce Herschensohn, as cited by Halberstam: "The Democrats always want a small army, but want to send it everywhere, while the Republicans want a very big army and don't want to use it at all.")

Though Albright's view was to be proved the correct one, Powell's concern for the lives of American soldiers is not easily dismissed. All too often, the officials and commentators calling for blood and fire have no personal experience of the frontline misery they are clamoring for—and frequently have surprisingly little empathy for those who will be put in harm's way, including soldiers and civilians. Powell, who endured two rounds of duty in Vietnam, is painfully aware of what battle is like. Ultimately, the truest test of a hawk's sincerity is whether he himself would volunteer to fight—or be willing to sacrifice the lives of his own children. Powell is right: G.I.s aren't toy soldiers. And unless a hawk can say he is prepared to make this ultimate sacrifice, he's on shaky moral ground.

Powell and the military elite weren't the only ones scarred by Vietnam, of course—an entire generation of Americans was. When President Johnson began escalating the war in 1964, I was a twelve-year-old student at a military academy in Los Angeles, the Harvard School. We drilled, took rifle practice, and fought battle exercises with the expectation that, after graduation, we would serve our country as junior officers in the rice paddies of Southeast Asia. We attended solemn chapel services in memory of fallen alumni; their heroic names lived forever on school

plaques. But as the war dragged on, and it became clear
even to ROTC-trained teenagers like me that something
was terribly wrong over there, that the majority of
Vietnamese—for whom we were ostensibly fighting—did
not seem to want us to win, some deep sense of patriotic
mission that stretched back generations in my family and
countless others was broken. Now, among the young men
and women I knew, the honorable path was not to fight in
this American war, as our fathers had when they were
called to duty decades before, but to fight against it.

In recent years, it has once again become fashionable
among the pundit class to denigrate those who protested
the war and to venerate those who chose to serve. But the
antiwar activists I knew and worked with did not make
their choices lightly or selfishly. The decision to break with
our country's policy was a wrenching one for us, and we
paid for it in various ways. Many of us, including myself,
were sentenced to jail for our protests; some, like a close
college friend, served two years in a federal prison for
burning his draft card. I was prepared to join him if my
number had been called in Nixon's macabre lottery system.
My early youth was a never-ending campaign of pamphle-
teering, marching, and, as the war spread its poison,
increasingly bitter run-ins with violent police assault
squads. But the deeper cost was the disorienting sense of
estrangement we came to feel from the country we had
been raised to love. Ironically, we saw the same alienation
in the young veterans we came to know as they returned
from the war and turned against it. The stories have
achieved mythological status and I'm sure some of them
are true—but no one I knew ever spit on a returning soldier. These men were even more haunted by the war than
we were; we felt they were brothers in the same nightmare.
Some—like my friend who decided to go under pressure

from his father, a conservative Florida mayor, but insisted on serving as a medic on a helicopter gunship—experienced things he could never put behind him and died a few years after the war ended, in a way that seemed suicidal. He had a Southern sense of valor, clearly intact under his wry veneer, that two decades after his death still brings tears to my eyes whenever he swims into memory. The point I'm trying to make is that antiwar activists were attempting to prevent casualties like this, senseless carnage that outlasted the war itself. And I came to regard these efforts as heroic. I still do.

The only members of my generation I have contempt for are those who loudly supported the war but found convenient ways to escape serving in it. I saw this syndrome develop while still a military student—as the war staggered on, suddenly the names of fallen graduates came to a halt. The conservative tycoons and politicians who sent their sons to the academy were finding face-saving ways for their offspring to dodge the war—the preferred escape hatch was enrollment in the National Guard. This allowed these "fortunate sons" (in the words of the acidic antiwar song by Creedence Clearwater Revival) to appear patriotic and not disturb their career trajectories, while saving their asses. It was an easy out made famous by two of the nation's most prominent fortunate sons, Vice President Dan Quayle and the current occupant of the White House.

This contempt is shared by Powell, who, Halberstam notes, "despised the class distinctions that had determined who had gone to Vietnam and who had not, which he called 'an antidemocratic disgrace.' " Powell wrote in his autobiography, "I can never forgive a leadership that said in effect: 'These young men—poorer, less educated, less privileged—are expendable (someone once described them as 'economic cannon-fodder') but the rest are too good

to risk.' I am angry that so many of the sons of the powerful and well-placed . . . managed to wangle slots in the
Reserve and National Guard units." This raises the question: What does Powell think of the war record of the
president he currently serves as secretary of state?

I continued to wear my antiwar record as a badge of
honor years after Vietnam, eliciting predictable sneers
from conservatives and mandatory respect in liberal circles.
The lessons of Vietnam guided me during my opposition
to President Reagan's murky war in Central America, even
through the Persian Gulf War, which I again marched
against, as a bloody crusade on behalf of Big Oil. Years
later, I came to see the Gulf War as more than this, as I
educated myself about the ghastly regime in Baghdad and
the horrors it had inflicted on its own people as well as enemies. By the time Milosevic and his henchmen began bom-
barding defenseless cities and filling concentration camps
and mass graves with undesirables, while his European
neighbors and U.N. "peacekeepers" endlessly dithered, I
had come fully round to a conviction I had not embraced
since I was a boy: America is not only capable of using its
unrivaled power for good—it must. When waves of
American bombers began striking at Serbian military
installations and power plants in spring 1999, I felt a kind
of unmitigated pride I hadn't remembered since those
long-ago days when I watched old World War II movies
without a sense of irony. As Halberstam documents,
President Clinton had to be pushed and prodded into taking decisive action—by aides like Albright and Holbrooke,
by General Clark on the military side, by trusted allies like
Tony Blair—and finally by the unrelentingly belligerent
Milosevic himself. But when Clinton finally did, it was his
finest moment as commander in chief.

The transition from dove to hawk is a political, intellec-

tual, and personal journey that many others in my generation have been making in recent years, some since
September 11. The length of this collective trek came
home for me this morning on the way to work, as I listened
closely for the first time to the lyrics of Neil Young's new
song, "Let's Roll," inspired by the words of United Airlines
Flight 93 passenger Todd Beamer as he and his brave comrades rushed the cockpit. Thirty years ago, I was equally
stirred by Young's bitter "Ohio," his antiwar anthem about
the Kent State student protesters who were cut down by
"tin soldiers in Nixon's army." (It was the one time the fortunate sons in the National Guard saw action during
Vietnam, to kill their fellow citizens.) But it's the simplicity
of Young's current song that sums up the world today: "No
one has the answers / but one thing is true / You've got to
turn on evil / when it's coming after you . . . Time is running out, let's roll."

For years after Vietnam, I wanted America to step back
from the world, and what I regarded as its arrogant—if not
imperial—need to impose its own sense of order on history.
But I have come to share the view of Robert Kagan, that "if
you are the president of the United States, you do not find
trouble, trouble finds you." Or as Richard Holbrooke told
Halberstam, speaking of Clinton's early desire to focus
almost exclusively on domestic issues (believing this was
the electorate's message in choosing him over the interna-
tionalist Bush): "What Clinton did not yet understand was
that foreign policy never lets an American president go."
There are inevitably times when the darkest powers of the
human heart find the means and opportunity to threaten
not just the world's peace but its sense of decency. And
while international coalitions or U.N. peacekeeping forces
would, in a better world, be the best way to respond to
these explosions of evil, the sober truth is that—from

Kuwait to Kosovo to Kabul—only the United States has demonstrated the force and the will to do so effectively.

I am no foreign policy expert, as is surely plain by now. But I believe it's incumbent on all America's citizens to learn as much as our busy lives allow about the world—and not just leave it to our best and brightest—because the United States' unique leadership role assures that all of us will feel the impact of the globe's crises, no matter how remote they might initially seem. I have developed my own criteria for when I think American intervention is justified; that is, when it's worth the cost in blood and treasure, not only for the U.S., but for the people we are trying to rescue. In my mind, there are three cases when resorting to military force is necessary: 1) When the United States is directly attacked—which it was not only on September 11 but in the 1993 bombing of the World Trade Center, as well as the explosions aimed at the U.S. embassies in Africa and naval ship in Yemen; 2) When an aggressor threatens regional stability and world peace—such as Saddam Hussein's invasion of Kuwait and Milosevic's assaults on Bosnia and Kosovo; 3) When a nation launches a campaign of genocidal extermination against its own people or those of its neighbors—as Milosevic did against the Muslims of the former Yugoslavia and the Hutu tribe did against the Tutsis in Rwanda.

Bloodbaths like Rwanda strike many Americans as not worth the cost of intervention, since they do not directly threaten our national security. But we do indeed have a dog in these fights. These orgies of violence are crimes against humanity—and unless they're stopped and their perpetrators brought to justice, they degrade the world we live in and embolden future Pol Pots and Interhamwes, the machete-wielding vigilantes who hacked to death nearly a million of their Rwandan neighbors in a 100-day spasm of gore, while the U.S. did nothing and U.N. soldiers fled the country. The tragedy of Rwanda, as a 1999 *Frontline* report on PBS documented, was that this low-tech genocide could have been stopped with a minimal show of force. Instead it was a "triumph of evil," as *Frontline* titled its report, "which the philosopher Edmund Burke observed happens when good men do nothing." When demonic visionaries are allowed to put their Grand Guignol theories into practice, the moral universe that all of us inhabit shrivels.

In historian Walter Russell Mead's terms, I have gone from being a Jeffersonian to a Wilsonian. In his new book, *Special Providence*, Mead provides a highly useful map of the schools of thought that have guided American foreign policy throughout the country's history, dividing them into the two above, as well as Jacksonians and Hamiltonians. Mead's graceful analysis, which seeks out the wisdom and flaws in each of these schools, has won strong praise from astute foreign policy practitioners like Richard Holbrooke and fellow historians like Douglas Brinkley and Ronald Steel, and deservedly so. His provocative theoretical architecture and lively writing style give average Americans the opportunity to examine the assumptions behind the country's foreign policy decisions, from the calamitous to the heroic.

Jeffersonians, as Mead defines them, shun foreign entanglements, particularly wars, which they perceive as the greatest threats to our precious and fragile democracy. Named after our third president, who feared for the future of our democratic experiment in a perilous world, Jeffersonians dread the corruptions of a militarized society, recoiling at Cicero's admonition to a Roman jury that "the law shuts up when weapons speak." Among the Jeffersonian school's more illustrious proponents, according to Mead, have been some of the "most distinguished and elegant strategic thinkers in American history—men like John

Quincy Adams and George Kennan—as well as passionate and proud democratic isolationists" and anti-imperialists like Mark Twain, Gore Vidal, Ralph Nader, historian Charles Beard, libertarian thinkers such as the scholars at the Cato Institute, and, he reveals in the book's conclusion, Mead himself. Jeffersonians cringe at the Wilsonian argument that tempests like Kosovo and Rwanda cry out for our intervention, that "the American national interest in an orderly world coincides with the country's moral duty." In contrast, Jeffersonians, who see the world as dangerous and unreformable, heed Adams's eloquent 1821 declamation that America should not go "abroad in search of monsters to destroy. She is the well-wisher to the freedom and independence of all. She is the champion and vindicator only of her own."

The Jeffersonians' greatest weakness—and it's a glaring one, Mead concedes—is their tendency to be on the wrong side of history. The Jeffersonian camp, which urged American neutrality far too long into the rise of the fascist juggernaut, was deeply discredited by World War II as well as by its opposition to the Cold War. Jeffersonians rose to prominence again with the failure of U.S. policy in Vietnam, but their ascendancy was short-lived. "In the 1980s many Jeffersonians had convinced themselves that American power was fated to decline," observes Mead. "The obvious upsurge in American international standing and economic power of the 1990s took them aback. Largely isolated in opposing the Gulf War, Jeffersonians took another blow when the war ended in an easy victory with neither the heavy casualties nor the political problems that many of them had predicted. When the Balkans interventions did not end in unmitigated, clear disasters, Jeffersonian croaking about the dangers of intervention, the arrogance of power, and the costs of imperial overreach

had lost most of their credibility. Jeffersonians continued to
cry wolf in the 1990s, but fewer and fewer people listened."
If he had not already sent his book to the publisher, Mead
would surely have added the Jeffersonian bleating about an
Afghan military morass and massive civilian casualties to
his list of this school's intellectual failures.

The Wilsonians and Hamiltonians are the two interna-
tionalist camps in Mead's map, and he says they represent
the current thinking of the foreign policy establishment.
But since the Hamiltonians concern themselves almost
exclusively with the creation of a global financial order
within which American business can prosper, rather than
with military matters, we need not dwell on this school here.
The Wilsonians, named for the president who believed the
United States had a moral and practical duty to spread its
values through the world, are according to Mead "more
interested in the legal and moral aspects of world order than
in the economic agenda supported by Hamiltonians." The
origins of this school predate President Woodrow Wilson
himself, observes Mead, stretching back to the Christian
missionary movement of the nineteenth century that lobbied Washington to adopt progressive policies toward
China, Siam, the Ottoman Empire, and other far-flung outposts. But it began its triumphant reign during the
Woodrow presidency.

"Fashionable though it has long been to scorn the
Treaty of Versailles, and flawed though that instrument
undoubtedly was, one must note that Wilson's principles
survived the eclipse of the Versailles system and that they
still guide European politics today: self-determination,
democratic government, collective security, international
law, and a league of nations," writes Mead. "Wilson may
not have gotten everything he wanted at Versailles, and his
treaty was never ratified by the Senate, but his vision and

diplomacy, for better or worse, set the tone for the twentieth century. France, Germany, Italy, and Britain may have
sneered at Wilson, but every one of these powers today
conducts its policy along Wilsonian lines. What was once
dismissed as visionary is now accepted as fundamental.
This was no mean achievement, and no European states-
man of the twentieth century has had as lasting, as benign,
or as widespread an influence."

Wilson's own war may not have brought about the
world he envisioned, but most subsequent Wilsonian interventions through the twentieth century and into the
twenty-first—from World War II to the Balkans to
Afghanistan—have helped extend the rule of peace, justice,
and democracy. And the commitment to "nation building"
in war-ravaged countries, which is an essential corollary to
the Wilsonian philosophy of military engagement, has also
brought harmony to the world, from postwar Japan to
Kabul's new U.S.-supported transition government.
President Bush himself, who scorned Clinton nation-
building in Haiti and the Balkans during last year's presidential campaign, has since September 11 become an
ardent convert to this strategy, as well as an overnight fan
of Wilsonian-style multinational consultation.

Wilsonianism's greatest difficulty is determining where
to draw the line on its humanitarian impulse. As Mead
points out, in a benighted and violent world, the calls for
American action can be endless. He paints a chilling picture of what a society dedicated to serving as the world's
policeman can become: "A global hegemon leads a hard
and busy life. Are the tribes revolting in Kabul? Is a coup
brewing in Manila? Is piracy on the upswing in the South
China Sea? Are Arabs bombing Israelis (or vice versa) in
the Holy Land? A global hegemon must determine if any
of the thousands of crises that occur in any random decade

post a threat to the hegemonic order . . . Moreover, the capital of a hegemon is invariably a place of secrets, many of them dirty. There are secret agreements with allies, the secrets of military planning, the secrets of a vast and active intelligence community and a web of agents. Many of the hegemon's allies are not particularly nice. In most of this sad world's bloody struggles, both sides are crooked, both drenched in blood, and neither attracted to the cause of liberty, virtue, or anything else that goes beyond personal and clan ambition. Inevitably the hegemon enters into arrangements with murderers and thugs; inevitably the hegemon seeks to make its allies more effective at murder and thuggery than their opponents.

"This is no Jerusalem, no 'City upon a Hill,' " a dismayed Mead cries out. "This is Babylon; it is Nineveh. It is the Augean stables, not an honest republic."

Serving as the world's centurion also repeatedly puts the global power's own citizens in the line of fire. And, particularly in a society like the United States that has abolished its military draft, this life-threatening service falls disproportionately on that class of society that Colin Powell calls "economic cannon fodder." Mead has a different way of characterizing this group. Most of those who serve in the American military come from what he calls the Jacksonian wing of American society—the descendants of Scotch-Irish warrior clans who settled largely in the South and on the American frontiers (now the Sunbelt) and the subsequent waves of immigrants who adopted this group's ardent pro-Americanism and rugged individualism. The motto of this populist and patriotic school, named for the war hero and champion of the common man, could well be "Don't Tread on Me." Jacksonians believe "that the U.S. should not seek out foreign quarrels, but when other nations start wars with the United States, Jacksonian opinion agrees with General

Douglas MacArthur that 'There is no substitute for victory.'" This culture, whose heroes over the years have been men like General George Patton, Ronald Reagan, Ross Perot, George Wallace, and John McCain, puts a high premium on self-reliance, courage, honor, and military service, which, Mead writes, is viewed by Jacksonians as a sacred duty. When the rest of America "dodged the draft in Vietnam or purchased exemptions and substitutes in earlier wars, Jacksonians soldiered on, if sometimes bitterly and resentfully. Failure to defend the country in its hour of need is to the Jacksonian mind evidence of at best distorted values and more probably contemptible cowardice. An honorable person is ready to kill or to die for family and flag."

Jacksonians also believe in all-out war once the firing begins, and they have low regard for international law and organizations, particularly ones that limit U.S. action. "Jacksonians believe that there is an honor code in international life, as there was in clan warfare in the borderlands of England, and those who live by the code will be treated under it," writes Mead. "But those who violate the code, who commit terrorist acts against innocent civilians in peacetime for example, forfeit its protection and deserve no more consideration than rats."

This would account for the daisy-cutter firepower directed at al-Qaida's caves and the high popularity of the Bush administration's military tribunals for captured terrorists. Author Michael Lind has argued that Jacksonianism is the most popular political philosophy among the American public at large, much stronger among ordinary Americans than it is among the elite, and he is certainly right. Mead, in fact, contends that the first President Bush lost his job when he stopped being a Jacksonian in his war against Saddam and declared victory without finishing the job, out of

Hamiltonian deference to our Saudi oil suppliers (who feared an unstable, and perhaps even worse, democratic government in neighboring Baghdad)—one more indication to Jacksonian voters that Bush was more concerned with his new world order than with average Americans.

Though my family roots are in this Scotch-Irish culture, I fell out with this tradition over Vietnam. I don't believe that an American citizen has a moral duty to fight every war its government declares if it goes deeply against his conscience—but he should be prepared to pay the price with a prison sentence if it comes to that. I also parted company with the Jacksonians on the Balkans war, which they saw as irrelevant to American interests, an example of Wilsonian do-gooderism gone amuck. We've come together again on Afghanistan and al-Qaida. But, as Mead points out, Wilsonian support for wars doesn't count as much as that of Jacksonians in the American political spectrum. It's the martial energy of the Jacksonians that political leaders need to enlist to successfully prosecute wars: "Every American school needs Jacksonians to get what it wants. If the American people had exhibited the fighting qualities of, say, the French, in World War II, neither Hamiltonians, Jeffersonians, or Wilsonians would have had much to do with shaping postwar international order."

Jacksonians have greater moral authority when it comes to making momentous war decisions because they and their children do the preponderance of fighting and dying. But this is not the way it should be. Placing the burden of military service on a warrior subculture is an unjust division of labor that, as Powell has argued, should be repellent to our democracy. This is why I have come to believe we need to bring back the military draft, stripped of the loopholes for "fortunate sons" that made a mockery of it during the Vietnam War. World War II ennobled America, not just because it was a righteous cause, but because it was fought by a democratic cross section of the country, from hillbillies to Hollywood stars, like bomber pilot Jimmy Stewart.

This brings us back to a question I raised earlier, one that is particularly painful for me as the father of two sons. If commentators—or any citizens—call for American troops to go to war, I think they must be willing to enlist themselves, or if they're too old for duty, be willing to picture their own sons or daughters in uniform. My boys are years away from fighting age, but as long as America serves its current global role, I know there will be wars awaiting them when their time comes. I don't think they should automatically enlist, regardless of the nature of the war. I've talked to my oldest son about Vietnam and why I opposed the war, and I hope he will deeply search his own conscience before he makes up his mind. I don't believe in "my country, right or wrong." But if the cause is compelling and just, I also hope he does the right thing and serves his country.

When my sons crumple in pain on the playing field, my heart loses its rhythm until I see they're all right. When they're sick and their breathing grows clotted at night, I sleep my own restless vigil. Both are prone to florid nosebleeds, and I can't even stand to see this blood pour from them. How could I ever agree to put their lives at risk, these two young souls whose destruction would mean the end of the most precious part of my life? How could any war be worth the life of your son—or your neighbor's? If you're debating the merits of a war in your head, and you don't get to this question, you haven't gone far enough.

Shortly before he released the patriotic "Let's Roll," Neil Young appeared in the somber, candlelit telethon *America: Tribute to Heroes*. The song he chose to sing that evening was the peace anthem "Imagine," in which John

Lennon urges us to think of a world where "there's no countries / It isn't hard to do / Nothing to kill and die for / and no religion too." So clearly old Neil is wrestling with a lot of conflicting feelings these days too.

The song has always moved me, and Young's high, plaintive voice, after all the nationalistic and religious killing and dying going on, made it seem particularly sad. But the fact is I can't imagine life without my country. My sense of myself, what I believe in, is so wrapped up with being an American that I can't disentwine them. Maybe that's a failure of imagination; maybe John's world is a higher one that future generations will someday inhabit, "and the world will live as one." But all it took for me was one look at the burning New York skyline to know that America was worth fighting and dying for.

Jacksonians conjure their own images when they think of America, some of which I share (Fourth of July barbecues, Saturday night high school football games, the flag snapping in the breeze) and some of which I don't (gun shows, SUVs lumbering through traffic, the smug look on Bill O'Reilly's mug). But I always swell with pride when my eyes fill up with the urban panoramas of great American cities, like New York or my own San Francisco. These jostling streets of polyglot races and creeds and fashion statements, of naked ambition and soaring dreams—what historian Ann Douglas hailed as "mongrel Manhattan"— are democracy's greatest advertisement for itself. And they're why New York's highest towers became a target for the most atavistic forces at work in the world today. Yes, the Jeffersonians have a point—global powers like America, with military, diplomatic, and corporate outposts from Mecca to Timbuktu, inevitably invite resentment and hostility. But the terrorists striking at New York and Washington were not just making a political statement, they were making a cultural one. The World Trade Centers truly were the world—just recall all the seven-continent faces of the people who worked there as they appeared in the *New York Times* obituary pages. The worldliness of American democracy—its openness to every type of human aspiration, even fundamentalism—is an affront to those who think better in caves.

So yes, some things are as precious as life itself, such as our way of life. The beacons of freedom, justice, equality, and human tolerance turn out to be not as inextinguishable as most of us in America grew up thinking. They can be put out, and they're put out in different places all over the world. And when this darkness encroaches too far, we must risk our lives, even our sons' lives, to push it back. America is a light to the world—even to the ex-Taliban fighters and *madrassa* students who dream of coming here to live and prosper—because each generation has been willing to fight to keep it alive, or in the case of many of my generation, to fight their government when they saw it had gone grievously wrong.

When it comes to destroying Osama bin Laden and his holy band of civilian-slaughterers, I'm an ardent Jacksonian. President Bush has it right: pursue them to the ends of the earth, until they're captured or dispatched to their feverishly awaited Paradise. I'm a Wilsonian when it comes to rebuilding Afghanistan and working actively with other countries in the region like Iran, India, and Pakistan to promote peace and democracy. (And so far Bush's team seems to have it right here as well. Memo to right-wingers who still oppose nation-building: Check out the American eagle on the presidential seal—it clutches arrows in one of its talons and an olive branch in the other.) And I'm a Jeffersonian when it comes to vigilantly defending civil liberties at home, which from Cicero's day to our own always come under threat in wartime. Here I part sharp company with the administration.

As Mead observes, the interplay between America's four schools of foreign policy thinking has made the country strong throughout our history. It is this supple give-and-take that has bestowed the "special providence" on our country that, Otto von Bismarck remarked, God reserved "for fools, drunks, and the United States of America." Yes, we might have ended up like the French during World War II without the Jacksonians' warrior spirit, but the republic might have completely shattered during Vietnam or slid into a nuclear war if the Jeffersonians had not finally forced the government out of it. There are surely many other Americans like me, who while firmly in one camp, continue to draw guidance from the others.

To his credit, for instance, *New York Times* columnist William Safire tempers his Jacksonianism with a principled commitment to Jeffersonian liberties. His opposition to Bush's assault on the rule of law since September 11 has been among the most eloquent and impassioned from the press. Conservative commentator Andrew Sullivan has also broken ranks with his political comrades on some issues since the war began, endorsing the Bush administration's modified Wilsonianism as it "has improvised an imaginative if precarious series of bilateral and trilateral alliances, each designed to solve a particular problem" arising out of the fight with terrorism. Sullivan has also acutely recognized the "theocon" element of the Republican base represented by the likes of Jerry Falwell and Pat Robertson as a growing problem for the GOP since September 11. "It is hard to fight a war against politico-religious extremism if you are winking at milder versions in your own political coalition," he noted in a smart essay on "The War and the Right" in the *New Republic*. "In a war with terrorist theocracy, America's political secularism—allied with its civil religiosity—seems one of the Constitution's sterling achievements, and not one that many Americans would want unraveled any time soon."

As the war in Afghanistan draws to an end—hopefully with the imminent capture or demise of the al-Qaida leadership—America faces its next global decision. Should we follow through on President Bush's ambitious call for an all-out war on terrorism, in particular seeking to destroy once and for all Saddam's regime? Or will this Jacksonian impulse to escalate the war cost too much blood and sorrow for an already extended Fortress America?

Mead would counsel that the Iraq debate should occur within a broader and long overdue national discussion about the global role of America. Ever since the decline of the British Empire following World War II, the U.S. has served, in Colonel House's phrase, as "the gyroscope of world order." But many Americans have not fully appreciated the costs of running a global system, says Mead—although it came home for us on September 11. *Black Hawk Down*, the new movie based on Mark Bowden's bestseller, surely raises the same question for the American public: When is it appropriate for the U.S. to use its troops? Certainly, Somalia teaches us, not when our soldiers are being used as nation-builders in a country gripped by warlords and chaos. Or does it? Afghanistan appeared to many skeptics to be the same dark alley. And yet in this case the majority of the country, after twenty years of fighting and tyranny, turned out to be more than ready to be relieved of its agony, even under the shuddering impact of American bombs.

Serving as the world's only superpower need not be the thicket of a thousand piercing thorns that Mead and other Jeffersonians fear. In truth, the U.S. has been very discriminating about where it has intervened in the past decade or so. As Mead acknowledges, the Pentagon itself has become a bastion of Jeffersonian and Jacksonian thinking, the two schools most reluctant to stick their noses in the world's business. The only clear example of an intervention debacle during these years has, in fact, been Somalia.

But even as I write these words, the drums of war are growing loud again, sounding out "Baghdad." And my first response to them comes from my Jeffersonian past: not again, not another war; when will Americans finally get to lay down their military burden, why should it be up to us to relieve the world of one more evil dictator, is he really the horseman of the apocalypse the war drummers say he is? The drums quieted briefly as America celebrated Peace on Earth. But they're beating again, and Americans will soon have to decide whether to heed them.

AUTHOR BIOGRAPHIES

MEERA ATKINSON
Meera Atkinson is an Australian writer living in New York City.

ERIC BOEHLERT
Eric Boehlert is a senior writer for *Salon*.

DAMIEN CAVE
Damien Cave is a senior writer for *Salon*.

CHRIS COLIN
Chris Colin is the associate editor of the Life and People sections at *Salon*.

JAMES CROAK
James Croak is an artist living in New York City.

JEFFREY EUGENIDES
Jeffrey Eugenides is the author of the novel *The Virgin Suicides*.

JANET FITCH
Janet Fitch is the author of *White Oleander*.

TERRY GOLWAY
Terry Golway is the city editor of the *New York Observer* and is a former Staten Island resident. The son, son-in-law, and godson of New York firefighters, he is the author of *Full of Grace: An Oral Biography of John Cardinal O'Connor* and *So Others Might Live: A History of New York's Bravest*, among other books.

SUZY HANSEN

Suzy Hansen is an assistant editor at *Salon*.

DANIEL HARRIS

Daniel Harris is the author of *The Rise and Fall of Gay Culture* and *Cute, Quaint, Hungry and Romantic: The Aesthetics of Consumerism*.

WILLIAM HARVEY

Violinist William Harvey is a freshman at the Juilliard School of Music in New York.

GARY KAMIYA

Gary Kamiya is *Salon*'s executive editor.

KING KAUFMAN

King Kaufman is a senior writer for *Salon*.

COLE KAZDIN

Cole Kazdin is a writer in New York.

SEAN KENNY

Sean Kenny is a British freelance writer.

CHRISTOPHER KETCHAM

Christopher Ketcham is a freelance writer in New York City.

M. A. MUQTEDAR KHAN

M. A. Muqtedar Khan is a political science professor at Adrian College in Michigan. He is on the board of the Center for the Study of Islam and Democracy.

Caroline Knapp

Caroline Knapp is the author of *Drinking: A Love Story*. Her most recent book is *Pack of Two: The Intricate Bond Between People and Dogs*.

Ann Marsh

Ann Marsh is a writer in Los Angeles.

Tom McNichol

Tom McNichol is a San Francisco writer whose work has appeared in the *New York Times Magazine*, the *Washington Post*, and on public radio's *Marketplace* and *All Things Considered*. He is a contributing editor for *Wired* magazine.

Laura Miller

Laura Miller is *Salon*'s New York editorial director.

Rick Moody

Rick Moody is the author of five books, including *Demonology*.

Asra Q. Nomani

Asra Q. Nomani, a reporter for the *Wall Street Journal* currently on leave to write a book, is reporting for *Salon* from Pakistan.

Phillip Robertson

Phillip Robertson was reporting from Afghanistan for *Salon*.

Lauren Sandler

Lauren Sandler writes about culture from New York.

JENNIFER FOOTE SWEENEY

Jennifer Foote Sweeney is the editor of *Salon*'s Life section.

KEVIN J. SWEENEY

Kevin J. Sweeney, an environmental consultant in Piedmont, California, served as press secretary to former Senator Gary Hart.

DAVID TALBOT

David Talbot is *Salon*'s founder and editor in chief.

JAKE TAPPER

Jake Tapper, a contributing writer to *Salon*, was *Salon*'s Washington correspondent in 2001 and the author of *Down and Dirty: The Plot to Steal the Presidency*.

A. R. TORRES

A. R. Torres lives in New York. Her husband, Luis Eduardo Torres, died on September 11, his second day of work in the World Trade Center. She is currently compiling his life story for her son and stepsons.

JOAN WALSH

Joan Walsh is the editor of *Salon* News.

STEPHANIE ZACHAREK

Stephanie Zacharek is a staff writer for *Salon* Arts & Entertainment.

ACKNOWLEDGMENTS

Salon is a tight-knit family of staffers and freelancers, many of whom deserve thanks for their contributions to this book. But we owe a special debt of gratitude to Max Garrone, Adrienne Crew, Ruth Henrich, Laura Miller, and Scott Rosenberg of *Salon* and to Suzanne O'Neill of Washington Square Press, who conceived the idea for this book and saw it steadfastly and enthusiastically through to completion. Thanks also to the writers whose work we have collected, whose physical and moral courage was in many cases put to the test in the course of their endeavors.